Laurens P. Hickok

Creator and Creation

Or, the knowledge in the reason of God and his work

Laurens P. Hickok

Creator and Creation
Or, the knowledge in the reason of God and his work

ISBN/EAN: 9783337220174

Printed in Europe, USA, Canada, Australia, Japan

Cover: Foto ©Lupo / pixelio.de

More available books at **www.hansebooks.com**

CREATOR AND CREATION;

OR,

THE KNOWLEDGE IN THE REASON OF GOD AND HIS WORK.

BY

LAURENS P. HICKOK, D. D., LL. D.

BOSTON:
LEE AND SHEPARD, PUBLISHERS.
NEW YORK:
LEE, SHEPARD AND DILLINGHAM.
1872.

Entered, according to Act of Congress, in the year 1872,

By LAURENS P. HICKOK,

In the Office of the Librarian of Congress, at Washington.

Stereotyped at the Boston Stereotype Foundry,
19 Spring Lane.

PREFACE.

THERE must be some point from whence the Universe may be observed, and the self-consistent whole be fully comprehended. To a spiritual discernment from that point the Universe will be known as a Cosmos of order and beauty, and such comprehensive knowing will be true wisdom. Intelligences from lower positions may be urging their way upward towards this point of vision, and may be esteemed wise proportioned to their elevation ; but the impulse which, from any stair, urges to a higher, is, at least, a *love of wisdom;* and so the spirit of true philosophy may be taking any step from the lowest to the highest. But the wisdom here loved and sought must be more than a mere apprehension of facts, even the comprehension of facts in their essential unity. To merely get facts as they appear, and carefully classify them, may be called science ; but except as it shall be sought to know the facts in their necessary connections comprehensively, the so-called science will have in it nothing of philosophy.

It will, moreover, be a delusive assumption to hold that Nature's intrinsic connections can be gained by experience, or by any logical deductions from experience. Appearances will be found in uniform collocations and invariable successions; but the fact of uniform appearances together in place will not warrant a logical conclusion of a substance in which they inhere, nor will the fact of appearances in an invariable order of sequence admit of the logical conclusion that they adhere together in a causal efficiency. Not less illogical must it be to rise from such assumed substances and causes to one absolute substance or cause. Philosophy and Theology must alike be impossible for any sense-attainment, or an understanding-judgment as a conclusion from sense. If we have not the faculty for an insight into experience which finds a deeper meaning than the mere appearance, then must we be incapable either to be wise or to love wisdom.

And so also with Revelation as with Nature. An assumed Revelation may be studied, and its facts arranged with much learning; but when a profound scepticism meets us, and drives us back of the facts, and asks for the validity of prophecy, and miracles, and inspiration, and even for the being of a God who can foreknow, and work miracles, and inspire human messengers, we are thrown directly back upon these old assumptions of Nature's necessary connections. No sense-experience puts within the consciousness anything by which logic alone can enable us to know that which beyond Nature supports and connects Nature ; and thus the logical understanding is driven helplessly to swing on the circle, of taking the Bible's God to make and hold together Nature, and then to take Nature's God to make and reveal the facts of the Bible. The student of the Bible allows himself to rest his faith, ultimately, on nothing which has not first appeared in sense-experience ; physical science is pushing eagerly and earnestly her free inquiries : many phenomena are encountered which run back into sceptical difficulties ; and seriously or mischievously these stumbling-blocks are thrown in the way of religious faith ; and then no theology, without a higher philosophy, can either pass on over them, or push them out of the path.

We must recognize a higher spiritual faculty than sense-experience, as an organ for a spiritual philosophy, which shall abundantly comprehend and confirm our theology ; and therein may all scepticism be fairly met and answered. The phenomena of Nature must be seen to be ordered by essential forces back of the appearances; and also faith in Theism must rest on truth known to be beyond Nature, and determining the order of Nature, though known by the insight of reason in Nature. So, seeing in experience what is conditional for it, we attain a comprehensive knowledge of Experience itself. And here only is the opening to a spiritual philosophy which may be competent to silence all sceptical cavilling with our theology.

As far as is necessary or desirable, the metaphysic for such a philosophy has, some years since, been given in the Rational Psychology. The physical portion, necessary in the completion of such philosophy, has never yet been adequately presented even in outline. This is here attempted: and after a critical examination of the leading theories of modern philosophy, exposing the main point in which with most there is an utter, and in the best a partial, deficiency, and therein opening the sure process to the knowledge of an Absolute Creator, the Creation is itself speculatively contemplated in its essential Forces, and these determined in their necessary connections. These essential Forces have their determined connections in all the mechanism of Inorganic nature; and then a life-power is contemplated as superinduced

by the Creator, which uses these essential mechanical
forces in spontaneously upbuilding about itself, and
for its own ends, the varied organic structures of the
Vegetable and Animal kingdoms ; when a contemplated endowment of animal sentient life with reason
introduces man in the image of the Creator, and
crowns the creative work with a Spiritual kingdom
in Humanity which has dominion over all.

The validity of the speculation, and the stability
of its connections, must be determined in the comprehensive unity and consistency with which it shuts
phenomenal facts together in a universe, and the certainty with which it puts the origin and consummation of the universe in the Absolute Thought and
Will of a Personal Creator. The importance to the
present age, so unphilosophical and thus so sceptical,
of a deeper interest in Speculative Philosophy can
hardly be over-estimated ; and perhaps by what is
here attempted, such interest may be somewhat
quickened and extended.

AMHERST, 1872.

CONTENTS.

PART I.

KNOWLEDGE OF A CREATOR.

CHAPTER I.

CHAPTER II.

CHAPTER III.

PART II.

KNOWLEDGE OF CREATION.

CHAPTER I.

CHAPTER II.

FIRST DIVISION.

ANTAGONIST FORCE.

SECOND DIVISION.

DIREMPTIVE FORCE.

THIRD DIVISION.

REVOLVING FORCE.

CHAPTER III.

THE REIGN OF LIFE IN THE VEGETABLE KINGDOM.

THE REIGN OF SENSE IN THE ANIMAL KINGDOM.

THE REIGN OF REASON IN HUMANITY.

CREATOR AND CREATION.

GENERAL METHOD.

THE Creator determines the creation. In the order of thought and being the Creator, but in the order of our knowledge the creation, is prior. Knowledge begins in experience, but as the Creator never himself appears in human experience, if our knowledge must be restricted within experience, we of course can never know the Creator. At the outset we are thus thrown upon the necessity of finding and using an organ of knowledge which may carry us beyond all that is given in experience, or our very undertaking to recognize a Creator, and speculatively contemplate the originating of his work, must be an absurdity. But in the use of Reason as a distinct organ of transcendental knowledge, we may consistently attempt to attain a knowledge of the Creator; following which, we may also consistently seek to know the work of creation in its incipiency, progress, and consummation.

The following will thus be our General Method: —

It will be requisite, in a First Part, to determine the extent of Knowledge within Experience; to recognize Reason as competent to carry our knowledge beyond experience; and then by Reason, to attain the sure knowledge of a Being who may be an Absolute Creator.

It will then belong to a Second Part to show that no one Space and one Time can be determined in common for all, without a knowledge of fixed force in place, and passing force in period; to contemplate how such distinguishable forces may be originated, and by their multiplication and interaction a material Universe may be consummated; and then how the super-induction of a life-power may build up all the organisms of the vegetable and animal kingdoms, and the gift of Reason may elevate the animal to the human.

The execution of the Plan must necessarily carry us up to the highest sphere of speculation; and yet a careful insight will be found adequate to guide our way, and take us safely through all the mysteries necessary to be solved in the adventurous undertaking.

PART I.

KNOWLEDGE OF A CREATOR.

A LOGICAL proof for the Being of God is an impossibility, in the sense that the very attempt to attain such proof involves a logical absurdity. It would be seeking for a primitive syllogism that might prove its major proposition. The first syllogism must necessarily assume its major premise. The being of the Creator must precede the being of the created Universe, within which all sense-experience must be found and all logical data attained; and hence this proof for the being of a Creator cannot come within the circumscription of any logical syllogism. "No man hath seen God at any time," nor has any man seen that which contains God; hence the being of God can never be distributed in the conclusion of a logical judgment.

We shall need, in this First Part, three chapters.

2   17

CHAPTER I.

KNOWLEDGE RESTRICTED TO THAT WHICH IS GAINED IN EXPERIENCE.

GRECIAN thinking controlled the Ancient Philosophy. Other processes of thought were foreign, and continued separate, or at most were held subsidiary to this. The philosophic stem, divided into two main branches, flowering in Plato and Aristotle, and which at length exhausted themselves, the one in New Platonism, and the other in Aristotelian Scholasticism. It is not for our purpose important that we here note their peculiarities. Much of their spirit appears in Modern Philosophy, but it has been by infusion rather than genetic propagation, since no seed from either branch of the old was a germinating source for the vigorous and prolific new shoot.

Modern Philosophy started in doubting, not for the sake of doubt, but that all doubting might be excluded from it. Even if amid otherwise universal doubt, one thing was indubitable — that there was *thinking*. Philosophy may throw itself upon conscious thought for life and deliverance from all doubt. Conscious thinking immediately introduces self-consciousness, and thus thinking Being, and the test for the validity of the being is the clearness of the thought.

But the thought of a most perfect Being is a necessity as clear as the thought of self, and thus the being of God is as indubitable as my own being. As thinking gives spiritual being, so sense gives material being, and clear sense-perception must be valid, for the most perfect being could not make senses which were helplessly deceptive without thereby impeaching his perfection. Spirit and matter, thus known, were also known as wholly disparate and utterly intercommunicable, and their concordant occurrences were referred to a " pre-established harmony ; " and all occasion for interaction was through the Deity, and known as " occasional cause." All distinct appearances were made modes and attributes of one Absolute Substance, in which all further thought was lost, since out of this abyss there can be found no emergent traces. The absolute substance stood utterly helpless; it could not move and strike, or, if stricken, it could make no rebound.

Philosophy, then necessarily, turned all its thinking into the channel of experience. Sense opens to us all we know ; and Sensationalism, i. e., Empiricism, is the source for all possible Human philosophizing. The well-known " Essay on the Human Understanding " presents the clear outline of the general system. Mind is originally destitute of ideas innate or imparted, and stands utterly void. Its experience is from two sources ; Sensation being an inlet from the outer world, and Reflection opening to what passes from the mind itself in its own exercises. We thus know material qualities and mental exercises, and can form judgments by comparing, abstracting, and combining, what is thus given. Reason is no faculty for original knowledge, but for inducing relative ideas and deducing concluded judgments. An abstraction of extended sensations gives place, and an abstraction of limits to place gives pure Space; and so also an abstraction of successive sensations gives period, and an abstraction of all limits to period gives pure Time. The idea of substance was a riddle, for abstracting sense-qualities and exercises leaves only space and time, and yet the qualities need the substances to be *in* space and time. Ultimately the idea of Cause induced a similar perplexity. If denied to be attained in some supra-sensible manner, then the ideas of substance and cause were necessarily inexplicable as having any reality. Sense gives sequences, and Cause supposes a necessity of connection in the sequences, and this assumed idea of necessary connection was explained as being the factitious result of the frequent repetition of the experience. Other ideas transcending experience perplexed the empiricist from time to time, and received his solutions as plausibly as practicable, or else were left as mysteries for future elucidations, or as incapable of human cognition.

And here it may be allowed that experience does give a common highway of knowledge, in which, for a short distance, all walk together. We wake in consciousness through sensation, and continued perceptions perpetuate consciousness. Past perceptions may be made present recollections, and these may be subjected in reflection to analysis, comparison, abstraction, and connection in judgments and general classification; and we may thus have each his sense-world ordered and arranged in his own experience, and each may say for himself what is, and what has been; but when we inquire, Why thus? and seek to know what *must* be,—no perception of sense, nor any logical judgment according to sense, can find an answer. All is within experience, and there is no organ to look through and beyond experience, and thus conscious experience itself can have no explanation. No sense can perceive how it perceives, and hence there can be no possible interpretation of our knowing, nor any settling of the validity of that which appears in conscious experience. Yea, the sense alone never seeks to rise above itself, and ask a reason for its own being and perceiving. That we irrepressibly have such inquiries, and can never be restrained from starting them anew after every repulse, and yearn some way to get round and over our encountered difficulties in knowing truths eternal beyond experience, is an abundant proof that man has a higher faculty than sense and logical judgment; and that some organ of intelligence is in humanity that the brute never had; and as it rises above sense in its inquiries, so must it be competent to go beyond sense in its knowledge, or its capacity for inquiring is worse than in vain to it. A sense-philosophy cannot satisfy, though such philosophy has become nearly all-prevalent. It is interesting in itself, and for our present purpose necessary, that we note discriminatingly some of its most prominent theories in their variety.

The notice taken of these theories will best subserve its purpose, if we disregard the order of time in which they were promulgated, and arrange them as they in themselves exhibit the promptings of reason more manifestly, though their authors recognized no distinct Faculty of Reason, except in some of the last examples given.

1. PURE EMPIRICISM IN THE POSITIVE PHILOSOPHY. — In the early age, as history opens, it is quite in course to find that the observation of the changes and movements in the world around has induced the conviction that some power above nature has controlled the changes and motions, and that the gods, though keep·ing themselves concealed, are the great agents in working out the passing events. Their voices are heard in the thunder and the earthquake; tempests and pestilences are the expressions of their displeasure; and prevalent health, prosperity, and fruitfulness are the results of divine benignity.

Longer experience, and with closer observation, assigns the powers at work in the material changes to some occult efficiencies within and about the objects themselves, and these secret forces and hidden entities in nature are moving the dead matter of the world about, and in the directions of their own energy. The

Theologic faith fades out, and then the Metaphysic age dawns in human history. Subtle discussions, abstract reasonings, and ideal speculations, in a thousand varied and ingenious forms, occupy the attention of the strongest minds through long generations.

But anon the metaphysic age passes as necessarily as had the theologic; since sharpened observation had attained to clear and positive consciousness of the phenomenal world, and the wise have learned to discriminate between immediate perceptions and fancied notions, or fictitious ideals. If these occult notions have any real entity, they are beyond human knowledge, and outside of all conscious experience, and science learns to care nothing about them. The Positive age is thus a sure occurrence in its time, in which the superstitions of the theologic and the dreaming fictions of the metaphysic age have become merged and lost forever, as controlling matters of interest and attention, in the age of Positivism. The sages of humanity have now the grand work, uninterruptedly, to get and spread the light of positive science; attaining, arranging, and classifying all that comes in to conscious experience. Humanity must needs have passed all these stages to the last, and, indeed, every individual mind has its theologic, metaphysic, and positive period, while in the last only, all illusions vanish, and true science prevails.

The order of procedure in positive science is from the simple to the complex, till we reach and make clear all the complications of nature and human society. The science of Sociology, in the family, the community, and the state, organizing all relations and occupations, and overcoming the resistances of nature, and the selfish inclinations and animal passions of the uncultivated races, finally introduces order, freedom, and social contentment, and opens the way to the indefinite development and progressive maturity and perfection of the human species.

By a strange personal experience, a religious *cultus* was superinduced upon the positive science, which it is taught will harmonize all the family of man in universal unity, as if Humanity had become itself one great Being. The religious age, spontaneous in its devotion, was originally exercised in fetichism, worshipping any rock, tree, or animal that fancy proposed. Then polytheism abounded; followed by monotheism as the mind rose to higher unity, till ultimately the true, living, thinking, feeling, loving, Humanity is the object and end of all worship; and the greatest names of history, as manifestations of humanity, are worthy of a qualified homage.

Positivism is thus in theory consistent with empiricism, and a consequent of it. It attempts to carry out its own adopted *dictum*, that the human mind has no function that can make itself objective to itself. Any single sense may as well attempt to examine and expound itself, as the entire consciousness to attempt determining the validity of its revealings. And yet with all this consistency in claim and theory, its whole procedure evinces the presence and perpetual prompting of the function of Reason which it so peremptorily discards. If there were nothing but elements given in experience and their use in reflection, there could be no attempt to overlook experience, and determine how much it might know. Perception, and judgment according to perception, would go on just as occasion was given; but from nowhere could come the impulse to examine experience, and learn how far the consciousness might spread its light. The brute perceives in sense, and judges according to sense, as truly, and often as exactly, as the man; but no animal ever manifested the capability or the curiosity to examine his experience, and determine the limits of his knowledge. That the Positivist is able to so emphatically assert his positivism, carries in it a sure evidence that there is working in him a higher intelligence than any sense-experience can reach.

And then there is, moreover, his constant assumption of Necessity and Law in nature, which can come from no element attainable in sensation. Experience may remember past observations, in the uniform combination of some qualities and invariable sequence of some events, and such order of experience may be transferred to an outer world, and called an order of nature; but this would then be only a way that nature was seen to have, and not any necessary behest that nature is forced to obey. Law is more than the fact of order; it is an imposition from a source that binds to order, and is a notion which only can flash in from a light that overshines experience itself.

And then Positivism has also its Religion with its *cultus* of sacred ordinances and ritual ceremonies. True in form to its restriction of all knowledge to experience, its religion has no higher deity than Humanity, and its most sacred shrines are the names of the renowned men and women of the ages, to whom homages, and festivals, and votive offerings are dedicated, and the calendar months are named from the most eminent, and the days of the week from other illustrious benefactors; yet even such a service could never be assumed as binding itself upon human observance, were there not in man a deeper claim than any sense can awaken. But because social life is itself of the reason, and has its rights and duties, it reaches beyond the wants which make the cattle herd together, and thus the *religion* Positivism inculcates, born of social ties and sympathetic claims, would never have been even speculatively instituted, were it not that already in the priest and the worshipper there is a spirit seeking supernatural communion, and *binding back* from all finite good to an exhaustless source of eternal goodness. While Positivism knows not its *use* of the reason, it still evinces the *working* of the reason, and that it has been deeply quickened and prompted by reason.

With the observed uniformities in experience, and

these in their connections taken as laws in nature, as if they were more than facts found, even as necessities imposed, it is true the human mind may accumulate its observed facts, and physical science may sort and classify them endlessly as experience attains them, while all philosophic inquiry is held in abeyance. Yet will not the enterprise of reason be ever so satisfied or repressed. The faculty is there, though unrecognized, and its living energies will prompt speculative inquiries into these uniformities and invariable sequences of nature. Science itself soon learns that it can make its way with far greater facility, when it is helped to a ready anticipation of its probable hypotheses by a given direction to the course of its inductions. Thus both the spontaneous impulses of the faculty, and the wants of science, will combine to urge on philosophical investigations: and humanity can never rest in barely perceiving and classifying the facts of experience, but must go beyond the positive in sense, and attempt, at least, to know experience as universally and necessarily determined. The ages will be seeking for the reasons why its passing experiences are ever thus, and this is nothing other than finding the ultimate truths in the insight of reason itself. Reason's insight is the last reason for anything, and man is never at rest till his clear insight and comprehending oversight sees' beyond the facts, and finds the facts themselves to be reasonable. No matter how positive the man may be in the observed order of his facts, and that he has it as the long experience of ages has given it; he wants to know the long order, not merely as positive fact, but as imposed law; and even the positivist himself talks freely of the *laws* of nature, and the *obligations* of society; for no man's speech can satisfy his inward conviction, which does not carry in it the meaning, that there are *à priori* bonds on all the facts of nature and communings of society.

It might thus have been anticipated, just as it occurs, that the reason should thrust up its irrepressible inquiries, and in ignorance of the source from whence the asking comes, the mind should set some lower faculty to the task of finding an answer. The sense and logical understanding are set to solve the problems the reason propounds, and which will really amount to nothing else than asking reasons for a fact, and then giving another fact in answer. Experience cannot ask for itself, why itself is so : the reason makes the demand, and experience can as little answer as inquire to any purpose. When it has given one fact to explain others, which must be its only way, there is still the same thing to be gone over. The reason can never stand on any last fact, and cease her inquiries. She must get above the fact, and see through the fact a transcendental principle, and no empirical answer can be other than illusory. And yet, notwithstanding the manifest absurdity of attaining any end in such a process, we shall constantly find modern philosophy very largely at work in the interpretation of experience by experience, and striving to grow wise, or at least evince its love of wisdom, by pushing the mystery of one fact back into another, till the remoteness quenches all further curiosity. The Positive Philosophy can never be truly positive, and attain and keep a fixed position, except by a perpetual delusion.

2. EMPIRICISM AS EXPOUNDED BY THE LAWS OF ASSOCIATION. — While Positivism seeks to repress all attempts at explaining why nature has her uniformities, and holds it enough to take experience as it is, and by careful study make the most of it, there have not been wanting other theories for accounting why experience is so orderly, even while admitting and strenuously teaching that our knowledge cannot transcend the sense-consciousness within which all experience must be. Assuming a Divine power out of and over all experience, it might be held as it variously had been, that this outside power did all the work of arranging, either by occasional interpositions, or by a pre-established harmony, or in an original Divine Constitution; while others dispensed with any outside agency, and said nature must have some relations, and as well those according with our own experience as any other, and we need only to consider all things as a "fortuitous concurrence;" and still others, admitting the present mystery, proposed in all humility, from imbecility of faculties, to lie still and wait for future disclosures. All explanation was arbitrary, or fortuitous, or hopelessly impossible.

An independent and acute scrutiny ascertained the impossibility of determining the necessary connections of cause and effect in experience, by any knowledge gained by experience. The sole purpose of any inquiry must be, not *to know* any such determined connections, but to explain why the human mind comes *to deem* the sequences in cause and effect to be necessarily connected. And the short statement of the explanation is the force of Habit. We find certain sequences occurring so frequently in the same order, experience has them so often and for so long a time, that, although no connecting link comes within sensation, yet the frequent repetition induces an idea or semblance of such link, and this becomes a belief, a confirmed conviction, that there is such interlinking, and all originating in habit. The common-sense conviction, in this way, of the laws of experience, becomes so controlling that no testimony of their miraculous violation ought to influence us. But such strength of conviction was only subjective seeming, and not at all any known necessity in objective being. This the clear-sighted philosopher well knew, and on it was built, with logical consistency, an impregnable scepticism. Experience can account for the common conviction that the connections in nature are necessary, but no judgment in experience can possibly show any validity for the conviction that there is any such necessary connection. All reasoning from the connections of cause and effect rest only upon the illusion

of habit, and never can be the confirmation of truth
and knowledge.

And now, closely allied to this, and indeed almost
a carrying out of the same theory a little more cir-
cumstantially and minutely, is that above announced
as resting upon the law of Association. There is the
same limiting of knowledge to experience, and in consistency with this, expounding our convictions of an
outer world and its connections, and our assent to all
necessary truths, on a similar subjective basis a little
more completely worked out and systematically arranged. This theory assumes that past sensations
afford the sufficient occasion for expecting future sensations in certain conditions, and that the order of
past experience becomes a law of association by which
the expected future sensations in experience are
regulated. The law of association is described in the
various forms that former experiences have determined for it, and these forms of applying the law of
association sufficiently account for our belief of an
external world, and its orderly arrangement in conscious experience, though we can have no knowledge
that such outer world is in existence.

Thus any one may say of himself: A little reflection teaches me that my current fleeting sensations
are of little account in my conception of the existing
world around me, but that there are possible sensations of innumerable variety, which under supposable
conditions I deem I could at this moment experience,
and it is to these possible sensations that I am obliged

to turn, as important in awaking me to the conception of an outer world. My actual sensations are transient, while these possibilities of sensations are permanent; and in giving to them distinctive names, they come to be apprehended as distinctive things. In any group of such possible sensations I have associated the whole from some one that was an element in a former group of actual sensations, and this associative process has furnished the connections in all the qualities of the thing, and from a natural forgetfulness of the associative process, the thing is taken as having these fixed connections from necessity. These abiding things, therefore, and not the transient sensations, I associate in fixed orders of succession, just as I have found my transient sensations succeeding each other, and it is to these permanent possibilities of sensations that, in the obliviscence of the association, I apply my conviction of necessary connection as cause and effect, and thereby make up my world from these connected possibilities of sensations. I can, at will, withdraw myself from the transient sensations that have been given me, by closing my senses, or turning the organ another way, but I cannot put from me these permanent possibilities of sensations at will, since I deem them to be abiding through all my changes.

I find others, moreover, manifesting their apprehension, not of their transient sensations, but of these permanent possibilities of sensations, as if their experience in this were in common with mine. In this way there is for me, and for others in common with me, a world of possibilities of sensations connected according to laws, and which must so be taken by me as a world existing external to me and others. The actual sensations of the city of Calcutta must, in any case, be fleeting, but the permanent possibilities of sensation, on condition of my sailing up the Hoogly by daylight, must be my existing Calcutta, ordered and arranged according to applied laws of association for me and others. Matter, therefore, is to be taken as a permanent possibility of sensations, as it exists in our consciousness; and such material world we may know, and believe to be real, but no other world can be our world of experience. The permanent possibilities of sensations outlast all our changes, and will be for others when we are gone, just as they are now for other beings in common with ourselves.

And as with the organic senses for matter, so with the inner sense for mind. The inner exercises may all in common be termed feelings, as they affect the consciousness; and the actual feelings, like the actual sensations, are transient, and little to be regarded as making up the known mental world; but the permanent possibilities of feelings must make up what I know as my one perduring mind. The one capacity for permanent possibilities of feeling which may continue through reverie, or fainting, or sleep, or bodily dissolution, is what must be known as the perpetuation of myself. There are some differences to be noticed between permanent possibilities of sensations and permanent possibilities of feelings, among which the most important is, that the former are possibilities to others as well as to myself, but the latter are a series of possibilities in my life to myself alone. But this permanency, as myself, may be determined as existing in other series of possible feeling, as otherselves also. Other figures of seeing and speaking possibilities I know, as I know my own seeing and speaking body; and I am conscious of modified bodily states followed by feelings, and these again followed by some outward conduct in myself. Now, the first as peculiar state of body, and the last as peculiar conduct, I cannot connect in myself except as through the intermediate feelings. My body is naked, and I put on clothes; my stomach is empty, and I take food; but I connect the first two by the feeling of cold, and the last two by the feeling of hunger, only in my consciousness. I get, in the observation of other seeing and speaking figures, the first and the last, but I do not get their intermediate feeling to connect them. Still, as I know their state of body and subsequent conduct to be as mine together, I legitimately infer the middle link of feeling to be present, and connect the two in them, as it does and must in me, and thus that they are sentient beings as I am. They have bodies as mine, exhibit acts significant as mine, which indicate feeling as mine, and thus that they are otherselves as I am myself. So it is competent for me to know other series of feelings

than my own; to know even a series that is superhuman or divine, from knowing manifestations of
superhuman or divine thought and feeling. I may conceive a thread of consciousness perpetuated through
an unending series, and believe in an immortality.
Mind, as a series of feelings, with the background of
perpetuated possibilities of feeling, is, therefore, an
object for our subjective consciousness, though we
may not be able, and truly are not competent, to know
such a world of spiritual beings actually existing.

But there is one part of this knowledge, in subjective experience, which the philosophy itself admits to
be wholly inscrutable by any experience. I remember the past parts of the series; I may expect future
parts; and thus the one myself is in all the series,
past, present, and future. The mental series is in this
peculiar. The material series is known only by others
than itself, even by the mental, and by that alone;
but the mental has its own thread of consciousness
throughout, as a series which is aware of itself. Here,
it is honestly recognized, that the theory faces an inexplicable mystery; since it cannot be expounded to
experience, how a past fact and a future fact can at
once be a present fact. And here, the determining
of a series, that shall know both its past and future to
belong to a present self, is ingenuously left outside
the theory, waiting some other means of solution.

But this law of association is made to reach much
further, and mediate a knowledge beyond the experience of matter and of mind as given in the fact of

consciousness, even to the determining of intuitive knowledge in mathematics. The necessary truth of geometrical axioms and demonstrations is made to be a matter of experience, through the medium of association. And just as we did let slip the consciousness of the associative process, in the connection of the sensations in substances and attributes, causes and effects, and deemed thus the connections to be necessary and immediately known, so also in our obliviscence of our associations from experience in mathematical truths, do we deem their relations to be necessary, and our apprehensions of them immediate intuitions. Thus we have found, invariably, that two things put together with two other things have made four things, and in the expectation of any future process of so putting two and two things together, we overlook the association of it from our past experience, and then think that we immediately see the two and two things together to be four things. The knowledge that two and two make four is from no known necessity in the case, nor any intuition of a universal truth; but only from association through former experience, which associative process we overlook, and deem the relation between the two and two and the four to be an immediate intuition. If when two and two things had been put together in our past experience, there had always been, by some jugglery or miracle, another thing secretly interposed, so that the summing up should have been five, then would the associative process have been accordingly in our anticipated future additions of two and two, and passing the association we should have acquired the mathematical intuition that two and two are five.

So again, our invariable experience has been, that on round bodies becoming cubes, they have ceased to be round, and that cubes becoming round, they have ceased to be cubes; or when bounded by straight lines, the invariable experience has been that more than two lines have been needed to make out the complete limitation; and hence the association from such experience puts the permanent possibilities of sensation after the same form, and letting fall from consciousness the association, we deem it to be an intuition, that there cannot be cubical spheres, nor spherical cubes, nor can two straight lines enclose a space. If our two eyes had been made invariably to give a cube with a sphere and a sphere with a cube, by some double vision in the consciousness; or had we never known two straight lines but as they appear together on a railroad track, when perspectively they approach each other on opposite sides of us; we should then have intuitively known that a cube must also be a sphere, and a sphere a cube, and that two straight lines must always enclose a space. The determining rule is the order of association according to former experience, and the permanent possibilities of sensations take on the same order, and passing over the association, we have left to us the supposed immediate intuition.

And now this is very ingeniously wrought out,

strictly in accordance with the psychology that knowledge is limited by experience. It is no reproach to the philosophy, that the externality and necessity of the uniform order of the objects of experience are only a subjective seeming, and no possible knowing; nor is it any conviction of logical absurdity to show, that such laws of nature in experience would be only laws of mental association, and that the other men here are only other as men are in our dreams, and their manifestation of similar feelings and convictions with ours is only a doubling of the subjective seeming, as when we might dream others · were dreaming as we dream; for all this is understood from the start; and since the human mind cannot push its knowledge beyond what is given in conscious sensation, the entire credit which the philosopher asks should be accorded to him is, not that he has shown there is any outer world, but how experience may seem to be outward, and orderly arranged; and that he has done this logically, from the data given in experience alone.

But the deep reproof to be applied to the philosophy is from another quarter. The inquiry it has made, and so logically answered, is what the rational mind cares nothing about. The whole business is a delusive play with fictions. The only inquiry made is, Why does our world of experience seem external and orderly connected? And the answer given is, That there are associations naturally, and even necessarily, generated by the order of our transient sensations, which inevitably induce such seeming. But when we admit all this, it is still of no interest to the philosophic mind. That asks yet, as from the first, Why this order of the primitive transient sensations, which has determined the association in the permanent possibilities of sensations? May there not here be an insight to an outer and orderly material world? Reason stands knocking at this door, and cannot be deluded into any interest with the logic that may seem to be pleasing itself about any mere seeming. It will wait here till this door opens.

3. EMPIRICISM IN THE PHILOSOPHY OF COMMON SENSE. — The Philosophy of Common Sense restricts all human knowledge to the elements given in conscious experience; yet in some of its varied theories it assumes much that stands out quite beyond all experience, and applies these universal truths in different ways to relieve itself as it may from the difficulties it encounters. At its inception, it rested mainly in the assumption that consciousness was valid and its testimony final, and consistently attempted by no speculation to go back of consciousness to find any confirmation for it. It sufficed it to say, that all scepticism must appeal to consciousness for the affirmation of its doubts, and if this were not valid, then its facts of doubting were as insecure as any facts immediately affirmed. Some sense may be so conditioned at times as to delude, but this would be corrected by other senses; and some persons may be deceived in their experiences, but the normal ex-

perience of the many will prevailingly control; and the collected, unbiassed decision of common experience must be the ultimate criterion of truth. Common consciousness, and logical judgments from the facts of consciousness, cover the entire field of our knowledge.

Further reflection modified these assumptions of the validity of the facts immediately given in consciousness. It came generally to be admitted that all the senses did not alike give immediate knowledge of an outer world. Temperature and taste, odors and sounds, are rather feelings within us than any attributes of things without us, and are primarily our sensations, and only secondarily the qualities of matter. The sense of vision and of touch were held more directly to give the attributes of outer things, and from them it was assumed that we attained immediately the primary qualities of the material world. And yet, in these two senses, there came to be recognized quite a difference in the directness of their knowledge. The nervous network of the organs of vision and of touch were taken as thoroughly interpenetrated and suffused by the living intelligent spirit, and here in the nerves, it was assumed, spirit and matter came physiologically in unity. Any impression on the organic nerve was thus held to be in immediate communication with spirit, and here the matter in contact was supposed to give over its essential attributes directly to the spirit's intelligence. And yet close reflection found color in vision to come from outer things through the medium of light, and must thus be a primary quality of the light rather than of the illuminated body. Extension was in the color, and from the light; and we could not thus attain directly the shapes of things, and only the shapes of colors which the light brings from the things. Two persons together do not see the same object in their vision of the sun, or a star; nor indeed do the two eyes of the same person see together the same thing; the two only see different mediate rays of light from the same thing.

The primary qualities of the real thing, it thus comes to be admitted, must be sought solely from touch; since only in the contact of the organ with the thing, can we immediately have its primary quality given over to the sense. Solidity was thus held to be a primary quality of matter, intrinsically in its essence, and given to the consciousness in the experience of its impenetrability by contact, and measured in amount by the comparative degrees of resistance. Extension also belongs to matter essentially, and is given over to the sense in touch, and measured by the extended nerve in the organ affected, relatively to other portions of the living body, in various ways of contact, as by the grasp of the hand, the sliding of the finger, or the sweep of the arm. The externality of matter was also deemed to be immediately attained by touch; but its outness was admitted as rather a relation between matter and mind, than a primary attribute of the matter itself. Thus common sense was held to have matter face to face, and immediately to take these primary qualities from it into consciousness. The secondary qualities were allowed to be only affections in us, and to give to the consciousness only the mode in which outer things in indirect ways affected our organs.

It might well be objected to any such theory of intuitive knowledge of matter, that the supposed extended spirit, in the extended nerve-organism, does not know any extension except in the affection. The eye has no knowledge of the expanded retina, except as the retina has its content for color; nor does the hand know extension, nor solidity, till first the impressed nerve has its sensation. The spirit does not know extension because it is diffused, as supposed, through an extended network of nerve-fibres. The nerve is still between the outer matter and the mind, and it is the affection of the nerve only that the mind gets.

The true answer, however, to such a theory of immediate knowledge by touch, is a direct denial. The thing in contact with the living nerve does not put over any part or attribute of itself into the nerve, and through that into the consciousness; it can only affect the living nerve, and become a sensation; and the quality of the thing is only the way in which it has qualified our sense, and not that any element of the thing has been immediately imparted. The claim that we immediately know its externality is an affirmation of its complete outness still, and that we only know it in the affection produced. The most that may be said is, we know the without by what is within; the thing by the sensation; and this can be no immediate knowledge. Even in contact, the whole thing is outside, and the affection only is given within, and the outer can only be known through the medium of the inner. Herein is no intuitive knowledge by touch, any more than by any other organ. All sense-intuition is the putting of the affection and the intellect face to face in the consciousness, and not the thing and the intellect face to face as object and subject. The insight of reason reads the true meaning of the sense-symbols, and knows the thing in the symbol, and can intelligently expound the primary qualities of extension and solidity; but the sense without the reason-function knows nothing beyond the quality, whether in touch or any other organ.

But even with this assumption of immediate sense-knowing, the common sense was helpless to connect the qualities in any ordered experience, and fix the objects in any necessary connections, and know nature as a universe. The appearances come within, and flit over the field of consciousness, as the cloud-shadows chase each other over the landscape, and no sense-faculty can find any determining medium for connecting them in the order of their coming and departing. To meet this exigency, there has been the assumption of a higher sense-faculty than any organic perceiving, and the affirming the human mind to have an original constitutional endowment for apprehending the connections of sense-experiences. Like the organic senses, this higher sense is incompetent to overlook and comprehend itself, and expound its mode of knowing, and its most confident convictions are simply inexplicable mysteries, as if they were inspired revelations; but the universal consent, in this common constitutional taking of uniform combinations and sequences in experience as necessarily connected, is assumed to be as safe a reliance as the direct testimony of consciousness. This is expressed in the various ways of " primitive belief," " universal assent," " dictates of common sense," in this eminent signification of a sense above organic perceiving; and by this higher form of assumed sense-apprehension, they attain their remedy for admitted organic deficiencies. Such assumed higher sense is a common endowment of humanity; and this may be cultivated to attain such judgments as follows: All objects of perception must be in space and time; qualities must have their substance, and events must have their cause; like qualities and events must have like substances and causes; nature's changes must be in orderly successions, and she can gain nothing new, and lose nothing old; and others like to these.

But such assumption, of some mysteriously working-sense, is only the manifestation of the distinctive working of reason which has not been recognized by them, and for whose legitimate insight they have

ignorantly substitnted a fictitious foresight of prophecy. The assumed Seer has a new sense opened
for these higher communications, and all inexplicable
and mysterious as they are, we come to put our faith
in these revealings of truth beyond ordinary perceptions in consciousness, and trust the surreptitious
connections as giving to experience an orderly and
necessary stability and uniformity. The whole is a
mere fictitious psychological invention.

There is yet a further method, when it is found
that the human mind cannot rise in its *knowledge*
above the relations given in experience, to open, by
a logical process, a way for the exercise of *faith*, and
therein to carry human belief quite beyond the possibilities of human knowledge. We may ascend in
our judgments from the conditioned to a conditioner,
or determining condition, and this in an indefinite
process, but can never reach an ultimate condition
which has no determiner. And now this "law of the
conditioned" is subjected to such logical process, and
in the following form, for the admission of faith beyond knowledge. There may be two contradictory
propositions, neither of which can be conceived as
true, and yet as contradictory opposites, from the
logical law of the excluded middle, one of them
must be true; and then on the ground of such a
conclusion, we may believe that to be true which
can neither be known nor conceived. And this is
specially applied to two supersensible truths, the

connections of nature into a universal whole; and the Being of a God above nature.

Of the connections of cause and effect into one nature of things, we may so form a logical argument. Of any perceived phenomenon just occurred, we cannot conceive that it did not previously exist in some form. But we can neither conceive of its beginning with time, and thus to include absolutely all time, nor that it had no beginning, and thus runs back through infinite time. Such is the impotence of human thought. But a beginning with time and a non-beginning with time are contradictory opposites; and we must conclude of this phenomenon, that it has either beginning or non-beginning. Both cannot be true, but one must; we cannot conceive of either, nor possibly know either; yet we must believe one or the other to be true. Our faith here may, and even must, run beyond all thought and knowledge. We may thus believe in the necessary and universal connections of cause and effect.

And so in reference to the being of an Infinite and Absolute Deity. We may say of his omniscience, that it must require a mode of knowing that takes in all the connections of universal nature, but we cannot conceive it either as running through the infinite successive changes, or as compassing the infinite successions all at once. The first is the Infinite, the last is the Absolute, and both alike unthinkable and unknowable; and yet by the logical law for contradictory opposites, as above, while both together cannot be, one of them must be. Our faculties are too limited to think or to know in this sphere, but logic opens it for human faith to enter. We must believe that the Being who knows the universe is either an Infinite or an Absolute Being, though he cannot be both; and our faith cannot find on which to fix.

In these forms the philosophy of Common Sense exhausts all its expedients. It first assumes consciousness to be valid and sufficient in the aggregate of the senses; then restricts immediate knowledge of the outer world to vision, and more specially to touch; then imagines a fictitious, inspired, and prophetic sense, that forecasts the successions of nature; and lastly, by logic, supports a faith that can rest on no thought, and can guide itself to a specific object by no possible reason. The whole absurdity and contradiction, in which this form of philosophizing ever issues, is from limiting all knowledge to what is given in experience. The unacknowledged faculty of reason they have, and it prompts them to get speculative truth; but they put the lower faculties of sense and logic to the vain task of solving the questionings of reason, and of course in their neglect of reason the issue is folly.

4. Experience of Force given in Muscular Pressure. — This is a philosophy which begins in experience, and affirms that all beyond experience is unknowable, and yet assumes to know very far beyond

that which sense, and all logical deduction from it, could ever acquire. It is thus unwittingly using the Organ of Reason without giving credit for it. Its prime *dicta* are, that to think is to distinguish and find relations; and thought can be conversant legitimately only with that which is relative; while the Infinite and the Absolute must to man be ever unknowable. The theory may be given in the narrowest compass as follows : —

The ongoing of nature is a process of evolution, the law of which is progression from the homogeneous to the heterogeneous, yet perpetually making the heterogeneous more and more definite and coherent. This is effected through continuous differentiations and disintegrations. An indefinite number of homogeneous molecules in mass will differentiate and disintegrate, and the mass become more heterogeneous in its portions; and yet these heterogeneous portions will become more and more definite and coherent, till the mass of star-mist shall become sun and system.

The explanation of this evolution may be thus given, in the closest outline. Passing the other senses and their given perceptions, even that of vision and its colored extensions, the sense of touch is taken; and this not as tactual merely, whereby temperature may be attained, but as muscular pressure apprehending resistance. The muscles press and are pressed, in which we become conscious of co-existent resistances. Pressure with counter-pressure, at a given

point, determines a position; through continuous positions, determines a line; through contiguous positions,
a surface; and through surfaces in all directions, a
solid. The correlation of muscular energy and equivalent resistance gives the knowledge of Force. The
muscular tension is in consciousness; the co-existent
resistances come into the consciousness; and then
these correlations of resistance are known as the matter touching and touched, and which essentially is
Force, and immediately known in conscious experience.
The force is not *in* the matter, the force *is* the matter.

Abstract the force, and Space remains; the matter
and the space differ, only as positions with and positions without co-existing resistance differ. Matter is
extended and resistant, and the resistance as solidity
is the primary attribute. Space is extended and
non-resistant, and extension is the primary attribute.
When the resisting positions are given successively
in an order of sequence not reversible, we know the
occurrences to have a fixed series; and an abstraction of the successive resistances leaves Time in
the consciousness. Succession with non-resistance is
Time. The change of matter through contiguous
positions in successive moments is Motion; and thus
matter, space, and time are conjointly conditional for
motion. The primary knowledge of motion is in the
conscious change of position of our own muscles, and
we mature this knowledge of motion when there is
no muscular pressure, by at once cognizing the concurrence of space and time with the movement.

4

Force is in this the deepest element, change of position the next, and the concurrences of space and time complete the complex cognition. Matter and Motion are concretes; Space and Time are abstracts.

Relative Space and Time is that which stands related to the matter in space and time, or which may have been abstracted from space and time; and the relative space and time are, thus, the forms of force, or matter. Absolute Space and Time is that vague notion of space and time, nascent in consciousness, as lying beyond all limits of relative space and time. The question is asked, Is the Absolute Space or the Absolute Time a form from some absolute existence? which question is affirmed to be unanswerable. And so also Relative Force is that which relates immediately to the experience of muscular energy. Absolute Force is that vague notion of force, nascent in consciousness, which is beyond all limited co-resistance to muscular pressure. The being of Absolute Force, it is argued, is demanded from the persistence of consciousness itself. Persistence in consciousness is the criterion of reality; and we always rest satisfied that the thing is real, which, in appropriate conditions, persists in consciousness. Muscular pressure is not permanently persistent, and consciousness itself persists only as changing appearances take place in consciousness. The purely simple, having no changes, could awaken no consciousness. When, then, muscular pressure with its co-resistance ceases, and all relative force is absent, consciousness itself must cease. But consciousness is persistent in the absence of muscular pressure and its co-resistance, for which sake, from the very nature of consciousness, a persistent absolute force must be present. This is *à priori* postulated for the persistence of consciousness itself; and it is the proud boast of this philosophy, that such postulate has been found by it to be a logical necessity for the continuance of consciousness. This persistent Absolute Force is thus affirmed to stand in its truth "deeper than demonstration; deeper than definite cognition; deep as the very nature of mind. The sole truth which transcends experience by underlying it, is the persistence of Force." "To this an ultimate analysis brings us down, and from this a rational synthesis must build up."

In this persistent absolute force we have the indestructibility of matter, and the necessity for continuous movement. The force is matter, and can be conceived as neither beginning nor ending, nor ceasing from evolution; and here is the basis for a synthesis, as experience may find that the system of nature has been ordered. Absolute force is that universal force in which all changes and conversions of forces occur, and in which all is conserved and held in correlation. Matter is convertible into other matter, into spirit, and then again from spirit back into matter; and the universe of matter and mind is but this universal correlative and persistent Force. A given series may illustrate the perpetual conversions of force everywhere occurring. The moving force which swings the iron-tongue, and strikes the ringing chimes, is converted to the vibrations of the bell; thence into undulations of the air; and thence into sound in the ear; and here the force is spiritualized into tune in the intellect, and then emotion in the sensibility, and then to some executive impulse in volition; and now becomes converted into organic movement, as irritated nerve, and contracted muscle, and tension of sinews, and leverage of bones; and thence goes out again in its endless round of correlative pressure through material changes. The myriad-sided movement is everywhere the pushed and pushing conversions and successions of reciprocal and equivalent forces; and nothing new comes in, and nothing old drops out of the one Absolute Force. That is the ultimate of all analysis, and if there be anywhere, in or out, an originating Personality, he must to man be unknowable.

Of this entire speculation, it is important to note that, with no higher faculty than it recognizes, it would never have been attempted, and could never have been accomplished. Experience never attains force; and sense-consciousness has neither interest nor capability to determine what may be the conditions of its own persistent being. Muscular extension may push and be pushed in experience, and in every instance nervous irritability may have its peculiar sensation; but with no insight of reason the peculiar sensation is all that is brought within consciousness, and never the force that conditioned the conscious sensation. An appetitive impulse or a rational imperative may consciously have prompted the muscular tensions; but the feeling we have of these prompting activities is but the footprint of the spiritual force, which in darkness has previously passed onward. The force itself from appetite or obligation never comes into consciousness. The insight of reason into the facts of consciousness first gets the forces which give meaning to the facts.

Even if it were possible to attain force from the experience of muscular pressure, we have no experience which could give persistent absolute force. And if experience teaches that consciousness is persistent only as changes persistently go on within it, still not consciousness, but a higher authority, must determine for us that these persistent changes were necessary conditions for the consciousness, and that an absolute force was necessary for the changes.

And then, again, even if we had the recognition of absolute force, and its conservation, or persistency, and that all particular forces are correlative; What use could we make of it in any philosophy which is to determine the orderly development of nature in experience? We cannot say whether the absolute force is personal or not, nor whether itself is the product of personal intelligence and will; all we know is a continual maze of reciprocal pushings and pullings, converting themselves from one form to another, and we can only watch and classify the changes as we may in experience, with nothing to determine whence they come or whither they are tending. We may call the movement an "evolution," and say that experience finds it to proceed from "the homogeneous to the heterogeneous" in ever widening multiplications, but we can cognize nothing of an *involving* that determines the assumed *evolving*. The philosophy, even with this surreptitiously assumed force, can only expect the future from the past, with no insight of what force itself is, which may help us to determine why the past has so been, or how the future must be. The upshot of all is still fact in experience, with no possible explanation of the fact; and no rational mind can satisfy itself by it. Reason must in phenomenal fact see the force, and what the force itself is, and in this it may expound the mechanics of matter, the spontaneities of organic life, and find a passage out beyond to the supernatural.

5. The Critical Philosophy. — It is peculiar to any mathematical judgment that a diagram may be constructed of pure points or lines, which shall present the truth intended as an immediate intuition in the diagram itself; and this truth in one diagram will be the same truth as universal for all diagrams of accordant constructed form. Thus I describe a line from one point to another, and at once in this I can see that the straight line is "the shortest" line that can be drawn between those points. And but this one diagram is needed to see from it that the same

must be true of all straight lines universally that may be drawn between any two points. And as in this, so is intuition in all mathematical axioms and demonstrations. The new predicate to be attained, which in the case above is " the shortest," is seen from the diagram, and only needs to be put in the form of a judgment.

But in a philosophical judgment the case is the opposite. I say, all qualities must have substance; all events must have cause; and yet I can make no construction that will express the new predicate of substance or of cause, and cannot, thus, intuitively see the substance connecting the qualities, and the cause connecting the events, and thereby judge that they must universally so connect the qualities and the events. And yet, destitute of such capability of intuition, we are perpetually affirming, in philosophical judgments as in mathematical, the conviction of universal truths. But when required to justify our philosophical universal judgments we find much difficulty. We cannot put them face to face with us as we do in the diagrams of geometry, and hence we cannot see how we get our new notions of substances and causes, nor how we may validly make universal predicates of them. This attained conviction that no consciousness, pure or empirical, could bring substance and cause to appear within it, and consequently, by no possibility, could the intuition give any necessary and universal connections of qualities and events in or by the substances and causes, opened at once a wide door for scepticism in both philosophy and religion, and no efforts of empiricism could possibly close it. The Critical Philosophy, altogether the most remarkable of our age, started at just this point, and made it the burden of inquiry, "How are synthetic Judgments *à priori* possible ?"

The "synthetic Judgment *à priori*" was the above philosophical Judgment as distinct from the mathematical, and the inquiry involved the necessity for a searching analysis of the entire process of knowing, that we might thereby attain to a knowledge of how we know. All such systems as we have heretofore been examining were miserably partial and superficial, compared with the profound speculations of the Critical Philosophy. The mode of knowing must regulate the objects known; and in this way was attained what could come in to human consciousness, and how this could be ordered in human experience. The analysis took the human intelligence as it is, and found its highest capacities and functions.

The Sense was found as capacity for receiving affections which must from somewhere be given; and that primitively it has the two forms of Space and Time, as inclusive of its capacity for a universal receptivity. This merely envisaged, or put its content face to face with the consciousness, and as thus faculty for immediately representing gave its objects as Intuitions.

These sense-intuitions were then found to be given over to the function of Judgment, that they might be ordered into a consistent experience. This function of Judgment was found constituted with four primitive forms for ordering the Intuitions, distinguished as those of Quantity, Quality, Relation, and Mode; and these each subdivided into three subsidiary forms, making the well-known twelve Categories as the basis of the human Understanding. The intuitions become fashioned and connected in these forms as the chick in the egg, or the embryo in the womb, and hence they were named *à priori* Conceptions, as teeming with the intuitions given to them, from whence the ordered intuitions issue in their respective kinds and varieties of Judgments. Intuitions alone are blind; conceptions alone are empty; but the intuitions ordered in the conceptions become intelligible objects in a consistently connected experience.

And now, it is practicable, in the use of the *à priori* forms alone, to attain a universal scheme for all possible human knowledge. The form of Time may be taken as generally inclusive of all intuitions, and so put into the pure conceptions as to give the pure schemes of all possible Judgments. This process was known as " the Schematism of the Understanding."

First, the moments of time taken as continuous units and given to the category of Quantity, will come out in general schemes of its three varieties of Judgments. The moments connected in a series will give the scheme for Unity; the unarrested flow of the series will give the scheme for Plurality; and the exclusion of all limits to the series will give the scheme for absolute Totality. These moments, again, put within the category of Quality, will give the schemes for all its varieties of Judgments. The moments as content in the conception will give the scheme for Reality; as content withheld from the category, the scheme for Negation; and as zero, where content meets a void of content, the scheme for Limitation. But more important for the connections in experience is the giving of time to the category of Relation. The perduring time will give scheme for Substantiality; the successive time for Causality; and coetaneous time the scheme for Reciprocity. In this way may be an *à priori* determination of all possible kinds and varieties of Judgments the human intelligence can have in experience, for the actual forms must be ordered according to these *à priori* schemes.

It is, however, to be carefully noted that this is all from an analysis of empirical fact, and its *à priori* knowledge of experience is still *à posteriori* to the Intelligence that is to have the experience. The mind is a fact already made, and such a mind may so know; but some other order of mind may be constituted to know objects differently, perhaps directly contradictorily. The Critic of pure Reason has still no Absolute Reason for determining an absolutely and universally valid knowledge. The only speculative Reason recognized is a regulative Faculty, directing the search for the Absolute; but inasmuch as no possible form of the Judgment can furnish a content to its empty Ideals, so the critical Reason must ever remain barren of all cognition of the Absolute. Man may know all of sense-appearance, and in the understanding may order this in an experience which he knows as nature, but he can never know the supernatural.

And it is also to be noted, that some outer "thing in itself" must be assumed to give affection and content to the sense-receptivity, or the sense can give nothing to the understanding that it may connect in the judgments of experience. This "thing in itself" was to the last insisted upon as necessary to be assumed in thought, though not it, and only the impressions from it, could be brought within consciousness. As thought only it was known as *noumenon*, and its imparted representative was *phenomenon;* the latter was the object as known, the former could never become object.

A Second Stage of the Critical Philosophy, rejecting the *noumenon*, or "thing in itself," as confessedly beyond all consciousness, held it necessary to come to the knowledge of what knowing is, by a careful analysis of the knowing-process alone. It supposed itself to be truly the philosophy of the first stage more carefully analyzed, inasmuch as that had taught that the one "I think" must accompany every representation in consciousness, in order to preserve the unity of consciousness; but when the Philosopher of the first stage somewhat indignantly and very emphatically discarded this interpretation, and insisted on retaining the noumenon, the Philosopher of the second stage intrepidly took his own way, only insisting that it was plainly *the* way the first should have taken.

Its explanation, in a very general form, is as follows: The multitude have their sense-representations, and put them in a connected experience, but they do not reflect on what they have done, and hence have no clear knowledge of their process of knowing. The speculative philosopher does not rest in this consciousness of common experience, but by careful reflection upon it brings it to a new and higher consciousness, in which he comes to know how he has the common conscious experience. A record of what is attained in this philosophic consciousness is "the Science of Knowledge."

The common experience is under necessity, for the representations come from somewhere into the consciousness without being ordered by it; but the reflection of the philosopher is wholly free, for he turns back upon his common experience from his own motion altogether, and voluntarily controls his own thinking. On going up to the dawning of any of his representations in consciousness, he finds them to have been dependent on conditions which do not come within consciousness, and reflection is cut short, for he finds nothing further to turn back upon. But where *reflection* can *know* nothing, philosophic *contemplation* of the rising representations in consciousness can cognize in them their determining conditions. The knowing is beyond proof; back of all data in consciousness, even below consciousness itself; and yet a knowing absolutely sure and valid on which all conscious perceiving and logical proving must themselves rest for their validity, and which will subsequently manifest itself as the affirmation of Absolute Reason.

We must not lose sight, that the end of the Critical Philosophy is the attainment of a complete theory of knowledge; and that as knowing is an activity, the philosophy takes the subjective stand-point, and seeks to determine the method of activity in the subject knowing. There may or may not be outer things; that is here no matter in question; if there are, and they are known, they must be known by the activity of the subject knowing; and whether outer things give their representation, or some other agent put them within the subject, it is still all the same that the active subject alone can know them. When, then, the philosopher reflects on some conscious experience, he finds intuitions there present in consciousness, and which come and stay there without his ordering, and yet they could not appear to him without his activity. A dead inactive consciousness could not envisage, and thus the activity must have been in order to the envisaging; and this too beneath the consciousness, for the appearance is the last which any reflection can go back to in the consciousness. Conditional for appearance in consciousness, was some previous agency envisaging it. That activity must have

its law, or method of envisagement, already in and with
it, or no ordered experience could be in consciousness; and thus conditional for conscious experience,
must there be an activity with its possessed method
or law. Rational contemplation cognizes that, on the
necessary principle of " the sufficient reason," a cognizing activity and its possessed law must already be.
This is solely activity; living movement; having permanent essence and identity in its law of working,
with no other substantiality; and this is actual and
real, and the only reality which the speculative contemplation can recognize. This is the true self, or
ego, not yet conscious of its own being. The philosopher has cognition of it in contemplation, but it
has not yet come to itself. The philosophic consciousness states it as already a doing; a deed-act, since
its very essence is methodical activity; and in it we
have the ego equal to self; ego = ego.

The ego's method of activity is self-limitation; defining its own activity, and thus terminating itself
in that which is not-self; the ego oppositing to itself
a non-ego, since no intelligence can be without distinction, or limiting its activity in that which is
some other. And in this the philosophic contemplation posits a non-ego not = ego.

The waking consciousness has in this a vague
recognition of self and something other; and one
more step completes the process. The confusion
now is, that two opposites, ego and non-ego, strive
for admission, and neither can be in consciousness

without the other; and they are opposites, and it must needs be, as would seem, that one exclude the other. The necessary method of the activity is here counter-movement from each side, and then the ego limits the non-ego, and the oscillation or return movement gives the non-ego limiting the ego. They are both now in full consciousness, discriminated each from each. The ego has found itself distinct from all that is not itself, and henceforth its activity is clear conscious agency.

When, in the full consciousness, the ego is taken as limiting itself in the non-ego, the occasion is given for the science of knowledge in its Theoretic Part. The philosopher sees that all the work is by the one real activity, and that the non-ego is but a self-separation or reduplication of the ego, and the product of its essential method in self-limitation. The common unreflecting consciousness takes the ego as subject, and the non-ego as object, and holds them to be distinct in being, and the latter as external to the former. The philosopher thus, knowing the truth of the higher consciousness and the illusion of the lower common consciousness, can expound them both, and has in his contemplative position full opportunity to give a record of the entire process of Theoretic Knowledge.

When, on the other hand, the ego is taken as limiting the non-ego by itself, the occasion is given for the science of knowledge in its Practical Part. The philosopher sees that in the being of the living activity with its essential law, there must be a prompting as a claim, or self-behest, to work out its whole method; and that what it thus should do, it can and spontaneously will do; and thus that, which potentially is in the ego, will become actually a reality from the ego; and nature, and society, and state regulations must follow in their development. But still, with all the practical reality, it is a real within, and not external to, the ego; and illusive as all is to the common consciousness, the philosopher cognizes the whole in its truth, that the knowing can have nothing outside of its own activity.

The reality of the world came from fulfilling, that is, realizing the essential law in the ego, and is thus the product and creation from this essential moral order; and this eternal Moral Order is the eternal God; creator, and governor of universal experience. There is nothing which does not "live, and move, and have its being" in this essential, eternal Moral Order. We can apprehend none other, be comprehended by none other, and truly need none other God.

A necessary inquiry was left here unanswered. The philosopher stands outside the common consciousness, and contemplates it as a panorama before him. Is the philosopher Absolute Ego? May there be many Absolutes? or is there an absolute ego inclusive of every ego and non-ego?

A very ingenious and elaborate speculation was here introduced, and held the Absolute to be essential activity in an indifference-point between subject and object, and with the All potentially in itself in that point. As a living energy, the Absolute discedes from the point, projecting itself each way, and becoming on one hand subject and on the other object; the subject and object thus standing to each other in consciousness as the two opposite poles of the one living energy — they identical in the Absolute, and the Absolute not in consciousness; but when projected as opposites, they were made distinct and definite in the consciousness, while the Absolute still remained beneath consciousness, and could be recognized only in an "Intellectual Intuition." The law or method of activity is essentially intelligent, the Absolute having the Universal in its grasp originally, then disceding and distinguishing into subject and object, then harmonizing or identifying the distinctions as subject and predicate in a judgment. There is thus the potential All in the Absolute, and by the perpetual system of thesis, antithesis, and synthesis, this is successively developed into the subjective and the objective, which are but two modes of view from opposite sides of one and the same life-energy, and of which there can be no more than two fundamental sciences, viz.: The Philosophy of Mind, in the self-consciousness of the subject; and the Philosophy of Nature, in the life and movement of the objective world.

But with all the enthusiasm which the brilliancy of this "Identity system" kindled in its many disciples at its first announcement, it soon fell outside the onward flow of speculative thinking, and fixes no distinct stage for itself in the continuous movement of the Critical Philosophy. The march went round it, and did not take this up into it. If the Absolute be one, how differentiate into the relative? If it could effect this, it must be at the expense of itself, becoming a *neutrum;* and even if held to be self-active, in distinction from an Absolute Substance, what advantage could come from this, since the Activity must be self-destructive? The piquant presentations of these weak points effectually excluded it, as a starting-point for attaining any advanced position. Such an Absolute, it was said, could give no reason for itself, but "came as if shot from a pistol." It was merely an occasion for identifying subject and object, and so "only as the night, in which every cow looks black." The same self-opposites perpetually returned to identity, "as if a painter took only opposite red and green to blend into all colors." The Author himself frequently modified his starting-point, and finally assumed for his Absolute a free personal Will.

A third Stage, however, was soon attained by a speculation from a more profound principle, and carried to a more comprehensive result. So far as pure thinking is concerned, this last speculation leaves little else to be done, and little also of itself that needs to be done over. Its method of graded movement in the subjective ego is much after the manner of the second stage, and yet the movement begins and concludes quite differently from the second or the first stage. It does not begin with a finite ego in common consciousness or philosophic contemplation, but the movement from the start is of the Absolute itself. A preliminary analysis of consciousness attains an absolute thought-process, from which, as *causa sui*, the dialectic may begin thought and consummate all thinking. The process, moreover, is of a logical instead of a moral order; the logic developing into ethic by the inward interest of systematic completeness, and not the pressure of duty. And still another point of difference obtains: Instead of the philosopher contemplating the process from the outside, and thus knowing objectively the subject knowing, it puts the organ within the process, and sees the entire consciousness in its own transparency. A very condensed statement of the whole will here be given.

The preliminary analysis above mentioned, or rather a traverse of the whole movement in consciousness, is known as the Phenomenology of the Spirit. It takes the immediate sense-appearance, and in close scrutiny finds perpetually perplexing contradictions arising, the explanation of which carries the process after truth to successively higher and more comprehensive attainments. Every new statement of truth is seen, when examined, to have its remaining difficulties requiring fuller elucidation. An outline of this chase of truth through consciousness is as follows : —

When we attentively examine sense-appearances,

seeking to know just what truly is and abides in the consciousness, we find all else passing away but a permanently abiding " this " in the appearances ; and a little further care finds that with a permanent " this " there is also an abiding "there" or a "now." Thus the immediate appearance may be a man, and yet anon the man has passed out, and a house, and then a tree, &c., appears in consciousness; and yet of all there was a permanent "this here," as *this here* man, *this here* house, &c. And so, again, the immediate may be night and pass away, and the immediate is then morning, then noon, &c. And yet in all the passing there has been a perpetual "*this now*" night, "*this now*" morning, &c., standing in consciousness. The "*this here*" or "*this now*" has been the true which the consciousness has kept while the appearances came and passed away. And yet the " this," here or now, is not the essentially true, for a further careful scrutiny observes that there is no " this " except as *I* behold it. The " this " means nothing but as in *my* consciousness, and the " *I* " is the essentially true for the immediate " this."

And still again, when we closely observe this *I*, we find it continually passing from appearance to appearance, and standing under them as the mediate in consciousness, so that the appearances are no longer *im*mediate, but are nothing except through the medium of the *I*. The true, then, is not an immediate beholding, but a *perceiving*, or taking through a medium. We have thus, in chase of the true, in this third scrutiny, gone quite over from immediate consciousness into another sphere, which gives the true reflected in a medium, and have thus passed quite through the *First Phase* of knowing, which is named that of Common Consciousness.

In passing over from Common Consciousness to reflected knowledge of the understanding, we stand at once in this position : knowing the ego as under all the appearances, and knowing them as only reflections from the ego, and so in the Judgment they are qualities in the substance or effects in the cause. They are the reflection, or other side, of the ego itself, and could not be in consciousness but for the ego, and so the ego could not be in consciousness except for them. And this is true both for what the common consciousness may deem outer or inner experiences, material qualities or mental exercises; for we now understand them to be alike reflections from the one ego. The ego is continually turning the reflection from side to side, for it cannot keep either in consciousness without the other, and it cannot have both at once as the true. This struggling, see-saw mode of knowing wants a more stable standing, and the ego is forced to find a point in which it may be conscious of itself without dependence upon its representations. Watching carefully the reflections from the two sides of itself, the ego notes the subjective to be the active force which holds all the representations, and the true essential Activity, while nature is but its reflected *alterum;* and herein the ego knows itself to be lord of nature.

And yet this control of nature is not satisfying, for there is ever a colliding with and conditioning by nature, and not complete freedom from the necessities and obtrusive interferences of nature. The logical interest prompts the process onward to the point of full liberty. This cannot be in the communings of the ego with nature, and only of like with like. Historically, the ego enters into communion with other egos, and all come thus to recognize both themselves and each other. Each knows his own freedom and acknowledges the freedom of others, and thus the ego comes to complete self-recognition, and passes wholly through the *Second Phase* of knowing, termed SELF-CONSCIOUSNESS.

The ego now knows itself in communion with other egos, and all the sympathies of social life come within consciousness. Still the satisfactorily true is not fully reached, and the interest of logical completeness persists in the traverse. Ego opposes ego, and the freedom of one encroaches on the freedom of all, and the true point of social equilibrium and stable peace is in the harmonizing individual will to the universal, and the one will in all is the only true for the consciousness. The atomic egos now dwell in the universal, and the Absolute Ego has the knowledge and consenting purpose of all wills in his. All nature and all humanity are now one in the Absolute. He knows himself as having all thinking and all thought in consciousness, and gazes steadily and eternally on pure Truth. This is the *Third Phase* of knowing, termed the UNIVERSAL REASON.

The Phenomenology thus terminates in a *causa sui*, which in consciousness is also *causa omnium.*

Now, he who has traversed the knowing-process of the Phenomenology, comprehends what he has done, and has an interest in taking the complete Idea attained, and seeing percur from the start *à priori*, the whole process he has been traversing *à posteriori.* He knows that every enterprising mind must also be interested in such *à priori* process of knowledge. He can now set the whole before all such earnest thinkers, and make the Idea he has gained dialectically work out for them all subjective and all objective knowledge, and finally all self-knowledge, and thereby present a complete and pure Science of Logic. He may then take the logical objective and thoroughly dissolve it into its elements, and therein present a pure Science of Nature. And then, again, he can take the pure Intelligence from Nature, and give it in all its stages from militant to triumphant, and thence on to absolutely regnant and sole originant of all thinking and knowing, and therein a pure Science of Mind will be presented. And of this it is which the Third Stage of the Critical Philosophy has essayed the accomplishment.

But while the speculatist who comprehends the Phenomenology knows that the possibility of all this is in the Idea, his logical interest induces to the putting aside the results of previous study, and permitting the Idea to work out its own fulness after its method, while he absorbs himself in the movement, and, with no forecasting, sees this rational Idea in progressive development. The record of such consummated development will be the Science of Logic.

This Idea, attained in the Phenomenology, we here take and put ourselves in it, even make our mind identical with it, and become clearly conscious of what it does. We before called it *causa sui et omnium*, but only for the sake of a statement; while, in fact, any statement in words must be a misstatement, for the Idea is comprehensive of all substance, cause, and universal thought, as their independent source. It is in itself the pure activity knowing, and in which process we are to see how all knowing is and must be; and we can best describe it as *the knowing activity in its Idea*. As ideal knowing, it is pure thought-agency originating thought, while thought yet is not.

The Idea has Being in its most void abstraction. It is, and that is all which can be said of it; and this is as if we had said it is nought; for it has no predicate we can connect in a judgment with it. We see that it and nought are the same; and yet in that seeing we see the Idea already in action, and our mind the seeing organ within it, and what we have to do is just to note what comes of the movement. We learned its method in the Phenomenology. It is, that it may become universal knower, and is thus necessarily a dialectic in attaining the end of its activity. All Affirmation is also Negation; and the negating of the negation is a more full Reaffirmation; and such is the rhythmical movement through the whole process. With the simple affirmation there is also a negation which distinguishes, and then the negation is itself nullified, and the distinction thereby brought to a higher unity. The movement is therefore in a perpetual tripartite gradation of thesis, antithesis, and synthesis; threefold in each step, three steps to each state, and three states to each successive stage; and then the two last stages are taken separately from the logical cycle, and made to round themselves in the consummated sphere of Absolute Knowledge. The content posited with each step is carried virtually along through all the succeeding,—"suppressed," i. e., pressed under and kept within the following gradations,—and thus the knowledge augments with each removal. But we again caution not to forecast, and only note as we move; we are here to forget everything, and begin knowing.

The Science of Logic.

Our intellectual organ is in the Idea, and yet knows nothing of it; but a glance first gives its pure *being:* we cannot say it is this or that, for it is utterly predicateless, and the same as nought. We can say nought is, as well as we can say pure being is; and in saying either we say just as much and as little for one as the other. There is no predicate to finish a judgment for either. But the Idea is already moving and merely determining without stating, and as yet the action is *simple determination.*

Being.

The determining movement passes into a separating, or to and from, movement between being and nought, and the synthesis in the oscillation is a limitation, in which there is a coming combination of the two that is simply *becoming*, and thus an entering into the state of —

1. QUALITY. — The Unity in the becoming separates itself, in the swing of being and nought over their mutual limitation respectively, and there is interpenetration, which, like the blending of pure light and abstract darkness that alone are invisible, has become a curdled something for incipient predication, and we can say of it, " this here," or " this now," and is a first step in qualifying, as simply *existence*.

The Analytic movement, again, distinguishes the elements in existence, as " being " and its " alterum ; " and their synthesis is the negation of their limit, or finitude, between them, and affirming infinitude ; which unity in a third somewhat is existence which has inner but not outer determination, and is a second step in knowing, as Being-*for-self*.

The analysis of being-for-self is its inward unity annulled into the elements of unit and void, for the negating movement, in annulling inward limitation, everywhere distinguishes and expels the elementary elements, while the reaffirming movement every-where condenses and attracts them, and the one being-for-self has its inner quality sundered into many, and thus quality becomes quantitative, and in this third step goes completely over into another state which is —

2. QUANTITY. — Thus far we have taken the tripartite movement *seriatim* in the steps, and through the three steps to the new state; but as we are not here teaching, and only outlining the speculation, we may henceforward particularize less, and generalize in a more rapid movement.

The Idea has now being no longer pure, nor merely qualified, but holding in itself finitude and infinitude, repulsion and attraction, and thus competent both for self-diremption and self-identification, the synthesis of which is Quantity; the many in the one. The one movement through the many is continuity; and the many checking-in the one movement is discretion; and the synthesis of the continuous and discrete is Quantity *in general.*

Quantity in general with a limit is *quantum;* and the quantity in general may have infinite quanta, and the multiplicity of quanta is *number.* A quantum outwardly determined is extensive; and innerly determined is intensive; and the intensive quanta of an extensive quantum numbered is *degree.* The intensive degree qualifies the quantity, — as the degree of cold qualifies ice, or the degree of heat qualifies steam — and such qualified quantity is the Idea in a higher state as —

3. MEASURE. — The relation of an externally determined quantum to its internal degree is Measure; and is thus the relation of the same to itself on its different sides, or of its inner self as referred to its outer self. The measuring movement may pass on beyond its limit, and be measureless — or it may withdraw indefinitely within the limit, abolishing its degrees — and in either case it loses itself; but the specific ratio of inner degree to extensive quantum measures itself. Its determined inner refers itself back to its outer, and thoroughly and exactly qualifies the quantity and specifies the thing. Quality and quantity become identical in the thing, and being is suppressed beneath its own reflection. There is no more immediate apprehension, but mediate reflection; and the movement passes from the stage of pure being as perceived, to reflected being in the judgment, and we now have Being in the higher logical stage as —

ESSENCE.

In this stage, the Idea has taken all determinableness of being in unity *within* the Idea; and the movement is necessarily henceforth reflective, and in perpetual change from side to side. Viewed psychologically, it is the working of the understanding with sense-apprehensions.

As mere Essence, it is source for reflecting; and in which reflecting and reflected are identical. The Essence as one must yet exist as twofold. The Antithesis may be of many varieties, and yet if one side of the antithesis be, the other must also be. They are such as cause and effect; substance and accidence; matter and form; positive and negative, &c. The common understanding holds them as *different* existences, and thereby logically annihilates all existence in contradictions and absurdities. They can only be as complementary in the *same* essence : and hence the simple essence, as source for reflection, is the *potential for all existence.*

But the possible reflecting is also the necessary reflecting; for the essence can be only in the reflection. The cause is not, except as going into effect; the substance is not, except in its accidence, &c. This necessity of reflecting is Force and its Manifestation; the cause appears in its effect; and the Idea moves the essential into its further state as the *phenomenal.*

But in reflection essence and appearance are reciprocal. The effect must be as its cause, and the accidence as the substance; and thus both must be in the hand of an Actual which grasps both in one; and in this the Idea has gone over into the higher state as *actuality;* in which all reflection is " suppressed," and the movement carried over into a third stage; and as simple actual it can be nothing other than the thought-process in its Idea, whose movement we have been all along absorbingly contemplating. We have thus clearly attained, and pass over within the still higher stage of—

The Idea.

The Idea has universal essence within itself as a self-containing and self-contained whole, with all its particulars indiscriminate and unformalized, except as in their logical law; and is thus *subjective Idea.* The movement then differentiates and successively "suppresses" the differences, as mechanical distinction in molecular exclusion and inclusion — chemical combination by annulling the complemental elements in a third thing — and teleological construction by adaptations to purposed design; and is thus *objective Idea.* From this, the movement carries the Idea into spontaneous activity as Life, intellectual activity as Cognition, and voluntary activity as Will, which is the knowing itself as the good, and producing itself into the Eternally good, and thus completing and resting all thought in Absolute Good, as the *Idea in its Identity.*

In this the Science of Logic is completed, and the finishing of this is really the consummation of the philosophy; for the logic has carried out the full cycle of all thinking. The Second Part, or Science of Nature, is but taking up anew the Objective Idea, and with minuter precision purifying Mind from its otherness in matter, and therein dissolving nature wholly into Intelligence; and then taking the Subjective Idea, and more purely sublimating Mind through social Law, Art, Religion, and pure Philosophy, to Absolute Reason, as the permanent gaze upon open truth itself. In this way the speculation has given to itself the figure of a full ensphering rather than of a progress circling into itself; but its entire wealth lies permanently invested in the Absolute Good, as the Idea in its own Identity.

The comprehensive inquiry we make then is, What is the intrinsic value of this Absolute good? The answer may be fairly accorded, That it is the entire compass of all knowledge, so far as the *subjective process* of knowing is concerned. The most searching criticism will find scarcely anything, perhaps utterly nothing, to object to it as a process complete of the science of *thinking*. And granting that, is giving to it all it asks. It never proposed to itself the doing of any more, but denies that anything more can be done. All knowing is but thinking; and all the real which thinking can get is the thought it posits. In the Phenomenology it begins with the immediate objective, but it soon excludes from itself all but the mediating movement, and finishes with the thought of an actual moving, which is itself subject to nothing but the necessity to a perpetual counter-movement. And in the Logic, it begins with the pure being in activity, and finds no other object but the otherness given in its own antithetic movement. To the thinking subject the posited thought is object, and a seeming outer or other than the subject; but the completed movement expels and explains the illusion, and we know that every object has been but some image reflected from the subject. The Reason has been fairly recognized, and set to watch the thought-movement, and thoroughly expounded the whole process of thinking; and then the speculation affirms there is no other knowing. And now what is it worth, intrinsically, as philosophy of *knowing overt realities?* The only true answer is, It is worthless; for it is not such knowing. It thinks, and *seems* to know; but in knowing that its thinking is but a seeming, it makes all knowing empty.

The Universal is in, and for, and brought out by, the Absolute thinking-process only; and the inclination, or force, or obligation, or will, which the Absolute knows is solely the prompting as an inner subjective logical law. The objects, with their space and time, can be in common for no other personality than solely for the subjective thinker. The Absolute is as the Oriental Brahm, thinking alone as he gazes silent and absorbed into his own body; and this body, as Universal nature, is but the reflex of this silent spontaneous cogitating. Here is all the being and knowing possible, according to this philosophy; and it cannot long satisfy. Even if our common conscious knowing be but an illusive seeming, it has many persons, with their common objects, in a common space and common time, which no mere subjective thinking can account for; since thus there is but the one thinker, with the objects and their one space and time solely in *his* consciousness. That Reason which has so wonderfully projected this transcendental *thinking* is competent, rightly applied, to real objective *knowing,* and therein attaining positive things as well as its own posited thoughts. Philosophy has not a comprehensive Science of Knowledge, till it knows a personal Absolute Creator, and an overt Creation as an expression of his thought held in stable reality by his will.

CHAPTER II.

REASON COMPETENT TO KNOW AN OUTER CREATION.

Speculation cannot rest short of thorough insight and complete comprehension. So long as facts anywhere merely appear, and are arranged according to experience only, the thoughtful mind will wake the inquiry, How the fact came? And why thus, and not otherwise? It will not suffice to explain why the appearance has such a seeming to us; the mind must come to know the real in the appearing, or its speculative inquiry will be irrepressible. Nor should any one choose it should be otherwise. The most earnest and untiring speculation is never dangerous if kept within the light of reason; but the most dangerous delusions and the most hopeless contradictions arise from the attempt to bring speculative truth within the conclusions of the logical judgment. Deliverance alike from scepticism and credulity, and reverence for God, and trust in his Revelation come only from the cultivated use of human reason. The deepest want of the most sceptical age is knowledge guided by reason. The first inquiry, then, is, What is, distinctively, reason-knowing?

1. THE ESSENTIAL PROCESS TO THOROUGH AND COMPREHENSIVE KNOWLEDGE. — The Sense has various organs which may all at once present their manifold content. This must be separately distinguished, and the distinctions accurately defined, and we thus have distinct and definite particulars appearing in consciousness, and known as phenomena. So far is sense-knowing, and here knowledge in sense stops short. It is confined to the particular appearance, and never attains the intrinsic essence nor the connected relations. The content in mass has been wrought into separate particulars, and they are in the mind's grasp as a manifold of disconnected appearances. The Sense-function may, therefore, be known as *the apprehension* of particular phenomena.

In reflecting on our sense-experience we note that the varied phenomena have appeared in groups, and that certain particulars have ever appeared in each other's company ; and that in other cases appearances have been consecutive in an invariable order, and we sort and arrange our mingled appearances, into the aggregate communities and consecutive series, as we have been taught from former experience. We come to think each appearance in the common group to be

an attribute of the aggregate whole, and each sequence a link in the perpetuated series, and so we
conclude the aggregate to be a common thing with
so many attributes, and the series a connected order
of established sequences; and herein the Understanding judges each to stand in identity with the common
whole, and makes each particular a predicate of the
whole as the subject. But as thus far the Judgment
is only in accordance with the facts given in sense-experience, and as the particulars have only invariably
appeared in such groups and sequences, there is no
known ground in which the attributes inhere, and no
known source to which the sequences adhere, and we
cannot verify our assumed identity of subject and
predicate in our empirical Judgments. It is mere
logical classification after the order of experience,
and at the most is the probability of Opinion with
no certainty in the logical conclusion. The Under-
standing-function may thus be known as *the sorting
of all phenomena according to the logic of Experience; or, in short, the *logical Judgment.*

By an insight of these grouped and consecutive
appearances, we attain the substantial ground and
the efficient source, which necessarily and inherently
shut the phenomena together in their respective com-
munions and series; and we therein come to know,
not merely in reflection that our experience has
been in such invariable communion and succession,
but that with such grounds and sources the experience could not have been otherwise; and that the

appearances in experience have been determined in conditions lying back of all experience. It is only in the possession of a faculty competent to such insight, that we can give validity to any Judgment, and make any logical conclusion thoroughly clear and completely comprehensive. Such is the faculty of Reason; and we may know its function as *the comprehension* of universal experience.

Here are the necessary and invariable steps in the process of knowing real existences. The Sense apprehends distinct and definite *Appearance;* the logical Judgment gives probable conclusions as *Opinion;* the finite Reason, so far as it attains necessary and universal principles, secures *comprehensive Knowledge.* Modern Philosophy has mainly ignored the comprehensive function, and that now demands special and careful contemplation.

The merely sentient animal is competent to intellectual action, through the first and second steps of this process: the empirical consciousness in man circumscribes itself within these limits; but since man has been endowed with rationality, though he may not have come to recognize distinctively what reason is, yet will its possession necessarily drift him on to speculations beyond Sense-appearance and Empirical logic. The prompting enterprise of his reason is irrepressible; and the hopelessness of the effort is equally sad to contemplate, when it vainly strives to repress philosophical speculation as too adventurous, or to satisfy the philosophic impulse by any induction and classification of the phenomena of experience. Even could he find all phenomena, and their order of occurrence in universal experience, the deeper want of his being would be still unsupplied, and the more facts he had, the more intensely would he yearn to know what forces determined them, and what principles controlled them. But in the exclusion of rational insight, he can legitimately employ neither essential forces nor ultimate principles, for they are wholly supersensible.

What is thus unconsciously within the man is perpetually denying to him any rest in merely logical conclusions from empirical data. Finding facts and classifying them by experiment may for a time amuse, but never can satisfy. His unconscious reason forces him somehow to deem the relations of sense-appearances to be fixed connections; and though quite illogically, yet is he ever assuming that his qualities have substance under them, and his sequences have cause between them, and thus he surreptitiously makes of his experience a fixed nature of things. Nor can he stop in nature, for his unrecognized reason must rise above it, and assume a first Cause; and then will come in, what to his infidel philosophy must be, superstitious reverence and worship. He cannot refrain from talking about natural laws and spiritual responsibilities, though his philosophy most resolutely denies that he can know anything about either of them.

Such prompting to reach beyond experience is a sure witness to a supersensible endowment, and a perpetual rebuke to the philosophy which struggles hard to get on with no acknowledgment of it. We may refer to any one instance of clear and quiet conviction, and a satisfactory resting in the knowing, and we shall ever find that this satisfied conviction is in the insight of a controlling connection, by which the manifold is seized comprehensively in complete individuality. The sense and the understanding may perfect the appearances, and complete the external relations in a concluded total, and we may *opine* what the thing is, compared with other experiences; but we only *know* its essential nature, when we have looked through its intrinsic connection and found the indivisible tie which holds the many in its one comprehension. Any Object, as a Bird or a Beast, may have all its phenomenal parts apprehended, and these may be sorted and arranged in body and members exactly and completely; but we know the animal only in knowing the living sentient bond that thoroughly individualizes the organism. We put together and name a House, as an outside construction of brick and timbers, but we comprehensively know the house only in the design which runs through it to its end, and the forces which grasp the whole in balanced unity. The manifold in anything may appear in Sense, and be classified as a whole in the Judgment, but its essence is comprehensively known only by the insight of Reason.

Without here regarding the distinction, whether this inner tie be that of the thought after which the thing has been constituted, or that of the forces which have constituted it by equilibrating themselves in it, we will adduce some plain examples of comprehension beyond Sense and logical Judgment, and in which is attained a thorough knowledge that the insight of Reason can alone secure.

The manner in which we use and interpret *expressive Symbols* is directly in point to exhibit the work of the Reason beyond Sense and Judgment. Animal cries are the impulse of constitutional nature, and are given in the same way under the like conditions, at all times, by the same species. A Symbol is an expression outwardly of an inner sentiment, and the expression must be wholly ruled by the inner sentiment, and thus hold the very thought or feeling within it if it is to become in any way intelligible. So the national seal, or flag, expresses the sovereign will and pledge of authority, and these are so put in to the symbol that another can take them out and interpret them. But Reason alone can so put in or take out, and neither Sense nor Judgment can. And so of class emblems, party badges, or religious rites and ceremonies, — they are all symbols outwardly expressing an inner meaning, and such meaning Reason only can give or take ; and hence symbolic speech can be a mode of communication only between rational beings.

The Symbol may be in modulated tones addressed to the ear, or colored characters presented to the eye, and the organs may take exactly and completely all that sense can apprehend, and the judgment may select and arrange the elemental parts according to any empirical classification, but it is meaningless form and outer letter only till the Reason put in and take out the quickening power of Sentiment, which is the soul of the whole systematic arrangement. There is then no longer any separate particulars. Every letter is one in the word; all the words are one in the sentence; and all the sentences are one in the speech; and that which the insight of Reason alone reads shuts every part together in a single. The animal organs might apprehend the whole as well as the human; the rational being alone can have the thorough insight, and take the comprehensive meaning. It is another thing to the Reason than it can be to the Sense-experience; and to this it is a perfect unit, dismembered and so far destroyed if a single element be taken from it.

So, also, we may instance the manner in which the reason reads *mechanical Forces in outer objects.* The sense-experience attains in any machine all the particulars of form, arrangement, and movement; but no sense, nor judgment according to sense, can know the moving force which actuates the working engine. The Animal Sense may get the consciousness of nervous and muscular irritation and contraction in its own body and members, and may perceive its attachment to, and the turning of, any arranged machinery which it may be working; but the power itself which moves its living limbs, and passes over into the turning machine, no animal sense can ever seize and hold up to its own gaze in the light of consciousness. But the Reason-insight penetrates the moving parts of the machine, and even the living motions of the animal body, and knows the force that wakes and works, first in the animal muscle, and then in the arranged machinery. Till this force is thus seen moving and working in every part, the machinery is but a mass of particulars, each standing by itself and isolate, but that force runs through all the particulars and makes them one, and the whole is completely comprehended by it.

And so, moreover, the Sense-representation can give the rising and setting sun, and take in all the revolutions of the planets, and the arrangements of the visible heavens; and observations and calculations therefrom may fill out all the scientific plan of formal astronomy; but no observation nor deductions from experience can bring into consciousness the force which holds the stars in their places or turns them in their orbits; nor know what force is, or how it works. Force is beyond the sphere of Sense, and all the heavenly bodies are separate bodies, and in the apprehension can be grasped only in imaginary constellations. But the insight of Reason penetrates the Sense-appearance and knows the forces which determine them; that without the force the appearance could not be, and that with such forces the appearances could be in no other manner. The forces are themselves the essential substances and acting causes, and as the Reason has them, they necessarily connect the separate phenomena together, and all the moving worlds make but the single universe. The intrinsic connections hidden from all Sense, and leaving matter to be *understood* only as experience *puts under* one part some other part, make to the Reason the world of matter more than understood, even thoroughly seen and .perfectly *comprehended* in its essential and necessary unity. The parts are but one in the reciprocal forces which shut them all together.

The Beautiful in any work of Art, or the True in any Geometrical Diagram, or the Good in Moral Character, might here be appropriately noticed as what the insight of Reason only can reach, and by which the manifold in either sphere is completely individualized and instantly comprehended. There will, however, be frequent occasions in our further advance for the better contemplation of these and other instances of supersensible insight. It need now only be remarked that the insight of Reason as the last step in Knowledge has truly in it, as brought along and retained, the whole content of the two former steps. It may be either as a piercing glance, or a steady gaze, which seizes the whole at once in perfect comprehension. The tie that, in uniting, cancels the manifoldness, holds still within it all that is individualized by it, and thus the Reason knows all in the one glance which catches the comprehending connective. Reason-knowing is perfect, instant, comprehensive, knowing at a glance, and is also incessant-knowing as a constant gaze. Both the outer and inner are together in thorough contemplation, and thus the Reason has in its grasp Absolute Truth.

2. SPECULATIVE ABSURDITIES IN SENSE AND LOGIC BECOME TRUTH IN THE REASON. — All men have reason, though few distinctively and clearly recognize it. Hence the irrepressible curiosity that reaches after explanations beyond appearances, and also beyond any conclusions which may logically be deduced from them. In his ignorance of Reason, and its appropriate application to comprehensive knowledge, the man resorts to the functions of Sense and Judgment, of which he has conscious possession, and seeks to answer those questions of Reason by his Senses and logical Understanding; hence the large amount of profitless and delusive speculations which abound in every age. This remanding to Sense and Logic what belongs to a higher function necessarily induces contradictions and absurdities. The lower faculty has been set to work out the problems of a higher, and self-delusion and self-contradiction should be expected. The whole is cured, and absurdities avoided, while truth is established, by carefully using the right and excluding the impertinent interference of the wrong faculty.

The whole sphere of Antinomies in the conflicting of different intellectual functions has been by others formally stated, but we need here to give only some leading examples.

Motion, and Change in degree of movement, to the

sense, have logical absurdities. The law of continuity is inviolable, and forbids a leap over any degree in the increment or retardation of motion. How then may motion begin? and having begun, how cease? Its degrees in velocity must each be either indivisible or infinitely divisible ; but if the former, no passing them can make progress; and if the latter, then can there be no progress except in an infinite time. And so with any change in rate of motion; the degree can be neither increased nor diminished without the like absurdities.

So with any knowledge of Space or Time. They must be subjective in mind, or objective out of mind. If subjective, there must be as many spaces and times as conscious minds, for each has its own. But if they are objective, they must have properties distinguishing them from non-existences; and yet of space, its only property is extension, and of time it is succession. But extended existing space must have another space in which to be, and successive existing time must have another time in which to pass. Are they then non-existences except in our subjective minds? If so, then existing bodies may both be and change, with no existing outer space and time.

And so again, the being of Matter is an absurdity ; for if matter is, it is either compound or simple. If the former, it must be infinitely divisible, and its infinite compounds have still infinite spaces and times. If the latter, the simples are entities which have neither inner nor outer, neither upper nor lower sides, and

can occupy no portions of space or time. So again,
if matter exist, it must either be solid or have voids
within it. If the former, then it must be incompressi-
ble, contrary to the fact; if the latter, then matter
must act on matter through voids of matter, which
would be effects where there were no causes. Is,
then, matter to be made conceivable as points neither
solid nor void? Such unextended points could neither
hold together from within, nor resist from without.
The very existence of matter is full of logical contradictions, which no work of the understanding can
solve.

And equally so with the existence of spirit as other
than matter. If immaterial, and thus free and responsible, we have the contradiction to nature and
nature's laws, which nowhere give liberty, but bind
in conditions without an alternative; and if such
order may be broken, then universal scepticism must
follow. On the other hand, spiritual liberty must be,
or conscious obligation and responsibility cannot be.
Without freedom, law is tyranny, and the stings of conscience an atrocious constitutional perversion, and all
penalty is savage cruelty. The speculation of the
ages has here been in dialectical conflict, and any
help from sense or logic is altogether hopelessly impossible.

Finally here, if we inquire, Whence is the Universe? all logical attempts to answer must run into
hopeless contradictions. The universe has necessary
being in itself; or it has been self-produced; or it has

had some external Creator. If we take the first, then, as necessary being, it must have been ever necessary and ever unchanging in its necessity, while now nature is perpetually changing. If we take the second, then the actual has come from a potential; but to be potential for a universe must be to have inner causality on conditions, and so already an existence, and running at once into the former absurdity of necessary existence with changes. We have then only the third, and if created by another, it first existed in that other; and we have just the same dialectic to percur which we have just gone through from the start after universal nature's origin. The very attempt to find an origin logically involves the absurdity of a first which cannot stand except as a second. If we call the first a Beginner, a First Cause, a Cause in Liberty, we have already seen the absurdities involved in each. If we say, he is himself the Infinite, it is ,but putting all finites into a larger, and somewhere stopping on a largest finite. If we call him the Unconditioned, it will somewhere be a resting on a conditioner that has already conditions put within him. If at length we call him the Absolute, logically we must find him so little absolved, that is so much bound, that he must bind all below to him. The logical Infinite is merely an outside finite, the logical Unconditioned is but an upper conditioned, and a logical Absolute has in it already the bonds you arbitrarily cease to look for from beyond. In many ways, yea, in all ways which transcend nature's experienced connections, a dexterous logician may astonish by taking you to insoluble contradictions from the plainest experiences. But in all such cases, it is a logical legerdemain in which the conjurer is his own dupe. He has put empirical logic to the solution of problems which it cannot comprehend, and which by following he must misapprehend, and to any one whose insight makes clear the point of his delusion, there is not even amusement in looking upon the empty absurdities.

But the case becomes very different when we put these speculations in the light that reveals, and at the same time dispels, the delusion. The reason never so deludes, and once to let the reason reveal the source of the illusion is forever to dissipate it. We will give examples from both the Sense and the logical Judgment, and from the former, both that of a transcendental *diminution* and a transcendental *expansion*.

To sense, a central point can be no object, except as limited all about ; and a surface also can be no object to sense, except as having limits on both sides. Every object of place must have outside and inside, upper and lower; and every object in period must have beginning and ending, before and after. Nothing is known by sense, that it does not intellectually construct ; and so to sense-experience a mathematical point, and line, can be no objects. But to the reason, a limit is an object as truly as the limited, the centre as well as the area, the diameter and circumference of a pure circle as clearly as a material rod or ring. Reason has objects to itself, thus, which can be no objects of sense; and hence, when it has its own peculiar problem for solution, there should be anticipated only confusion and uncertainty, if it allow the sense-objects to be mistaken and used for its own. And from just such mistakes, the absurdities as above adduced take their rise.

Thus, for a first instance, reason may affirm, that there must be an Axle in the revolving cylinder which itself does not turn. And it may make it its problem to find and recognize such stationary axle. If, now, the constructing sense-faculty offer assistance and be permitted to delude by interposing its object, then must there occur absurdities in self-contradictions. The sense-object as axle of the revolving cylinder has an outer and inner side, and has been defined by an agency that has gone all around it. Hence the sense-axle must be itself a cylinder, and have still within it the axle which does not revolve. But every axle to sense, however far it may make analysis, must be a constructed object, and make necessity for an infinite divisibility, and thus introduce the absurdities of conflicting and unequal infinites. And to the sense, such proposition must have such self-contradiction.

But, if we will exclude all such sense-mistaking, and let reason alone work her own problem, there can occur no absurdities. Every diameter of every circular plane in the cylinder revolves about its mid-point, and on opposite sides of that mid-point the movements of the two portions respectively of all the diameters are in opposite directions each to each. The mid-point is a limit between opposite movements, and can itself have no movement; and as being the same for all the diameters of any one circular plane in the cylinder, it becomes a limit at which all the radii of that plane meet. So the contiguous points, limiting all the radii of all the circular planes in the cylinder, become a central line as axle to the cylinder, and which can in no part have any revolution. And now, this axle to the cylinder, as object for the reason, is a limit, and not a limited; it needs no diminution and can have none, nor can it open any occasion for introducing contradictory infinites. The contradiction came from the antinomy between sense and reason, and when the distinction of faculty is known, and reason is allowed to do her work in her normal way, there is no antinomy nor absurdity. And so with all the contradictory infinites that may come in, as above shown, in space, time, motion, and rest, &c., they never trouble except in the mistaking of a sense-limited for a reason-limit.

Thus, when we approach the infinite by a process of *diminution;* but a different absurdity occurs when we go after an infinite in a process of *expansion.* The solution keeps to the same rule of putting the right function to the execution of the proposed problem.

7

We may have an extending line and an enlarging circle, and neither can reach to limits which may not be surpassed. To the sense no object is definite till its construction is completed, and the longest line and largest circle may still be as infinitely augmented as the least. The point has no more an infinite expansibility than the largest circle, nor is it capable of infinite. extension any more than the longest line. The reason, however, can say of space, that there must be a whole which is inclusive of every part, and it may make it its problem to attain the knowledge of space as infinite, and therein know space to be an absolute whole. But if here there be allowed the interposition of sense-construction, and a mistaking of sense-object for reason-object, there must occur delusion and absurdity. The sense-object must be limited all about, and there can be no known space except as a line is drawn through or around it. The reason has space with no limits, the sense has space only within limits, and the confounding of objects so heterogeneous must involve endless contradictions.

But all possibility of such contradiction is excluded when the reason keeps its own object and does its own work. While, as an object of sense, space comes within consciousness with the construction of any object in place, and the space goes from the consciousness with the loss of the construction in place, and no space is known except as some space is limited, yet to the reason space itself is object, with no limits

in or about it. Reason knows Space itself as concrete
whole in itself, and every part adhering to its contiguous part with no possibility of sundering, and that no
part is movable from where it is, and transferable to
any other part of space. There cannot be the putting
of any more space into space, nor the taking of any
space out of space, nor the adding of any more on
to space, and thus there is no void of space to the
reason from within or from without. Space is a unit
to the reason, prior to any sense-construction of place,
and there can be no *extra* space which is not already
concrete in the one space. This reason-idea is the
true Infinite, excluding all finite. So soon as we
conceive of a sense-limited within space, we have
spoiled the infinite and put two finites over against
each other. Exclude all sense-place, and space itself
is one limitless, changeless absolute, having neither
contradiction, absurdity, nor mystery to the reason.
The finite is as irrelevant to the reason-object as is
the infinite to the sense-object. The contradictions
come from misappropriating objects and functions.
The reason works normally here, but the sense cannot here be employed without exposing its incompe-
tency in perpetual absurdities.

We next take an instance of logical connection in
Judgment, with its necessary absurdities, and the
removal of the same effectually by the normal use
of the Reason

The sense apprehends only the appearances, and
these separately and singly. When the logical judg-

ment would put them together in things and events, it must go according to the order of past experience, and the connection of the facts as found in experience must be taken by it as the order of nature. As the order has been found to be, such must be assumed as nature's law; and the future is to be expected to go on uniformly as the past has done, though no inner condition is known why the next event might not be contradictory, and violate the law. One substance must sustain another, and one cause must produce another, and there can be no conceived coherency save as one fact is interposed to support or draw another. But the reason may say that nature itself is a unit, and has all its balancing statics and working dynamics in its own being, and it may make it its problem to find its determined persistency in connection with its perpetual mutabilities.

If, then, the logical faculty be allowed to operate, the world must hold its rocks and mountains, and the elephant must hold the world, and the tortoise must hold the elephant, and thus onward. So also, the planet must control the satellite-revolutions, and the central sun must control the planetary revolutions, and a higher centre must control the solar systems; and we can have no alternative to perpetual interpositions with no ultimate. And so also with the series of conditioned sequences; the logic must leap from step to step with no final landing-stair. But if we exclude the impertinent logical interference, and let the reason do the work with its insight of conservative, correlative, and equivalent forces, the universe will stand in balanced stability, and move in complicated harmony, with no possibilities of disaster, nor absurdities of impossible expedients. Every part of the universal force pushes and pulls, just as *it* is pushed and pulled; and no part can be lost, nor stand isolate, nor tip unequally in any direction. The whole is determined from its own centre; and every substance has its stability, and every cause its efficiency, in its own place and in connection with the whole.

And here, if reason asks further for a Creator of this universal force, which is substance for all that stands and cause for all that moves, and excludes the logical faculty from interfering in the question, the answer will be both consistent and prompt; while if the logical faculty meddle in the matter, the whole is confounded with assumptions of a First cause, that has its necessitated conditions within it at the first, as truly as in any subsequent member of the series. The reason knows a Cause in Liberty; guiding himself by what he knows is due to his own dignity; and can thus begin and go out to an end in his own determination. And therein he is both originator and finisher of the work that shall most glorify and honor himself.

In all cases, the Reason has sufficient light in itself to guide in its own work, and eliminate all the absurdities of the meddling Sense and logical Judgment.

3. Distinction between knowing Thoughts and knowing Things. — Both science of Thought and science of Thing, are alike complete comprehension in reason, and thus both are true knowledge. But a prime difference between them is in this, that the science of thought is of that which is wholly within and essentially subjective, while the science of thing is of that which is overt and essentially objective. — One may have in thought a mathematical triangle or circle, and while the figure may condition other figures in subjective place and period, it cannot resist and react upon other figures themselves. I can put two equal triangles or circles to coincide in thought with each other, and the one will then be wholly lost in the other. All the energy is in the thinking, and no energy goes over into the thought to give to it any rigidity or stable consistency. And in the same way, one may have in mental conception any color or sound, and which may have its conditioning relationships of place and period with other conceptions, but the mere conceptions may be modified in any way among themselves with no mutual resistances and interferences. The conception has in itself no hard consistency, and all the energy is in the subjective thinking process, with none put over and persisting in the stated thought. — But when one has the plan of a house, or other complicated structure, in subjective thought, and he essays to put the plan in execution as a fixed thing, there is an energy other than the thinking demanded, even an

energizing which moves muscle, and applies hard instrumentalities in shaping and placing materials together; and only in overcoming the resistance in the material elements can the thought-out plan become an existing thing. The subjective thinking energy which made the plan has been supplemented by an executive will, whose energy has gone over into a controlling arrangement of resisting elements, and made them overtly to express the plan as now an existing thing. Subjective thinking-energy, supplemented by subjective willing-energy, has been put into essentially objective materials, and the product is an objective existence in common for all intelligences. — But still further, one may trace the growth of a grain of wheat from its first germinating to its perfect maturing, and while the insight of reason will detect a thought diffused through the organism of the plant, yet has not the subjective thinking put the ideal into the plant, nor has the subjective will supplemented the thinking and forced the component elements in construction, but an actual living germ has by its native energy built up the plant, and forced the component elements to their outer expression of the hidden idea, which the seed originally contained.

Here, then, are three different processes of thought, and all have the complete comprehension of their manifold parts in one, and are each thus a true knowing. The first has no other energy than the subjective thinking, and is *pure thought* only. The second has the energy of the subjective thinking; but another subjective energy than thinking, even an executive willing, must overcome the resisting energy already in the elements and arrange them according to the thought, and the product is an *artificial thing*. The third has the ideal thought as seen already in the object, and which has been put there by a power in nature itself that has built up the outer object by the inner working of its own forces, and is thus a *natural thing*. But while all these have true science, whether of thought or thing, inasmuch as all have the many comprehended in a single, yet can these objects be known as *created* only in a qualified sense, except in the last case, which is a true creation. The pure thought is a creation only as we say a creation of the imagination, or the creations of genius; the artificial thing is a creation only as a construction from created materials; but the natural thing, though in its generations a propagated thing, is truly a created thing, and all its energies of elemental material, and organizing instinct according to original type, are product of absolute thought and will first springing into being from the one All-creating source.

A stated thought, no matter how objectively it may obtrude itself upon the subjective consciousness, as in dreams, or hallucination, or prolonged reverie, is no created thing; nor should any logical process in positing its steps from stage to stage be termed a creating, since nothing is so produced and stablished that it can stand out from the subject thinking and become a common possession for other thinking subjects. A created thing has not only the imparted thought of the creator, but superinduced upon the energy thinking is also an energy imperatively willing the thought to stand in hard and rigid resistance to any encroachment. Only thus can the thought become essentially overt, and fill its place and period as in a common space and time for other beholders. The resisting energy must be in the thing and constitute its very essence, and not be merely the subjective energy of the thinking process. We can thus have no true knowledge of created things, except as we comprehend them in the very essential energies which constitute them; and we can have no true knowledge of their creator, except as in the things we see the thought the creator has put there, and also see this superinduced power that has fixed the thought in stable consistency against all aggression. It is not created thing without thought, for then it could be no object for intelligence; nor is it mere thought, for then it could not become common object; nor yet is it mere thought put into hard material, which would only be a new fashioning of old material; but it must be the creator's thought, fixed overtly for all by the creator's imperative will.

Other and beyond the science of thought, and the science of artificial thing, we have here the science of nature, as essential thing in itself, and know how we know the particular things of nature, and universal nature itself, as one thing. The manifold in Sense is sorted in the Judgment and comprehended in the

Reason, and is seen to have already an energy in possession and exertion which works the unity above and distinct from the thinking-energy. The dewdrop and the crystal have their expressed thought, but beyond. the manifested ideal in their formation is the essential force ensphering the drop and solidifying the crystal angles, and completing the things by an inner energy different from thinking. And in the same way of an inner force the worlds are formed, and all worlds made a universe; expressing a thought, but working out the expression by an energy that supplements all thinking. The mechanical forces in nature, and the organic forces in living bodies, work after an ideal; but their work is other than idealizing. The Creator has thought, but he has willed this into overt existence by an energy distinct from thought. A creator of realities is other than a thinker of ideals, and more than a former of material bodies, — even an author of matter itself.

CHAPTER III.

REASON KNOWS THE CREATOR.

ALL knowing takes the manifold in mass, distributes the particulars according to their sort, and comprehends them in a single individuality. The Sense, in common experience, takes the manifold; the Judgment puts the particulars into their classified sorts; and the Reason gets the inner connective bond which makes the sorted manifold a concrete individual. But we are now to know in the Reason only, and thus this invariable process of simple apprehension, and assorting judgment, and individualizing reason, is to be the work of reason exclusive of sense and logical understanding, and must necessarily be quite peculiar; and this peculiarity it is now the special design to notice.

In the Rational Psychology and the Introduction to the Rational Cosmology respectively, different methods were taken for attaining the Absolute Being; but with no expression of opinion concerning the comparative merits of either, a third method will here be taken to know the Absolute as Creator in the very being of Reason itself.

1. A CREATOR MUST BE INDEPENDENT OF ANY IMPOSED CONDITIONS. — Given an Acorn in its essential germ, and from experience we infer a preceding oak; and so also, given an Oak, and from experience we infer a preceding acorn. But experience finds nothing in either the acorn or the oak, which conditions the successions that experience has observed; and all that it can reveal is the sequence of acorns and oaks as a fact of as long continuance as the history of experience is recorded. It may call one prior and the other successor, but this will be wholly arbitrary, for nothing distinguishes in this respect the one from the other. Taking the oak and looking back, the acorn

has been prior; and taking the acorn and looking back, the oak has been prior. Experience cannot teach which is essentially prior, nor that there ever has been a prius, nor say why at all acorns and oaks succeed each other. It gives the bare fact of succession from its history, and explains nothing.

Experience under the promptings of a rational endowment, even while the distinctive characteristics of such an endowment are as yet unrecognized, will have put a somewhat between the acorn and oak, or in them both, which will have settled the conviction that the succession observed has by that somewhat been made necessary; and it may call that interposed somewhat the cause of the succession, and attempt, perhaps, thereby, in a *quasi* philosophy, to explain the fact of successive oaks and acorns. But in this restriction of all knowledge to experience, the necessary connective cause must be remanded to experience for its validity, and if admitted that no sense can bring it into experience, there must still be the supposition of some sublimated sense-object, which some finer and nicer organ might seize and envisage. But even if so attained, it would be only a fact found, that this sublimated somewhat succeeded one and preceded the other, and could explain nothing of necessary connection, and only add itself as a new item in the sequences which will need its necessary connection as much as the mere sequence of oaks and acorns.

And admit now, which we may hereafter present

for clearer contemplation, that the reason, as higher faculty, may by its insight into oaks and acorns know this somewhat we term Cause to be wholly other than any sense-object, and that it carries intrinsically with it an efficiency to make the one to come out of the other, this deeper reason-insight might then philosophically explain the necessary connections; but even that would only so far be expounding nature, and would be no knowledge of how such efficiency came into nature, nor could at all teach how oaks and acorns came into being, or any other objects in nature, that they should need necessary connecting causes. Even should reason be able to go further, and see in the oak or the acorn that which determined that this and not the other must be prior, this would not explain how that prior came to be, nor satisfy the reason, whether the prior were oak or acorn, that such determined prior made both itself and all the others. We should herein get the philosophy of nature, but should not by anything in nature so get the knowledge of nature's Creator.

An assumed *first cause* must still be conditioned cause, in the same way that an assumed first acorn must be conditioned to produce an oak and not a chestnut, or an assumed first oak must be conditioned to bear acorns and not chestnuts. What is to come from the cause must necessarily be already essential in the cause, and this as truly in a first as in any successor of the series. The question of creation is, How the first can begin to be? and if conditions are imposed upon it, it is creature, and not creator. And the same is true of *substantial being* standing under and conditioning the qualities. When the steam has been condensed to water, and the water again changed in congelation to ice, the respective qualities have been conditioned in their substances, and whichever way we follow the change, we must put under the new qualities the new substantial ground; but the question now is, How substance itself begins to be? If it have already conditions under it, it is created substance, and not creator of substance. Both in assumed first cause and first substance the conditions are already there, forcing us to go higher; but experience cannot transcend conditions, and hence no empirical data can give a creator in the conclusion.

2. THE FINITE REASON CAN FROM ITSELF KNOW THE UNIVERSAL. — With no sense-content, and no concluding in logical judgments from empirical data, the pure reason-knowing is solely from itself. Looking into its own being, it determines immediately from what it knows in itself what also must be conditional that other beings may be known. The reason-knowing is not looking on and around, but in and through, and thus is not Apprehension, but Insight. When sense-objects are given, it sees in them that space and time are conditional that they themselves may be; and when sense-objects are connected in things and their changes to a series of events, it sees in them that substantial and causal forces are conditional that such

ordered connections should be. But when no sense-objects are given, and no conditions of space and time or substantial and causal forces are determined by any insight, there is a sphere of knowing other than that which belongs to space and time, substances and causes, viz., a pure reason-sphere in which the conditions are attained solely by the finite reason having self-insight. The reason thus knows solely in reason's own light; and in this sphere it is that the finite reason knows the Universal Reason.

Finite reason standing alone in its own individuality has its peculiar measure, and so its self-insight has its peculiar clearness, compass, and systematic consistency, and so, too, each finite intelligence has knowledge peculiarly his own, and not another's, and wherein the knowing is relative to himself, and is not properly universal. Thus there is a good meaning in which mathematic or philosophy or spiritual truth is individual, and peculiar to each particular conscious insight. But there is a higher and equally valid meaning, which excludes all individual peculiarity, and in which there is but one mathematic, one philosophy, one truth for every rational mind. In such acceptation there is no particular appropriation, but the known truth is universal. Individuality stands in some other ground than the being of rationality, for there is one reason common to all humanity. Individual finite reason, looking into itself, and knowing its own peculiarities, is competent to see in itself also a universal; and to know that conditional for its valid knowing, besides the finite and relative reason which is its own, there must be a Universal Reason which is not its own, but only as it is common to all.

In this Universal Reason, the finite and individual reason can see, there must be the ground and source of all truth. Each mind's truth must have, for its validity in the knowing, that which is true in Universal Reason. Only in this universal can anything particular be stable. No individual reason can be allowed to stand indifferent to, and much less in opposition to, the Universal; for what is not positively for, is essentially against Universal Reason, and in that has become unreason, and must be everywhere repudiated and rejected by reason. But that any known truth stands full in the Universal Reason is sufficient for its validity. The last and highest reason for the validity of any knowing is, that what it knows is Universally reasonable. All demonstration is defective which is not carried back to its root in Universal Reason; and all testimony is insufficient to give knowledge to faith, till the testimony is seen to be squarely in accordance with that reason which is one for all. Individual mind thus knows the Universal mind; *that* it is; *what* it is, in attribute and essential perfection, though no finite can measure the fulness of the Universal. So it is that inspiration affirms we " know the deep things of God " by the spirit given to us. Not in that God-consciousness in which God is illumined to himself, but in our endowment of reason we see the being of the Godhead. The individual human knows from within himself the Divine Universal.

3. THE UNIVERSAL REASON IS A PERSON. — All complete knowledge involves the taking of manifold elements, separating and sorting them, and finally comprehending them in Unity. So the individual finite reason, if at all, must know the Universal Reason; and the finite may so know the Universal as to see in it that the Universal must be personal. The following successive positions, carefully and intelligently taken, will carry the insight from Reason in Universality to Reason as a Person.

Universal Reason must contain all elementary truth, and all assortments possible of the Universal Elements, and all consistent comprehensions of sorted particulars in Unity; and in this the Universal Reason has in possession all possible Ideas. The original Ideas are subjective in Reason, and so uncommunicated, and in themselves incommunicable.

In such origination of Ideas, Reason is essentially artistic, and cannot be satisfied with a solitary perpetual gaze upon its subjective Ideas, but must have a calm urgency towards expressing them. And also, in such origination, Reason is essentially good, and must have a loving interest in communicating the Ideas. Such urgency and interest must induce an ethical behest for their overt manifestation; and for this, Reason must itself be competent, or as unsatisfied it will become unreason.

8

An actual expression including communication of ideas involves both Idea set forth and Idea taken, and thus a reason-giving and a reason-receiving, and so there must be several rational beings, and each apprehending the Idea in common, and which alone can constitute a standing together in community. Intelligent recipients of the original Ideas must, therefore, be brought into being in the likeness of the Universal Reason, and therein competent to participate in the conscious possession of the thoughts of Universal Reason.

These severally existing intelligences cannot commune with the Universal Reason while the original Ideas remain in subjective secrecy, but the Ideas must be set forth in an existing, outstanding Universe; and while the intelligences must be in the image of Universal Reason, the stable existences must also be in the likeness of the original Ideas; and in this whole work we shall have the complex Universe in the two worlds of matter and of mind, in which Universal Reason has expressed the Ideas, and to which the constituted intelligences come in participation, and thereby the Universal Reason and the constituted intelligences may stand together in satisfactory communion.

The finite reason sees in such Universal Reason complete self-possession and self-sufficiency. All possible resources are within it, and it can be helped or hindered by nothing without. It stands to itself throughout in perfect freedom. No force can compel, no want can constrain, no master can coerce its movement. No necessity can apply to it a physical *must;*

nor authority impose upon it a peremptory *shall;* and
only the *ought,* as that which is due to its own dignity,
can prompt and guide its agency; and so its work is
not at all what it must, or what it shall, but solely
what it *will* accomplish. Such inner disposing of all
inherent possessing and outer communicating is WILL
IN LIBERTY; and the whole is comprehensively held
within its own law of freedom. Its spring to action
and its end of action are both wholly within itself, and
its being and doing is alone in its Eternal reasonableness. It summons its powers in requisition for its
own Excellency's sake, and sends them to the attainment of its own honor; and thus its own mandate,
sounding through its whole being, makes it eminently
and discriminatingly to be *Person.* In this view we
are henceforth to speak of Reason as *He* and not *It.*

4. THE PERSONALITY OF REASON IS ALSO ABSOLUTE.
— " He is before all things, and by him all things consist," and thus nothing outside of him can limit, constrain, or in any way impose conditions upon him;
and in this meaning it is that we say the Person of
Reason is Absolute. He is absolved from all coaction
from every quarter. The Universe depends upon
him, but has no reagencies holding him under any
duress. His absoluteness relates to a variety of
particulars which may be separately considered, according to their peculiarities. His *being* is absolute,
as wholly underived and independent. His *sovereignty*
is absolute, as amenable to no authority. His *agency*

is absolute, as beyond all force. His *blessedness* is absolute, as beyond all possible perturbation. We will subject these particulars severally to the insight of reason for its abundant confirmation. Carefully and clearly contemplated, the absoluteness of Universal Reason in these respects cannot have the shadow of a doubt.

1. *His Being is Absolute.* It is impossible to suppose a source from whence Reason should be derived. If Reason once was not, then only unreason was, and the only source whence Reason could come would be the absurdity of his origin from unreason. He cannot be supposed not to be. To say that reason is not, would involve the necessity that still reason should be, in order that the declaration might have any true meaning. To say that once He might not have been, is to suppose that his opposite must then have been; and the opposite of reason cannot be supposed without at the same time supposing reason as the determiner of what his opposite is.

Again, Reason is not on account of something else, nor by the help of something else, nor through the sufferance of something else. However others may be, or whether others be or not be, yet reason must be; for his supposed non-being is an impossibility, inasmuch as, if his non-being were affirmed to be true, this very truth would still confirm that he is. The truths which the light of reason gives are no products of power, but are independent of power, and are liable to no interference from power, and these truths which are beyond all power, and by which all power must be controlled, cannot themselves be but as reason also is.

We say, therefore, of the Universal Reason, that he is self-existent, not in the acceptation that his self makes his existence, but that being is so necessarily his that no applied power can make him not to be. Nor are these absurdities, from any supposition of the non-being of reason, the result of any logical illusion, for it is not logic that has at all been here in use, and only the insight of reason; so that the function of reason itself must be perverted to absurdities and contradictions before it can be admitted that the being of reason is dependent on anything. That there is reason for anything, yea, that there is reason for doubting everything, still leaves it impossible to doubt that reason himself is. The Absoluteness of the being of Reason is thus guarded on all sides by endless absurdities and impossibilities that he should not be. His appropriate name is, " I am."

2. *His Sovereignty is Absolute.* Absolute sovereignty does not imply arbitrary sovereignty. Sovereignty imports Authority, and this is the same as being authorized, or rightly founded. We cannot therefore say of the sovereignty of Universal Reason, what we have just shown of his being, that it is every way unlimited and underived; for that would involve the intrinsic absurdity of Authority unauthorized. Such an Absolute would admit of going opposite ways, and to opposite ends, and yet be Authority still; and

which can be nothing but the absurdity of Arbitrary Authority. Authority must be authorized; supported and justified by reason; hence of authority we cannot say, as we said of being, that Universal Reason is beyond all conditioning control. Still the sovereign authority is Absolute when it rests only in the being of reason himself.

A logical process to get ultimate Authority for Sovereignty would involve necessary absurdity; for it would derive Authority from a source that would still come from another, and no assumed last source could be ultimate. But the Universal Reason knows his right to reign in sovereignty from just what he is in his own being. Knowing himself, he knows it is his to be sovereign, and not subject. What he is, in his conscious intrinsic excellency, authorizes him to take the throne and hold the sceptre, and absolves him from all allegiance to any other sovereignty. He truly reigns in his own right, and cannot rightly alienate his sovereignty. Finite reason, superinduced upon sensibility, legitimately reigns sovereign over appetite; but legitmate as such Authority is, it cannot be said to be Absolute. The Supreme Reason must have absolute sway when the finite fails, and only where the finite is the same as the Absolute are they concurrent. The Supreme is ultimate, and thus an imperative that finds no outer source to give to it authority, and no higher right to take it away. The Supreme Reason has no sensibility to gratify, but a high behest to fulfil; and knowing what is due to himself, he is conditioned from within his own being, and absolved from all else; and such is Absolute Sovereignty.

3. *The Agency is Absolute.* No part, nor the whole of universal Force can act unconditionally. It cannot absolve itself from mechanical necessities. The equivalence of forces, and the conservation of force, determine that all motion must be as already moved, and in force there can be no first mover, as spontaneous originator of movement. All movement is conditioned to some previous motion. But the universal reason can begin action from himself. Without force, and even against force when force is, and thus wholly independent of all constraint, the reason can see in himself what is due to himself, and can start and guide his action accordingly. This inner behest, that the reason should act for his own worthiness' sake, or, which is the same thing, for ultimate reason seen in himself, gives occasion for action without another to move to action, and thus to put forth action that shall make both force and motion to begin. Action from a conscious inner claim is self-action; personal action; voluntary action; and when it can come from no higher claim than his own reason, it is Absolute Agency. Such action is purely spiritual, and such agent is Absolute Spirit.

4. *The Absolute Spirit is Absolutely blessed.* It is happiness to have a constitutional sensibility, and this sensibility gratified. But no happiness can be absolute. It depends on condition of constitution, and

congenial applications to it, and is thus necessarily a thing made, and must be as it happens to be made. Nothing of happiness can be properly blesseduess; much less absolute blessedness. Blessedness belongs to nothing but Reason, and is found only in the satisfying of the inward behest of reason. Gratified sensibility is happiness; fulfilled imperative is righteousness, and as a fixed disposition it is holiness; and steadfast holiness may be known as conscious Blessedness. It has its own approbation, and the known approbation of reason everywhere.

But human blessedness is conditioned and limited many ways. Even when the holiness regulating appetite is persistent, the bliss has no tranquil security. The sentient appetite tends to excess, and must perpetually be watched and guarded. Such a militant state cannot have unalloyed blessedness, even in persevering holiness. Even as angelic spirit, with no sentient craving, there is still the opening for temptation, from spiritual excesses and iniquities, to ambition, pride, envy, hatred, so that an angel must guard his virtue and perpetually rule his spirit, and can never reach a state of unasking tranquillity in his holiness.

Not thus with the Supreme Spirit. He has perpetual integrity, security, and serenity. There is to him no possibility of assault from without or from within. Nothing better to him can be than fulfilling the claims of reason; truly glorifying himself. He, therefore, "cannot be tempted of evil." He cannot turn to any good that shall to him be so good as the maintaining of his integrity, and thus ever maintaining and ever being reason. He is above all possible conflicting interferences, and is, therefore, Absolutely serene and tranquil in holiness.

The only conceivable source for disturbance is in the sin and suffering of his creatures. His revealed representation of himself is as if affected thereby disagreeably; even as grieved, pained, and angry. These representations are in conformity with human conceptions in like cases, but do not betoken divine infirmity and distressing inner commotion. Every feeling is still prompted by reason, and in its reasonableness has security for unalloyed blessedness.

5. THE ABSOLUTE CREATOR IS TRIUNE. — The Absolute Reason knowing the universal in his thought, and therein possessing the Universe in Idea, has three distinct agencies in operation. The universal has been taken in its manifoldness; has also been separately arranged according to its elementary sorts; and the sorted particulars have been further grasped in unity. There can in no other method be comprehensive thought, for this process is that of rational comprehension. Essentially in reason there are three subsistent agencies, and these unite in giving to reason its own determinations, and the very essence of reason is this threefold acting. But so projecting the Universal Plan, or originating the Universal Idea, is not properly the creating of the Universe. The

Idea must be in the Creator preliminary to his creating, but the expressing the Idea in overt, stable consistency, is alone the proper creating work.

Strict simplicity can neither think nor will. Thought involves comprehension of ordered elements, and Will involves disposition relative to rational ends, and so neither thinking nor willing can consist with pure simplicity. We cannot think of, reason itself cannot know, a thought or a will which is solely simple. If, then, the agency which plans an ideal universe cannot be in simplicity, more emphatically may we say that the agency which is to give rigid reality to the Idea cannot be simple. The agency must be several, and the products must have their severality; and yet the agency must also be joint as well as several, and the product must be a unit of severalities. We can bring neither a creating work nor a created world into any mode of being known, except as in the creating and creation there be a manifold in Unity. And already in the essence of Absolute Reason we have found the severality and the unity of Agency which are necessary conditions for the creative work. The attainment of the Universal Idea in its comprehension required three agencies, and the setting of the idea into fixed reality will demand the same agencies.

The Idea is already in actual thought, and the Will which perpetually maintains the actual thought, as the archetype of the universe, is one constant, conscious, free activity. This is the superintending, guiding, authoritative agency of the whole creative process, and may be known as the Paternal Activity. It upholds, and rests in the upheld idea, and with this agency alone, all is hidden and secret in the counsels of the originally planning agencies.

Creation is an outer manifestation of this inner plan, and giving to every element of it its particular expression. The idea as thought is to be stiffened and hardened in the expression to an impenetrable existence, and to such end an overt energizing must go forth into it, which shall fix the elements fast into permanent things. A distinct conscious Will must enter the Idea, and while flexible as thought, must give the Idea exact expression which shall also be impervious to any other agency, and make the Idea "stand fast" in rigid consistency. This energizing will is a constant, conscious, free activity, distinct from the thought-activity which states the idea, and yet it is its exact counterpart in every element of the idea, and may be known as Logos, Word, or Son, " by which the Father made the worlds."

But the rigid realities, all made to exactly express the elemental thoughts in the idea, must further be connected through and through in comprehensive unity. An energy aside from that which makes them steadfast must move them together in concrete consistency and order overtly, as the plan is connected and consistent innerly; and which, too, must be a constant, conscious, free acting, in joint fellowship with the above idealizing and realizing agencies, fashioning the chaotic material to a comprehensive universal Cosmos. This last forming agency may be known as Holy Spirit.

Each of these separate agencies has its own respective conscious Will; the wills distinct, but the consciousness in each a peculiar appropriation to itself from the one consciousness in Absolute Reason; and such conscious will can be named by nothing so appropriate as Person. Yet while distinct in free activity, they are not distinct in their substantial being, for they are the three subsistent agencies we have already seen to be essentially in Reason itself, and go to the completion of its one being. Absolute Reason is essentially threefold, and as Creating Reason necessarily in threefold personality. The Creating Spirit so knows his creating, since thus is it in conformity with his essential rationality. Conscious free idealizing is first, and all-controlling: conscious free realizing is second, and all-expressing: conscious free individualizing is third, and all-comprehending: and only as human reason can see the divine idea in the real, and this in its real comprehension, can man know either the Creator or his creation. Divine Reason knows concurrently with his creative work; the human knows in the work the thought and will of the Creator. The Father, whom none seeth, has the hidden ideal; the "Word, with God and was God," expresses the ideal in reality; and the Holy Spirit fashions the worlds and binds them in a universe, and so "garnishes the heavens." Creation, correctly contemplated as from the Absolute Reason in essential triunity, loses its mystery, but augments its majesty, in its pure rationality.

6. THEISM DISTINCT FROM ALL FORMS OF PANTHEISM. — Absolute Personality recognized will give Theism, and exclude Pantheism, no matter what the connections of the parts of the universe to each other, nor how directly the universe may come from the Creator. The product of the person will be other than the person, and the personality of the Maker as Absolute will exclude all external conditioning and derivation; and thus on the one hand the creation will be a really objective existence, and on the other the Creator will be true Deity. But all methods of develment, or evolution, will involve Pantheism and exclude Theism. The unfolding in any way is but a gradual disclosure of the one already existing thing; and before the development, the one is the All, and after the development, the All is still the one; and neither the one nor the all can get any distinction of being. When the one absorbs the All, it will properly be termed Pantheism; and when the All hides the one, it will more properly be termed Pancosmism; but in each case the whole is without proper Personality, and is virtually Atheism.

There are two general forms of Pantheism, each having some modifications, but all will be sufficiently noted in making the general discrimination. One comes from logically following out physical law, and may be known as *logical* or *physical* Pantheism; the other comes from finding a perpetual dialectic in all progressive reasoning, and striving to overcome this by a transcendental synthesis, and which may be known as *dialectical* or *transcendental* Pantheism.

The *first* form recognizes the uniformities and in. variable sequences of experience, and logically infers the future from the past, and the distant from the nearer observation, and concludes nature to be a perpetual orderly series of concomitant and successive events, and all conditioned in their connections by what precedes to what must infallibly succeed. The material world has its connected physical causes and effects, and the linked series are inviolate, while the mental world, in its intellectual, sentient, and practical life, has its own history of passing events connected by motives and moral influences, which make the whole to be strictly uniform and rigidly inviolate. Matter and mind go on in their counterpart series, and together make a universe of concurrent events by which all sentient experience has its regular laws, uniformly rewarding and punishing as the laws are kept or violated. Often the violation and penal result are seen to be the direct steps to a further advance, and the sins and retributions are really as necessary means of progress and coming melioration as the virtues and rewards. An unerring power is everywhere silently and constantly at work, and which no man really helps or hinders, and which as truly works out human destiny as material changes;

and man's wisdom is, so far as practicable, to fall in and work with it, and always to rejoice in it.

All anxiety about supernatural agencies is but a weak superstition, leading invariably to philosophical, social, and moral perversions. There is no God out of Nature; and only a God in Nature, wisely working all nature onward in the track of destiny. No personality who begins and consummates can be discovered; the inner power works out the development.

The *second* form of Pantheism is exceedingly profound and thorough in its dialectical process. It finds thought in its very spring and source to be dialectical, having a necessary antithesis in its deepest notion. All Affirmation is as truly and necessarily also Negation in its opposite aspect, and whatever position be taken, the immediate counter-movement must pass onward to its own Negation. To prevent direct self-contradiction and thus absolute scepticism, or rather utter nescience, the reason must be brought in to see in its higher light, that the antithetic negation is not a direct denial nullifying the old position, but in fact an opening to a common synthesis between them, wherein they come together and close themselves in higher and richer unity than before. This new position is then at once a spring to a new form of negation, and this to a transcendental synthesis enriched by retaining all the former; and thus on, by a perpetual repetition of new outlays and richer incomes, till the cycle comes round into itself; and then afterwards opens into a broader circuit, till the last cycle of all enclosed cycles, when the reason is brought face to face with itself, in divine self-consciousness and universal being.

This process of Absolute Thought is held to be a true exposition of the eternal essence antecedent to and in the work of creation, and giving the very fibres of the universe, around and upon which all of nature and of humanity are set. Thought is all that is — the highest and only knowledge and reality. It is God and the Universe ; God knowing himself, in thinking the universe. And here the error is not in the dialectical process, or the transcendental order of the higher rational logic ; for that is the most thorough, profound, and rigidly conclusive possible. But it makes the thinking to be all. God and the universe are in the thinking, and there is neither Creator nor created but in the thought. There is no overt agency that forms and fixes a solid world on these thought-fibres, and holds it there palpably and overtly, as the expression of the thought and the manifestation of the will and wisdom of the Thinker. It is Absolute Thought in self-development ; the world-spirit, solely intellectual spirit, thinking itself into a universe, and thereby coming to the knowledge of itself in this universal knowledge ; a complete Pantheistic Thought-development.

To meet and demolish the first form of Pantheism demands a clearing of the mind from all the illusions of sense and experience, when attempting to carry our knowledge by them over into the region of the supernatural. If all philosophy is exhausted in examining nature, and only assuming that the observed order of facts in nature is the sole warrant for supposing any intrinsic connections in nature, then must nature's ongoing be the ultimate to us, and the end of logic is, that the only God is nature. But when we have known that Absolute Reason acts originatingly and electively from the claim of its own excellency and to the end of its own dignity, we have at once a personal Cause in Liberty, who is above nature, and both the Author and Finisher of Nature.

And to convict the second form of Pantheism of its partiality and incompleteness, we need to note that it can have no Space and Time in common with human conscious experience. In it, the Absolute thought-development makes its own space in the statement of its thoughts in infinity, and its own time in the succession of its thoughts in eternity ; while all particular appearances in nature are but the stated and passing out-thoughts of this Absolute thinking-process, and can have no space and time of their own, and stand only in the subjective space and time of the Absolute thinking.

But in common conscious experience, there is in each consciousness its own space and time, with which another does not come in communion, and also the consciousness of a common space and time in which all have their determined experience. This can be explicable only in the truth that nature is persistent

Force in changing forms and thus determining its own space and time for every conscious experience, leaving each with his own subjective inner experience to a space and time of his own with which no stranger can intermeddle.

This reason ground-work of persistent and changing Forces is yet to be known as standing out in clear intelligence; and in it we shall find both a creator's thought and a creator's upholding will, establishing the thought in exact and palpable perpetuity. Such a creation is the product of a Creator, who has his distinct personal being beyond the creating acts which express his inner thoughts.

PART II.

KNOWLEDGE OF CREATION.

Design and Method. — Nature has been studied long and patiently in the light of experience; broad inductions have been made, and general judgments concluded; and within their varied categories all facts of observation have been arranged and classified. Scarcely does a phenomenon now occur which has not already a name indicative of its assigned relation, and a place appropriated to it in the scientific catalogue. But convenient and useful as the empirical classifications may be, like the alphabetical arrangement of the dictionary, they have no known connections intrinsically determining the places and periods of their appearing, since the essence necessitating the manner and order of appearance is ignored, for this is held to lie in a sphere quite beyond the reach of human attainment. And yet science is very familiarly, if not ostentatiously, dealing with these unknowable essences, as substantial forces and efficient agencies, working out in their inevitable sequences the results which appear. Certainly, the substantial forces and living agencies never appear in human experience, and if we may use them at all in expounding phenomena, it must be by the exercise of an intelligence transcending all sense-experience.

And now, not with Creation as a fact accomplished are we here interested, whether as actual appearance or as force and life working out that appearance; we go back to the Creator we have found, and seek, in and from him, the origination and established existence of the Force and Life which stand everywhere beneath the appearances coming up in human experience. The essence is to the appearance as the meaning is to the word; the sentiment is given to reason in the letter, but the meaning was before and determined what the letter must be, and both the meaning and the letter have their source in one Author.

Creation in appearance must be in Space and Time; as standing or moving in space and time, creation must have essential Force; and to hold and use force in organic construction and agency, there must be Life. To know these at all, must solely be in the insight of Reason; and we now assume what the issue will show, that creation given to experience may be determined by what Reason may know of Space and Time, Force, and Life.

This Second Part will thus need three chapters: —

Chap. I.   Reason-knowledge of Space and Time.
  "   II.   Reason-knowledge of Force.
  "   III. Reason-knowledge of Life.

CHAPTER I.

SPACE AND TIME.

1. THERE ARE MANY DIFFERENT KINDS OF SPACE. — There may be pure intellectual constructions of geometrical diagrams, that shall stand in the consciousness of the one who constructed them only. These diagrams of right lines, curves, and angles, making purely subjective objects, will have extension, and relative distance and direction each from each as standing in their places, and all together will be included in one space ; but as the diagrams are in the subject, so the space in which all are is wholly subjective. When such pure diagrams fade away and fall out of consciousness, the space in which they stood falls away from consciousness also. If, again, another set of pure diagrams be similarly constructed, they, too, will have their subjective space, and which in like manner will pass away when the diagrams pass out of consciousness. Now, it may be said of each such set of figures, that they had their own space, but it cannot be said of the first set, that its figures together were in the same space with the figures of the second. There have been two spaces as truly as two sets of figures, and the same person may have as many dif-

ferent spaces as he shall have separately constructed sets of figures. And then, too, any number of persons may construct in their own minds their separate sets of figures, and thereby each may have his numberless distinct spaces, and neither one can put all his subjective spaces into one space, and much less can any one put all the subjective spaces in all persons into any one space. Here, then, is one kind of space in which stand the person's own pure figures, and which may be known as *Subjective* Space; and yet this one kind may have infinite separate spaces in the separate constructions of one, and of all.

So, also, the visual organ, morbidly or from pressure, may have colored spots of different light and shade floating within it, and each spot will have its own outline defined more or less completely. With the spots in the organ, there will also be a space in which the spots appear, and all the spots will have their relative directions and distances each from each in that one space. If the eye become clear of these floating phantoms, the space in which they were goes away as the spots disappear. Should then another occasion give other colored spots, they would have a common space, but not the same space as the former. And so other eyes may have their spots and spaces, and on divers occasions, and these spaces will be diverse, and can never be put into a common space. Here is another kind of space as solely *Organic*, and its separate spaces may be infinite.

And in the same manner with *mirrored spaces*

which may be endlessly diversified; as also *dreaming* spaces, and *telescopic* spaces of different lenses, and ordinary *phenomenal* spaces, and *remembered* spaces; in all these varieties and sub-varieties, their diversity can never be brought into a common unity.

2. THERE ARE DIFFERENT KINDS OF TIME. — As extension has its space within which to stand, so also has succession a time in which to pass. Thus, in all the before-mentioned kinds of space, if in each a series of sequences occur, there would be as many kinds of time, and which could none of them be made to stand in a common time.

So, a person may be absorbed in an inward train of thought with an intensity that shall prevent all note of passing outer occurrences. There is a subjective time in which the successions pass, and such time is only for the man thinking; and to him this absorption in his own thinking may pass off, and he again note the occurrences of outer events; and such changed orders of sequences may be frequent, and each will have its ordered times that cannot be in a common time for them all; and many men may each have such *thinking* times, and thus still less can these many men bring all their varied times into any one time.

And so with *dreaming* times, and outward *appearing* times, and past successions made to be present in *remembered* times; they all differ in kind, and may all be in all men, and no one can arrange them all in any one time.

We may thus say of space, that there are many kinds of spaces, and the many cannot be put into any one space ; and of time, that there are many kinds, and the many cannot come into any common time. And yet, we perpetually speak of space and of time as each one Space and one Time. With this notice of the many spaces and times, it might seem impossible that we should know the one Space and one Time.

3. THE CONSTRUCTIONS OF SENSE GIVE EXTENSION AND SUCCESSION ONLY. — The constructing agency works in the light of consciousness, and hence knows what it is doing, and what it has done; but its knowing is only in the doing, and in the product of the work, and not anything *à priori* of the doer, or of the content as material used. Hence the attending, or intellectually constructing or defining agency knows only the extensions and the successions which its conjoining acts have put together, and it works the same in one field as in another. It may be in pure subjective consciousness constructing its mathematical diagrams, or with any content or morbid affection in any sense organ, or from a mirror, or in a dream, and the line or figure it describes will be the extension that it knows, or the sequence that the progressive movement joins will be the succession that it knows, and merely as constructing agency, the products are

either extension or succession, and that is all that appears in the consciousness. The distinguishing agency may discriminate the contents used, and thus may separate pure lines, or colored lines, or tangible lines, &c., as also pure sequences, or colored sequences, &c., from each other; but all that has any bearing upon the knowing of space and time is in the constructing, and not in the distinguishing operation. Were there, then, nothing further than merely sense-attention, the only apprehension there could be towards the taking of space and time in the consciousness, would be that of Extension in conjoining points, and that of Succession in passing through points, let the points as content used be what they might.

4. The logical Judgment gives Place and Period only. — When the conjoining sense has apprehended extension and succession, the logical understanding can further operate upon the appearing extensions and successions, and thereby carry the intellectual work further on towards the cognition of space and time. The limited extension of any kind, say here of a colored cube, or the limited succession of any kind, say here of consecutive red, orange, and green colors, may be subjected to the function of abstraction, and if the colored cube, as content in sensation, be taken away, there will remain its pure Place in the consciousness; and if also the consecutive red, orange, and green be abstracted, there will remain

their pure Period in the consciousness; and thus by abstraction we come to cognize place and period. But in this process we know only the place which the cube filled, and the period which the movement through the red, orange, and green occupied.

But such abstract places and periods may now, in a similar way, be apprehended in any number and variety, and the arranging and combining Judgment may give to them any possible conjunctions, and so far as the combinations go, there will be known the place filled by all, and the period occupied by all. But the knowledge cannot go beyond the places so filled and the periods so occupied. If there is a chasm in the extensions or successions, that chasm cannot be known as place or period; and if the extensions or successions terminate, there cannot be known either place or period beyond the terminations. So much place as is filled by all known places is known, and so much period as is occupied by all known periods is also known; but nothing of place or period is known beyond this. Places within a larger place, and periods within a larger period, we know by regular logical process; but we cannot carry our logical conclusions any further than we fill place and occupy period. All that the logical Judgment can possibly know of space is a place filled with places, and all that it can know of time is a period filled with periods, and which at the utmost is a knowledge of place and of period. The place known still is extension; and the period known still is succession ; and the extension cannot be space, for it wants a space within which the extension may stand; and the succession cannot be time, for it wants a time within which the successions may pass. No possible extension is space, for it must itself be already stretched out *in* space, and no possible succession is time, for it must already itself be passing *in* time. We might, on the other hand, analyze the places and periods, and strive to get out of place into space, and out of period into time, by diminishing; but the most we could reach would be the points in place, and the moments in period, and these would still be *in* space and time, and not themselves space and time.

5. THE REASON ONLY CAN KNOW SPACE AND TIME. — It is the office and prerogative of Reason to look into all that Sense apprehends and Understanding conjoins, and shut all together as comprehended in one. And just this the reason does in its knowing of Space and Time. Where the apprehension is of diverse points or diverse instants, there may be constructed limited extensions and limited successions, and the understanding may conjoin the particular extensions and successions according to any appearances in experience. The places of the extensions and the periods of the successions may be thus conjoined to any amount of place and period, and it will but put box over box to make up a nest of boxes, or link upon link to make a chain of links.

But the biggest box the understanding may conjoin will still be in place, and that place not space, but *in* space; and the longest chain the understanding may put together will still be in period, and that period not time, but *in* time. And this space which holds all places, or this time which contains all periods, is respectively object only for the reason. That, according to its comprehending function, shuts all places in a single which is space, and all periods in a single which is time. And this the reason does with any extensions constructed in any places, and any successions conjoined in any periods, and thus gives its kind of space for the kind of place, and its kind of time for the kind of period, whether of subjective, organic, mirrored, &c., spaces, or whether of thinking, dreaming, &c., times. The space and time are no aggregates of places and periods, but are each a concrete single, with no limits, internal nor external.

To the reason, thus, space and time respectively comprehend each its own manifold in one, and that one can no more be separated into parts than the parts can aggregate themselves into a single. Limited or divided space and time is as much an absurdity and impertinent assumption to the Reason, as limitless place or limitless period is to the logical Judgment. The limited place cannot be, but there must already be the limitless space in which it may be; and the limited period cannot be, but already there must be the limitless time in which it may be.

Space and Time are no abstractions, nor generaliza-
tions, nor logical deductions, but necessary comprehensions of the reason wherever there are diversities
in extension or in succession, the former for space
and the latter for time.

6. Sameness of Space and Time can be known
only in the Continuity of the Extension and Succession. — The dreaming space, and the dreaming
time, are each one and the same so long as the extensions and successions in the dream continue, but
the space and the time are both lost when the extensions and successions in the dream cease. What
makes two dreams is the two spaces and times in
the dreams, and these will occur in the sundering of
the extensions and successions. And just so with
our waking experience; the space and the time are
one and the same while the extensions and successions in phenomena continue, but the waking space
and time are as truly cut off in going into a dream,
as the dreaming space and time on awaking from the
dream. Whenever the extension or the succession
in consciousness stops short, the space and the time
are gone; and when they again begin, a new space
and a new time begin; and we can never put the
two spaces in one, and the two times in one, till we
somehow bring the extensions and successions to
join themselves across the chasm. Each man has
as many spaces and times as he has interruptions
of conscious extensions and successions, and he can

only bring his experience into one space and one time by somehow knowing that the extensions and successions still continued while he was unconscious of them.

And so of any two men, or of all men; they cannot know that their separate experiences are in the same one space and the same one time, except as they somehow know that they all have the same continuity of extensions and successions. Every man would live only in his own space and his own time, and could have no common space and time with his fellows, did he not somehow know that his and their extensions and successions were the same. The space and the time go with the extensions and successions; coming with them, staying so long as they continue, and dying out when they fade away from the consciousness. Make the extensions and successions Continuous, and you will have the same space and time for one man and for all men.

7. This Continuity of Extension and Succession can only be known through some Permanent in Nature. — In every man's experience, phenomenal extensions and successions are frequently being interrupted, and he cannot keep his own space and his own time one and the same by his phenomenal experience.   All men have each their varied phenomenal extensions and successions, and they could never live in communion in the same space and time, if all rested upon their phenomenal experiences.   The

history of different generations has necessarily frequent and long breaks in the continuity of phenomenal extensions and successions, and we could never keep the same space and time for the ages, if we had only the fragmentary records of past phenomenal experience. The fabled Wandering Jew, that carries the curse of immortality from the Crucifixion to the Judgment, might keep awake in perpetual consciousness of surrounding extensions and passing successions, and carry down one space and one time from the first, till space and time should be no more; but even his one space and one time would be for himself only, and no other could commune with him in his one space and time, any more than they could in the awful experience to which his impiety had doomed him. And so it must be with the Absolute logic of the Critical thought-process; it has the one Space and one Time for the Absolute world-spirit, but no other spirit in its free and philosophic dialectical movement can come within the Absolute space and time, or have any other than each his own space and time.

It is only in the knowledge of a Permanent that keeps its own place, and gives its own phenomenal extensions to the same man in his experience, and to all men always in all experience, that can give the same space to one man, and a common space to all men. And it is only one perduring source of all successions for one man and all men, that can give the same time to one man, and a common time to all men.   When all come to this Permanent for their extensions and successions, then all have one common space and one common time.

8. THIS PERMANENT MAY STILL ADMIT OF GREAT MODIFICATIONS OF THE ONE SPACE AND THE ONE TIME. — This permanent in nature, which will give its extended and successive objects for one and all, still gives its Space and Time for the phenomenal experience only, and as the phenomena may have their peculiarities from peculiarity of organic constitution, so the Space and Time may have corresponding peculiar modifications. The appearances in the heavens above and on the earth beneath are the sense-affections in all organs, from the same permanent efficiencies that constitute the heavens and the earth in their inner essence, and must thus give the same impressions relatively to the same organs; and in this respect all will be in the same space and the same time; but the different constitutional organism may give the appearances to be quite different to different men, and indeed at different experiences to the same man.   Just as the same landscape will give its different appearances through changed media, so the same substantial world may give different affections through varied organs.   The eye of one may differ from another as telescopes differ, and the auditory apparatus may differ in different persons as drumheads differ in tension and vibration, and thus the subjective affections may be widely dissimilar; and

where the extensions and successions are unlike,
there the spaces and times will be unlike. The
space of the same landscape seen through the
changed ends of the same telescope may be said
to be in both cases the same space, but the modifications are quite wide apart in the two cases. And
in a similar way, the successions may be largely
modified by making the same motion appear through
differently magnified representations. Even, thus, in
a common space and a common time, the extensions
and successions having modified appearances, the
common space and time will have also their modifications.

9. THE EXTENSION AND SUCCESSION IN THE SUBSTAN-
TIAL ITSELF GIVE, IN THE REASON, ABSOLUTELY ONE
SPACE AND ONE TIME. — Here is still a deeper view,
and here space and time come out one and the same
for all intelligences. The substantial world persists
in perfect conservation through all its inner changes,
and aside from all peculiarity of organism, the reason
gives sameness to nature's places and periods. This
secures the knowledge of the one Space as containing
all the places, and the one Time as containing all the
periods of the one substantial, universal Nature.

And yet, it is to be carefully noted, that as place
and period pass away in the passing away of phenomenal extension and succession, so would the
reason-space and -time pass away in the annihilation of Universal Nature. The reason-space and

-time is known in the insight of the essential, *noumenal*, extension and succession, and if these cease, their space and time cease from the reason-consciousness. The absolutely self-same space and time, respectively, of universal nature for all intelligences is still no absolute space and time for all possible universes. Were the present Universe conceived as annihilated, and all her extensions and successions abolished, then must the veritable space and time of this Universe pass away in its annihilation. Were we to conceive that another Universe came into existence, this would have for all rational intelligences its absolutely self-same space and time for all, but no one could put the spaces and times of the two universes into one space and one time, nor possibly say where or when one universe was, relatively to the other. No consciousness has both in its one light, and only the one that is; and we should be obliged to suppose two reasons, with each his own universe and its space and time, and neither reason to have any communion with the reason, the universe, and the space and time of the other. This last supposition of two independent absolute Reasons, and their Universes, is a self-absurdity, and thus an inconsistency with the very being of reason, and making absolute unreason, and cannot therefore be supposed.

That there should be one common space and common time, it is now seen that there must be one substantial, permanent, universal Nature, giving its phenomenal extensions and successions to sensible experience, and standing itself in its own place and period, which is veritably Absolute Space and Absolute Time, and that no mere thought-world can have such common space and time.

CHAPTER II.

FORCE.

1. FORCE DETERMINES PHENOMENA. — A game of billiards may be so played before a mirror that each appearance shall have its duplicate. All the phenomena are grouped together, and the events succeed each other in the mirror as in the open vision. The extensions and successions are alike, and the spaces and times are alike; the one is but the repetition of the other. We might conceive the mirror and the reality to be so arranged, that by the sight alone we could not say which was the direct and which the reflected appearance. In such a condition we could not explain any of the phenomenal connections. We could not say what gave the sticks their length, the balls their volume, nor, on the contact of sticks and balls, what gave the balls their motion. We might see that the balls always went when hit, and always moved in the direction they were struck, and might talk of the

necessity of such connections, and call the invariable uniformity of appearance *laws* of Nature; but it would be mere uniformity with no known necessity, and simple invariableness with no known law for it.

Should we, by observing the frame of the mirror or other circumstance, come to know which was the direct and which the reflected appearance, and should observe the invariable uniformity of extension and succession in the two appearances, we might probably go over here with the same talk of necessity and law in reference to the connections of direct and reflected appearance, as in reference to the connections of the phenomena among themselves; but these necessities and laws of reflection would be mere uniformity of fact, with no known determination why they were so.

We might go further with the sense, and apply the auditory organs — hearing the balls hit; and might also apply the sense of touch in muscular pressure — feeling the balls to be hard, and the muscles to be under tension when the hand pushed the stick against the balls; and we should here augment the number of invariable uniformities. We should have muscular tension when the stick went towards the ball, and sound and motion when the stick and balls met; and again we might talk of necessity and law, but we should still have only uniform fact, and no known necessity and law for it. That there is sound when the balls hit, and that the balls are hard, no more determines any necessity for motion when they hit than when the motion followed the contact in the mirror. The mere animal sense cannot learn statics and dynamics, and determine phenomenal connections, any more through all the organs than through any one. Nor do the phenomenal contraction of the muscles and the feeling of the tension when the hand moves, and pushes the stick, and impels the ball, give any more knowledge of necessity and law by the sense and logical faculty, than the appearances in a looking-glass.

But the reason sees from all these, and, indeed, in a small part of the phenomena, that a present Force is conditional for these uniformities, and determines all these invariable connections. A force stands permanent in a place, and determines all the phenomenal extensions; and this force changes its place, and determines all the phenomenal movements; or it may be that force modifies force in its place, and thus determines all phenomenal successions. The meaning seen, the lesson read by the insight of reason in these phenomena, is, that a force is present determining every phenomenon in extension and succession, and necessitating and giving law to every connection. To the reason, the force is as validly known as the phenomenon is to the sense, and all the particular phenomena, whether of reflection, or open vision; of extension in place, or of motion from place, or alteration of appearances,—all are closed together and completely comprehended in the insight of the single force that has accomplished the whole result. The force is known after the phenomena, but known to have been before the phenomena.

This force, which exists before and determines all phenomenal extensions and successions, cannot itself be phenomenal; the force affects the sense, and the peculiar mode in which the affection stands in the sense-consciousness is the appearance, or phenomenon; and so as the force qualifies the sense, we have quality in sense and substantial force in reason. The reason sees in the affection that the force is conditional for it, and is the essential thing that the quality means. Phenomena do not perpetuate their extensions and successions, nor can they determine their own interconnections; the substantial force alone can perpetuate and connect sense-appearances. Science is getting fast hold of the deep significance that matter can stand alone in extension, and work out itself its successions; but just so far as science recognizes such truth, it is obliged to modify all former notions of dead matter, — an inert matter moved by force, — and say out unequivocally, Matter *is* Force. But so saying, science is transcending experience, and entering the sphere where the insight of reason can alone guide the footsteps. If we use force at all, we must employ the function of reason, and not sense, nor logical conclusions from sense; and when we so come to know that force is, and what it is, we may also know what creation is, and the essential connections of the created universe.

2. THE ELEMENTS OF FORCE. — So far as the sense-apprehension alone is in exercise, phenomena are all the objects known; and, to sense, phenomena are all there is of matter. As they alter or move, it is the common assumption that some force has somehow been applied, and thus it is supposed that matter is one thing, and that force is distinct from it, and moves or modifies it. These two suppositions cannot go together. If sense give all the elements of knowledge we have, we shall have nothing to do with forces; and if force be recognized as a cognition of reason, we shall need and shall know no other matter; and the force itself will be all that matter is, and the matter itself will do all that force does. The phenomena will, it is true, be altered by the force, but this is because the phenomena come of the force through the medium of the sense, and are the mode in which the force affects the sense and determines the sense-experience. All matter and all phenomena may thus be here disregarded, and only the being of Force considered, since the force is the matter, and the phenomena give only the way the sense is affected by the force.

Should we conceive of some agency operating in an utter void, as perhaps gravity or magnetism, and so acting simply and singly, with or against nothing, we could not contemplate in such activity that it was an existing force. It must act from or against another, or we cannot recognize that it has a standing in place, or a passing in period, and it cannot manifest itself in any form of existence. As simple activity, the reason may recognize it, but not sense, and as such reason-object we may name it *impulse*. The reason can further discriminate such impulse as having in it an efficiency that will manifest itself on reaction with another, and know this as *energy* in the impulse, distinct from the efficiency or energy in the source sending out the impulse. That source might energize in remembering, or imagining, or even thinking, and the activity would carry along no energy, manifesting itself in reaction with another remembering, or imagining, or thinking; but if the source energize in executive willing, that activity as executive Will carries over from the source an efficiency in itself, and which abides with it, and must manifest itself in reaction when meeting in antagonism another executive activity. The energy in the impulse is not itself force, for as yet it can have no overt manifestation; but meeting and counterworking with another such agency, the two become a third new thing as Force. This may be in any way of meeting another, as of impulse meeting impulse, or meeting an already existing force, and such meeting and counterworking of the impulse changes it from simple energetic impulse to an existing efficient force.

The limit in which the antagonism occurs will become a taken and fixed position, and will give occasion for organic impression, and may thus induce phenomenal extensions and successions as in place and period; and in its own fixed contemplation by the reason, it gives occasion for estimating direction and distance by all intelligences; and also for estimating motion and succession by all intelligences; and thus for knowing one common space and one common time.

Again, an *expulse* may be sent out, and as a balance to its expulsion another must be sent out in the opposite direction, and two such divellent activities from a common source will be persistent in position, and necessary each to the other's expulsion as an equilibrated agency; and such diremptive action from a given limit will be also force. Heat or light that should simply go off in a single activity could not be conceived as in position, or determined as having succession; for there would be no fixed point for determining anything, and we could not say whether the single activity were impulse or expulse. But when it is contemplated that the two activities are disrupted in their source as if each reciprocally energized to expel the other, and these together keep their source in equal and persistent activity, they will constitute a recognized force, and give occasion from their luminous or thermal limit to determine extension and motion, and thus fix their place and period. The light or heat centres in diremption would have a space and time in common for all, as truly as the magnetic or gravitating centres in their antagonism. Such expulses may be contemplated as going out every way from a common limit, or the impulses coming in every way to a common limit, and both are forces giving a space and a time, respectively, in common for all.

Another activity may be contemplated as turning these antagonisms or diremptions upon their central limits, by the direction given to the new impulses or expulses that constitute a new force in the limit and position of the old; and such activity meeting and turning the old forces will be itself also a true force.

We have thus three forms of forces, one with impulses counterworking in the limit, and which may be known as *Antagonist* Force; one with expulses divellent from the limit, and which may be known as *Diremptive* Force; and one in originating the new in such a manner as to turn the old on the limit, and which may be called *Revolving* Force. In the order of contemplation, the impulses are sent together and make the antagonism; the expulses are sent apart and make the diremption; and the new force crowding into the place of the old makes the revolution. But impulse and expulse and newly generating force may all counterwork with each other respectively, and such mutual counterworking will in all cases be Antagonism. And the counterworking is the force; and out of the force is simple impulse, or expulse that has energy which can be measured only by the force in its place of counterworking.

Force is thus essentially the combination of two activities implicated in action and reaction, whether in their place of antagonism or diremption, and such implication of the duplex activities is not a mere limit, as mathematical plane, between them, but a limited, as a bodily plate, which has both upper and lower side; the action and reaction truly filling a place, and standing bodily in its own place, excluding other bodies. It is more than simple being. The impulses and expulses have being, yet they can have no appearance in experience; but where they act and react, there is interpenetration; mutual implication; and so a standing in place and perduring in period, and thus the being becomes *existence*. While the impulses and expulses out of the place of their implication are spiritual activities, their combination is force, in which the two, as antagonizing or divellent, become one, and such force is overtly substantial and causal. It has been *made*, and so is *fact;* it has a standing *in re*, and so is a *reality*. Expulses and impulses may so interwork to make all distinguishable forces, and then forces may interwork in endless compositions, resolutions, conversions, and correlations, while the universal energies shall have persistent conservation. We contemplate them as in three Divisions, viz., Antagonist, Diremptive, and Revolving Forces.

FIRST DIVISION.

ANTAGONIST FORCE.

1. CREATION OF FORCE. — Creation is used here, not as any modification of an old, but wholly an origination of a new thing. Something is made to stand where there was nothing, and thereby giving original existence. It does not involve any violation of the necessary truth, "out of nothing, nothing comes;" for a Creator is, and from the Creator creation comes. The attempt is, from the knowledge of force, to attain a rational determination of its Origin.

Force may be perpetually converting itself into other forms, while maintaining perfect self-conservation and exact equivalence; but such rising up of new forms is only a change in old forces, and what we now contemplate is, the first putting of force where no force was. From previous speculation, we know a Creator spiritual and personal, incognizable by sense, but who is now to manifest his "power and Godhead" in the creation of Force, and arrangement of it in a material Universe.

The interaction of forces modifies their state and place; but we may here pass by changes of inner state, and contemplate motion as change of outer place, and from this shall better be in position to determine the creation of force. Matter at rest does not originate motion, but must be moved; and such motion in experience indicates previous force. How shall we attain the knowledge of a first Mover?

I draw a weight to me, or cast a stone from me; and when I consider the action, I note that my feet in contact with the earth has given occasion for an antagonism by which equal momenta in opposite directions have been imparted to the earth, and to the weight or stone; and this in each case alike, except as in the pulling, the foot-fulcrum has been on one side of me, and in the pushing, it has been on the other side. The great inequality of mass gives only the motion of the weight, drawn or thrown, to be noticed, and I can follow the moving successively through the working levers of my limbs, the contracting muscles of my body, the irritation of the nerves, the excitement in the ganglionic centres, the affection in the cerebral sensorium, and if we include the animal heat expended, we shall then get through the manifest material movement, and come at length in the reason to the insight of a sentient agency, which is out of all empirical observation. Can this insight go further than the sentient impulse?

A man and a monkey may alike throw the stone, and we trace the successive movings of matter in the same way, in both the man and the brute, out to a sentient impulse that stands beyond sense-observation. And in this the man and monkey may still be alike. The sentient impulse to gratify some appetite may be the moving spring in both, and as this is in constitutional nature, and must prompt according to its degree of intensity, what is already in nature moves the stone in the case of each. But the man may do the deed from a motive the animal cannot have in consciousness. He may know the claim of reason in either taste, or science, or duty; and in the interest of beauty, truth, or right, may begin and perpetuate a movement on nature, which starts from a source beyond nature, and may resist and control nature. This reason-claim can overrule appetite, and overcome inertia, and gravity, and friction, and set static forces in motion. It has not made new matter, but it has begun changes in nature which can never be eliminated.

The rational spirit of Man may thus begin an activity from itself, which shall originate motion in matter, and so use and control material and sentient nature as to manifest that he has, what the Animal has not, a supernatural principle of life and action. He can control himself as artist, philosopher, or moral agent; and both think and act freely against nature. He so far creates as to originate his own ideals of beauty, truth, and goodness, and express them as his own in the world of matter as really as does the divine Creator. And yet, though man may use nature, and put his own ideals upon matter, yet can he not create matter. He moves matter only by using matter already created. His spirit is incarnated in matter, and can put out no overt energies which must not meet matter, and can neither go through nor around matter. His will acts on nature only through the medium of his own materiality, and though he literally moves the world with every tread, yet can he not step out in the void, and put his will into his own ideal, and make a new reality and add it to old matter. His permanent changes in matter make no additions to matter.

And were we to suppose a finite spirit free from all corporeity, if that be possible, the creation of its ideals and the will it should put within them would make them impenetrable to another will only to the extent of its own energy and within its own sphere of activity, and could only stiffen ideas into consistency within his own subjective sphere of thinking and willing. But with the pure Absolute Spirit, we have no such hinderances to the supposition of his creating. In him is the Universal source of all idea and will; and the putting an overt energy of his omnipotence into his idea makes it impervious to any other will than his own. It must truly be subjective to himself, and within his own degree and sphere of thinking and willing; but so also will all other creatures be. All must live, and move, and have their being *in* Him; and yet intelligibly they must stand *only in* Him, but *out of* each other; all immediately within the God-consciousness, but only mediate to any other consciousness.

The Absolute Spirit was, while yet the material

worlds were not. All elemental Ideas, and all possible combinations of them, are his; and that interest which comes from seeing that it is the most satisfactory in the end of reason that the ideal be expressed in overt reality is also his. But neither the elemental nor the combined Universal Idea is force. It stands only in thought, and has not been fixed in steadfast thing. And the most simple element for thing in any form is, as has already been noticed, the meeting and antagonizing of two single impulses in a common limit. We, now, suppose the Creator to fill the simplest idea of force with such antagonizing impulses; and the Idea is no longer mere thought; an energetic will has fixed the thought in its own counterworking steadfast in the void, and the place, empty of all but thought, is now filled by a force which will not let anything but itself stand in it, without first moving itself from it. It is the first element of matter, or rather matter itself in its primal essence. The equal antagonism holds the force at rest in fixed position, or an excess of energy in one impulse over the other necessitates perpetual passing out of place, which is motion. Here is sufficient occasion for common extension, and thus a Common Space, and common succession, and thus a Common Time. And space may to any extent be so filled and periods so pass, and we shall have therein a World making its own history.

The antagonizing impulse is to be conceived as

God's product, just as the stone-throwing impulse was the man's product. The latter moved matter in meeting it, the former made matter in meeting another impulse. And just as the stone-throwing impulse, though the product of the man's spirit, is not the spirit, so the force, though the product of God, is still not God. The limit between the material and spiritual, the natural and supernatural, is in the impulse. Where that meets in the limit and antagonizes, matter and nature begin; above that is the region of the spiritual and supernatural, spaceless and timeless except in thought-statement and thought-movement only. The completed creation will demand the cognition of the three distinct conscious agencies before considered, viz., the free idealizing, and the realizing, and the formalizing agency; but for some time to come, we shall need but the conception of simple impulses counter-working in their limits of meeting, and thus becoming Force, in order to an insight of many Principles and Laws which must determine largely human experience in connection with the material universe.

2. It is competent for Force to affect any Sense-organs. — All sense-organs have their peculiar appropriate arrangements, and their living nerves for conveying the irritation from any impression to the central sensorium. The organ being properly constituted, it is open to the application of force in some form, either direct from the body of the space-

filling force, or through some medium between the body and the organ. The combined forces that fill their place, and constitute body, cannot put themselves within the organ, and through that into the consciousness, and therefore forces themselves cannot be made to appear, in any sense; but they may make their impression upon any organ superficially, and such impression stimulates the nerve, the affection in which we term sensation, and which is intellectually brought into full perception. The organ is the medium between the force and the intellect, and the affection in the organ by the force is the immediate object of apprehension and intellectual construction; so that the constitutional essence of matter is perceived by no sense, and only the mode in which the organ has been affected by the matter. Hence it is that we rightly term all sense-appearance phenomenon, while the force, as matter in itself, and which cannot appear, is termed noumenon. The noumenon is the object of the reason-knowing, while the phenomenon is the object of the sense-knowing. The usual distinction, in less technical form, is "the thing in itself" and its "qualities." The animal sense knows only qualities, and without the comprehending insight of reason, it could not be known that there is any object beyond the quality. There are those who say that the sense is so constituted that we know the thing in itself by it, and this, though lacking in essential discrimination, is true on the whole. The sense is so constituted that in it the reason knows the thing in itself, but the animal sense knows only the appearing quality. The phraseology gives the truth as a whole, but it wrongfully ignores the agency of reason, and ascribes to the agency of sense more than any sense can accomplish. No consciousness ever embraced the essence of matter as "thing in itself," and the reason does contemplate what is in consciousness, so as to know that this truly means essential matter beyond appearance.

This discrimination of cognitive Faculty makes consistent the use of the terms Substance and Accidence, Cause and Effect, Action and Reaction. The reason knows the persistent force giving determination to the appearances in simple apprehension, and comprehends them in one by it; the comprehensive force is Substance, and the sense-appearances are Accidence. The reason also knows that a substantial force becomes changed by interaction with another, and that variations of appearance in the apprehension are induced by it, and comprehends the varying accidence in the changed substance; the interacting substances make the determining Cause, and the varying events are its Effect. And so again, the reason knows that the interacting substances modify reciprocally, and that as one changes the other, this one is also changed by the other, and thus the varying accidence in each is shut in concurrent communion; and such comprehension of interacting forces and mutually changed appearances is Reciprocity. The reason sees, in the knowing processes of the above three cases, a perfect accordance with the action of the knowing forces, and that the knowing subjectively and the being objectively exactly correspond.

And thus it is plain that the existence of such space-filling forces gives occasion for impressing any kind of sense-organs, and awaking sensations within them in endless diversity, and thereby multiplying appearances in experience as various as the organs affected and the forces impressing them, and according to the direction, rapidity, and intensity of the stroke. As is the peculiar sensation, such must be the perception; and as the organs in different persons are alike or similar, such must be the sameness or similarity in their perceptions; and if the organs of some are morbidly or congenitally varied from the normal standard, such must be the defect or derangement of their perception. The perfect organ being given, the existing Force has only appropriately to strike it, and the content is given that the sense knows according to its phenomenal quality, and in the quality the reason knows the substantial matter in its essential nature. Thus all appearances in all experiences come from the same universal forces, and are connected in one Space and Time.

3. FORCE DETERMINES MOTION.—The elements of force make it an object for the contemplation of the reason of much the same clearness as the intuition of a pure mathematical diagram. We may construct

the direction of the energizing impulses, and fix their
limit of counterworking, and the comprehension of
the separate energies in the antagonism makes it
easy for the reason to determine what must be the
necessary and universal result. The force has an
intelligible nature, and must develop its action according to its constitutional being, and resting and
moving will be according to laws which abide in the
forces themselves. We do not seek now to follow
any phenomenal changes through their processes,
since they are but the effects of force, and could
give only the appearance after the fact; but we contemplate the force itself in its essential nature, and
can foretell what must be, step after step, from the
determination of principles as *à priori* laws.

When the impulses just balance their energies in
the antagonism, by resisting in action and reaction
equally, they must therein rest constant in one position. The literal import of rest is balanced resistance. Where so purposed and constituted by the
Maker, the force keeps one place permanently, and
such is properly a *static* Force; a standing steadfast
in its place. When unequal energies counterwork,
their mutual resistance is force to the extent of
their equal energizing; but such force cannot rest
in one place, since its constituent impulses do not
stand equally in energy one against the other. The
impulse that has an excess of energy must prevailingly impel from its side, and drive the static force
from its place in the direction of its energizing.

The force in this way must successively pass from position to position, and such passing through contiguous points is generated Motion. What to the sense is an absurd because self-contradictory demand, that there should be a first-mover, is here made self-consistent and wholly intelligible. In matter as given to the logical understanding there can be thought no first-mover; for the mover must already be in motion, in order that it may move another. The reason-object as Absolute Spirit can have no loco-motion, inasmuch as he can be never known as occupying place. But the Absolute Spirit can originate force with unequal impulses, and this must immediately generate motion. The force moves, but the Mover does not move, and in this force motion begins.

An addition of energy on one side must drive from, and a subtraction of energy on one side drives from the opposite side, or may be said to draw to, and loco-motion is ever from the push or pull of unequally energetic impulses. A Force thus unbalanced, moving from place to place or pushing in its own place, is a *dynamic* Force, and may overcome the rest of a static force. A static stands, a dynamic drives or draws. Designed movement may so be generated when before there was no motion. In the light of such necessary truths all the Laws of Motion may readily be determined. We know them not as gained in experience, but as they must be before and in all experience.

i. *Motion from simple excess of energy must be incessant, uniform, and rectilineal.* If one impulse be of greater energy than the other, it must still be counteracted by the weaker to the amount of energy which the weaker has, but the excess of the stronger has nothing to balance it, and it must immediately impel the force as balanced into motion, and as nothing interferes to check the motion, it must be *incessant.* The excess of energy gives its amount of impetus at once, and thence onward follows up as the force that is balanced proceeds, and never comes to any repetition of impetus. The motion must, thus, be not only incessant, but also *uniform.*

The excess of energy gave its impetus at the start in its own direction of working, and which necessitated the movement of that balanced force to begin in that direction. As thenceforth there can be no repetition of impetus in any direction, so the motion must be incessant and uniform not only, but also must be *rectilineal.*

The whole perpetuated motion is determined in the instant impetus, and henceforth, without other agency, nothing of the motion varies. All the above must be as true, in the case of all aggregate forces in their one body, as with the forces in one point, for each point will have the same determinate law, and the whole must move together as the one, incessantly, uniformly, and rectilineally.

Again, the same determinate law must prevail in all transmissions of motion by the impetus of different bodies. If any aggregate of forces occupy places individually *in a body at rest,* and other forces moving in body come in contact in the direction of their balanced antagonism, the moving forces bring just their excess of energies, in their direction of motion, to the forces at rest which work in the same direction, and thus give to them their instant measure of impetus in the same direction of working, and therefore the forces at rest must take on an incessant motion in the same right-lined direction, and in uniform progression from that point of contact. And if forces *moving in a body* come in contact with those *moving in another body* by reason of greater velocity, the excess of energy on the one side of the antagonism in the swifter body will add a greater degree to the excess in the slower body, and thus instantly quicken its motion, but thenceforth that quickened motion must be incessant, uniform, and right-lined. And so must it be in all cases of simple excess of energies.

ii. *That motion which any superinduced force would give must be compounded with the motion which the original force already has.* Not here, as in the first law, is there perpetually a uniformity of the excess of energy and of the direction, but there is a combination of impulses or of forces, and also the introduction of that which in one case modifies the rate, and in another case the direction, of the motion. Another degree of excess in the antagonism is given, and thus the uniformity of the velocity must be lost, or there is an impulse transverse to the old antagonism given, and thus the rectilineal movement before the greater energy is gone. The degrees and the directions of the energies must be compounded.

We may here take any physical force moving under the determinations of the first law above given, and now superinduce a new force acting upon it. In one case, it may be precisely *in the line* of the old antagonisms, but in contrary directions, and of different degrees of energy. If in the direction of the weaker energy of the moving forces, and yet not of sufficient energy to balance the excess of the stronger, it must then retard the movement. If sufficient in energy to just equal and balance the excess, it must wholly suspend all motion. If sufficient to give to the weaker side of the antagonism a stronger impulse, then the excess of energy changes sides, and the old motion is not only suspended. but turned back, and must be retrograde movement. If the superinduction be on the side of the more energetic impulse, there must be accelerated motion. If the retardation or acceleration be by a force that gives its impetus singly and at once, then will the measure of the motion be determined in the instant impetus, and thenceforward the motion must be uniform. But if the retardation or acceleration be from a force which perpetually renews its impetus, then must the motion be perpetually retarded or accelerated. In all of these cases it is manifest that the old motion is to be compounded with the new motion given, inasmuch as these compound motions are the resultants, necessarily, of the combining of the old and new forces, and thereby modifying the excess of energy which generates the motion, though in the above cases there can be no change in direction except as it may be directly retrograde, but must always be in the same line.

In another case of compounding, the superinduced force may be applied *transversely* to the old antagonism. In such case there can be no balancing of the antagonisms, nor a direct reversing of the excess of energy, nor merely an increasing the weaker or the stronger impulse, and therefore the composition of the forces and their resulting movements can have nothing to do with the uniformity of movement, but must necessarily modify its direction, inasmuch as the new transverse force will not allow the old excess of energy to go any way up or down the old line of working. This old excess of energy will continue in its old direction, and the superinduced force will come and continue in some transverse direction, and the first law of motion cannot have an unhindered application. The movement cannot be in the line of the old more energetic antagonism, for the superinduced force now thwarts this by intersecting its line ; and no more can the movement be in the line of the new force, because the old excess of energy continues working in its former direction, and must thwart the superinduced force.

This new force may come in any direction on either side of the line of the old antagonisms, but in any way it must be in the same point with the old impulses at their counterworking. That superinduced force is, then, as a third impulse meeting the antagonist impulses in their point of contact, and interfering in the results of their working, and the motion induced must be determined by the compounding of those impulses. The excess of the antagonist energy, and so the motion, was before on one side and in one direction of the antagonism, and the new is tending in its own direction, and they can now neutralize and balance themselves in but one common point between them. That common point will give its excess of energy as a unit, and move the force accordingly, and the perpetuation of the impulses must perpetuate successively the points in which they balance each other, and the motion must be through these points successively, from one to another, and thus the line of motion must be through the points in which the compound energies shall balance each other.

The rate of motion and its direction, which the excess of energy on one side of the antagonism has induced, being given, and then the rate of motion and its direction, which must be induced in the excess of energy on one side of the force which is to be supplied, being also known, we must compound the two according to their respective velocities and direction, and this will give the velocity and direction of the newly acquired motion. This compounding of the excess of the energies must put the resulting line somewhere between the lines of direction which they separately make. The forces may be either repellent or tractile, and their resultant, both in degree and direction, will be the diagonal of the parallelogram which is formed by drawing a straight line in the direction of each of the forces, so that the two straight lines shall be proportional to the degrees of the forces; and then, from the end of each line, there must be drawn a line parallel to the other, thereby completing the parallelogram. The common resultant of any number of forces may so be determined, by taking them two by two to the last. The excesses of energy being equal, the resultant bisects the angle; if unequal, the resultant must be on the side towards the line of the greater, making the sines of the angles with the component forces to be inversely as the forces themselves.

If the excesses be equal and opposite, and there be no generation or accumulation of force at the point of antagonism, they must equilibrate perpetually, and no motion can occur. But if there be a generating of new forces perpetually at this point of antagonism, there will then be a peculiar composition which must give its peculiar but still very determinate resultant. The physical fact of the equilibrating impulses, as a static, has the further metaphysical fact of the originating new forces continually, as dynamic growth, in the same place as the existing force. The direction of the continually generating forces must be determined by the antagonism of the impulses working in that place. The spiritual source is as a constant energizing in the limiting point of the already antagonizing impulses, and sends out a perpetual growth of antagonizing impulses in that limiting point; and while resisted by the old impulses, and yet issued out in growth against them, these impulses of the new must in this condition, at first, be determined to an antagonism transversely with the old, and perpendicular to them in their common point of working. The constant accumulations of the new impulses must, at length, bring their antagonisms into all directions, and ensphere them about this point. The Spiritual source is Himself independent of place, and cannot be determined as in any place, but He creates new forces in the same place as is the old force, and the compounding of old and new in their working must equilibrate in the beginning in perpendicular antagonism, and ultimately in ensphered antagonism.

The method, as above given, of compounding the motions of two forces, which motions are generated by their respective excess of energies on one side of their antagonisms, is applicable to any number of superinduced forces, and any variety in their excess of energies. In each case the old motion must be given, and the resulting motion from the composition of the first superinduced force must be found, and this will then become the given motion. This, then, must be compounded with the motion which the second superinduced force would secure as its resultant, and this, then, is a given motion to be compounded with a third superinduction, and thus onward to any number. The resulting motion will ever be the compound of that which either force applied in succession would give together with that which had before been given in the original, or any aggregate of superinduced forces. The first Law determines the direction of motion, from the perpetuity and constant direction of the excess of energy which generates it. The second Law determines the direction of motion, from the compounding of the aggregate excess of energies in all the forces which conspire to generate it.

iii. *The rate of motion must be directly as the dynamic force moving, and inversely as the static force moved.* The static force is the intensity of energy with which the antagonism holds itself in position, and the dynamic force is the excess of energy in one side of the antagonism together with the intensity of the counteraction. In the static both impulses equally energize and resist each other, and the degree of the energies which rest against each other is the measure of the force. In the dynamic both impulses energize and resist, and thus constitute a force; but one impulse is of superior energy, and thus perpetually displaces this force, and the excess of the energy, together with the intensity of the counteraction, measures the dynamic force. The impulses may be of greater intensity in each point of a small body, so as to equal a less intensity in the many points of a large body; and thus it must follow that it is not the volume only, but the volume and the intensity, and which will be the mass, that measures the resistance to motion; and that it is not the mass alone, but the mass and the excess of energy that measure the capability to overcome rest and induce motion.

When, then, one force acts upon another, the two are combined into one which is exactly equivalent to their sum. The static element of this new force in combination must be the sum of the static elements of the two compound forces; and the excess of impulse of the new force is found from the consideration, that when combined with the new static element. the resultant must be equal to the sum of the two component dynamic forces. This determines the excess, and consequently the rate of motion which measures the excess (when the static force is given), to be directly as the dynamic and inversely as the static. Of course, when there is no excess of energy in one of the antagonist impulses, the force is a static; but when this is moved by a dynamic, its rate of motion is determined by the same law. The whole body moving may be called the dynamic force moving, and the whole body moved may be called the static force moved; and the Third Law of Motion is exactly expressed by its being directly as the first and inversely as the last. The complete conception of the static and dynamic force contains the complete determination of the Third Law of Motion.

In this Third Law of Motion is involved the conception of Momentum, Virtual Velocities, Inclined Plane, Acceleration of Falling Bodies, the determining Principles of Fluid Pressure, and the Revolutions of Planetary Bodies. All the laws of Elementary Mechanics are eternal in the forces.

4. THE ATOM IS CONSTITUTED FROM THE CREATED FORCES. — Single forces may be created in any number and put together in any variety of modes, but for the future uses of the atom, it is necessary that it be constituted from the forces in its own peculiar mode. The forces are the component elements of the Atoms, and the atoms are to be the component elements of the Universal worlds; and these atoms, therefore, must so be constituted as most completely to admit of expressing the divine Idea in the created universe; and its future uses in the construction of material bodies demand that we have full contemplation of its own inner construction in every particular. We might conceive of two Atmospheric currents meeting in antagonism, and so interpenetrating by mutual action and reaction each with each that they should form together a sphere of their own in the midst of the surrounding atmosphere; and even the conception might be extended to the resistances the currents should give to their interpenetrating reagencies on each side, turning them into circuits, and so making the sphere a whirlwind; and still more, that at the limit of antagonism, the turning reagencies might drive each other in opposite-handed circuits, and so make the spherical whirlwind to have its contrary direction in its two hemispheres. And

as the counterpart to such conception, we might well take the antagonizing impulses as they act and react in constituting a single force, and contemplate their interpenetrations to be so driven in and turned at their creation, that they together should constitute such a sphere with contrary circuits in its opposite hemispheres, and such would be precisely the atom which we shall subsequently see is needed in filling out the uses the atoms must subserve in material nature.

But such conception cannot so definitely be made and put in pure intellectual contemplation, as to give the thorough insight needed for an adequate comprehension of the atom in its coming subserviences in universal nature. We must necessarily take it, as if the Creator made it in successive instalments, and follow out the process as it were step by step. He may instantly create it in his own way; while to our comprehension, we must carry the individualizing bond through the process to the result, item by item, in our way of insight. This will make it necessary also to contemplate the Atom, as well as the Universe, to have a threefold agency in its Creation; viz., the voluntary idealizing, and realizing, and consistently fashioning the full product, and which cannot be contemplated as effected by a purely simple act.

We follow this method: The first created force is that of two impulses antagonizing in their common limit, and which is midway in the line of the two

12

impulses as they come together in contact from wholly indefinite distances. The next created force takes precisely the place of the first, both in its impulses and antagonizing limit, the first having been made to revolve on its mid-point to give place for the second. Thus the two forces of course intersect each other's impulses in their common place of antagonizing, and then both are made further to revolve together on their common mid-point to give the same place again for the third force to be created in it, and which third force also intersects the first two as they had intersected each other, and so onwards successively. But the revolving, instead of being in a plane, is designedly from the start made to commence turning across the plane, so that in half a complete revolution the impulses of the first force coming up to, shall just pass by, the impulses of the last made force, and intersect them across the plane in the common centre. Then, continued revolvings and creations of new forces will give to the moving impulses a spiral course, and from the contrary movements of the impulses that stand on opposite sides of the plane an opposite-handed helical movement also, till at length the impulses of the first made force will come to stand perpendicularly to the plane at its centre, and a sphere will have been completely constituted. No further forces can then enter, for the revolving is now blocked in the fulness of both hemispheres. The revolving force which began also stops in it, but to which we will turn our attention again in the

Third Division. The complete spherical Atom is thus constituted in its own peculiarity.

5. SUCH CONSTITUTED ATOM HAS ITS OWN NATURE. — Nature (*a nascor*) is a *being born*, and implies a perpetual passing out into new forms of existence. The new births are outcoming events from former growths, and the whole is but an evolution or development of what was originally given from the supernatural. The supernatural is spiritual, and has in it neither birth nor growth, but it originates from itself that which perpetually passes out in changing forms of being. The successive births were put originally in its constitution, and nothing comes from Nature which was not from the first put into nature. Hence we say of any overt existing thing that it works, acts out its changes, according to its nature. The connected necessities of cause and effect pass on according to inner constitutional law, and from itself there is no alternative to the order of development.

And here we note of the so constituted Atom, that it has already in it that which to the insight of reason determines its outcoming births and growths. Its nature is already put within it, and this has come from the independent self-originating source above it. Nature finds its beginning in the atom, while all above the atom is supernatural spirit.

The impulses are overt activities with given intrinsic energy of will from the central spiritual source, and their antagonism in each pair involves

action and reaction; and so their respective places
of antagonism cannot be mere plane, but complex
implication in a limited form of upper and lower
sides, and outer and inner standing, necessitating
the force in each case to be a bodily plate, filling
and holding its definite place impenetrable by any
other. But all these single plates of force are turned
every way into a sphere as they constitute the Atom,
and which in their composition must constitute the
centre of the atom to be a core to its body of in-
tensor energy, and the periphery of the atom to be a
shell of diminished energy, in the one solid body, as
the plates of force every way crowd each the other
towards its own centre, which is their common centre,
and where the intensest energy must be, and this centre surrounded by its shell of weaker intensity. But
outside the shell of substantial forces as atomic body
single impulses come in on all sides from indefinite
distances, as simple spiritual activities, impalpable to
any sense, and capable of manifestation only in the
movements of such forces, as from time to time may
be thrust in from without among the lines of their
agency. The Atom has its determined space, but its
surrounding impulses give no determinate place, and
only come in towards the place from distances wholly
indefinite.

Such concentrated, self-balanced, self-contained
Atom is an independent miscrocosm; a little world
distinct in itself, substantially existing in its own
static forces, and possessing its own intrinsic laws of

causal efficiency, either as acting upon or reacting against other existing atoms. It fills its own place, and excludes all else from its place, and has ever in it its own unchanged identity, however removed from place to place or compounded with other atoms. Its intrinsic essence is mechanical force, and its action and reaction must ever be according to the necessities given in its constitution. Knowing essentially what it is, we can beforehand say of it what the old philosophy determined of Universal Nature, that to it *non datur casus; non datur fatum; non datur saltus; non datur vacuum.* Its Maker is not excluded by it, nor precluded from changing or annihilating it, for he has access to its being at its central source; but its constitution, and law of being and working, nothing can modify except the spirit who originates it, and to that creating Spirit all atoms stand in utter dependency and complete subserviency.

6. The Forces constituting the Atom determine what is its Inertia. — Inertia is literally negation of energy, and in this literal meaning it is quite commonly applied to matter; and so matter is held to be passive, and itself dead to all energy. Yet matter does stand against and obstruct other matter, and does also interwork and change other matter; and this fact contradicts its assumption of passivity or dead inefficacy. It is then assumed, that while matter is itself passive and dead, there is, distinct from matter, force applied to or put in matter, and this force makes the matter obstruct

or change other matter. But here comes in an absurdity in the thought itself, for if matter be dead and inert it is inconceivable that force may be applied to it in any way so as to act on, or in, or by it. It can neither receive, nor retain, nor transmit force. The matter is taken to be wholly inert, and thus the force, and not the passive matter, must be the doer of all that is done, and the matter is as nothing aside from the applied force.

Denying all energy to matter both contradicts experience, — for when matter is stricken it strikes back an equal blow, — and is absurd in thought, since it assumes that passivity may modify force. It cannot, then, be understood of inertia that the matter is destitute of energy. The inertia of matter is indicated in this, that the matter does not change its state of rest or of motion from itself. When at rest it so remains, and when in motion it so continues, till something from without is done to it; and then the force, which overcomes rest or modifies motion, does either of these in inverse proportion to the mass of matter. Such facts seemed to evince that matter itself resisted change of state, and this dull stubbornness was called inertia; and yet, as reluctance to change carried in it a latent power to hold itself in the same state, the very inertia had a hold-back energy which was called *vis inertiæ*. This apparently contradictory notion of an inertness, made and continued so by its own energy, has kept the conceptions of rest and motion, and the multiplication of motion by mass in momentum. helplessly obscure and vague, always perplexing and often deluding and perverting.

But when, in the insight of reason, we know the material atom to be constituted of antagonist forces, it is quite competent to see exactly what, in the resting or moving matter, inertia is; and, as previously considered, that it is determinative of the Third Law of Motion. The material atom is a sphere of static forces, with their impulses persistently resting against each other at the centre in equal energies, and as the energies are in constant balance the matter is in constant rest. But an added excess of energy on any side deranges the balance, and a movement of the matter must ensue, and the same continued excess must necessitate the same persistent rate of motion. Yet as the applied excess of energy must reach and overbalance each resting pair of energies in their intensities by dividing itself among them all, so the rate of motion must be in inverse ratio to the aggregate balanced energies in their intensities, and in this is the essence of inertia; since proportioned to the balanced energies in their intensities is the hinderance to overcoming their rest; and the same applies, on the other hand, in hindering motion when the matter has its energies unbalanced.

So matter is never inert, for its essence is energy; but the intensity of its energy makes and measures the hinderance to any modifications of its state of rest or motion, and that is known as its inertia;

since the excess of energy that moves from **rest,**
or restores to rest, must come from without itself,
and in that the matter is passive.

7. THE ATOM DETERMINES GRAVITY. — It is the
crowning glory of Inductive Science that it found the
Law of Gravity. The name of Newton is immortal
from this discovery. It can detract from the philosophy nothing, nor bring any disparagement to the
fame of the Philosopher, to see precisely the degree
in which that discovery has increased our knowledge
of nature. The hypothesis suggested to Newton's
mind, by the falling apple or otherwise, was, that in
all matter there is a tendency towards all other matter; and when this was extensively tried by experience, especially in application to the complicated
variations in the moon's motion, there was no hesita-
tion in accepting the hypothesis as fact; and the ratio
of this tendency was further found to be directly as
the quantity of matter, and inversely as the square of
the distance. Such general formula enables us to go
out to the matter of all worlds, and determine its motions and the places it must occupy in reference to
other matter. In this broad fact we comprehend a
large amount of other particular facts, and bind the
many in unity within this one fact. We hence term
it the law of gravity, not because we know any principle that so determines it, but because it is a broader
fact than we have elsewhere found, and more single
facts may be included by it. But this broader fact

has no interpretation. For all we know, the proportions might have been otherwise, and we can find no reason that guided in the making.

Sometimes the explication is sought by saying that matter *seeks* other matter in this ratio, as if the apprehension of some sentient craving would relieve the mystery. This assumed social affinity between portions of matter is in the same way, as it was early said of the water rising in the pump when the air within was exhausted, only as this last was a repulsive sentiment, that nature *abhorred* a vacuum. But this higher fact of gravity, becoming known, included and expounded the rising of the water in the pump. The gravitating energy of the atmosphere upon the water about the pump forced this within the vacuum made in the pump, and we now smile derisively at the horror of nature for a vacuum, which belonged to the unreasoning simplicity of an older philosophy. But when we talk of the *attraction* of matter for other matter, and that the atmosphere *seeks* the earth, we use the same kind of false analogy, and manifest as ignorant a simplicity as the men of an earlier philosophy. The atmosphere no more seeks the earth, and the earth no more attracts the atmosphere, than the pump sucked water because nature abhorred a vacuum. Seeking and abhorring, attracting and sucking, each involves the same gross solecism. The pump removed the air from its inside space, and the outside force pushed the water into it; and two material forces, put within the energies of their component impulses, have their contiguous energies diminished, and their opposite energies augmented, and the two forces are thus pushed towards each other by their own energies. As the determination of the atmospheric pressure revealed the power of the pump, so will the determination of atomic energies reveal the power of gravity.

And yet there will remain a great difference in the two cases, with the advantage immensely on the side of the latter. The former found its explication in a higher fact, but that higher fact was left utterly unintelligible, and the whole was as truly mysterious as ever. No fact can be explained by another fact that is itself inscrutable. But in this latter case of gravity, we do not leave it an unexpounded fact, nor merely run it back if we could under some bigger fact, but we determine this fact by the known eternal law of its constitution. We read in the fact how the Maker made it. If God's created matter is in essence substantial force, then must every atom press towards every other atom, directly as the intensity of the force, and inversely as the square of its distance.

A clear contemplation of the constituted atom unanswerably verifies the law in both sides of the ratio. The solid centre and shell of the atom is on all sides surrounded by the simple impulses which constitute the atom, in their antagonisms at the centre, and their interpenetration by their action and reaction. The solid atom has every way its surrounding impulses. These impulses work in upon the atom from wholly indefinite distances, and all make together a sphere of utterly an indefinite magnitude. The impulses out from the atom have nothing that can affect the sense and give appearance, except as something may be interposed which shall constitute an antagonism at the point of interposition. The impulses all work to the atom, and can never set back from the atom. The intensity of energy in the impulses determines the density of the atom, and its volume, and these make up its mass or quantity of matter. Inasmuch as all the impulses are balanced in the atom, so the energy of impulse in any line upon the atom is equal to that in every other line ; and as the aggregate of all intensity is the quantity of matter, so the energy towards the atom in any one line, and also the aggregation of energy in all lines, is in each case as the quantity of matter. But this impulse in the one line to the atom is but another name for gravity ; hence the energy of gravity in all matter must be directly as the quantity of matter.

In reference to the other aspect of the ratio we note that from the nature of the given force the atom is a sphere with its intenser solid core, and its less intense though solid peripheral shell, so made by the interpenetrations of the forces in their plates and the composition of their pressures spherically in common. Hence the shell of the atom, inappreciable in thickness, enspheres its central core, and in all its parts presses upon the central core with the same intensity, in the aggregate, as the intensity of antagonism in the central core. And then again, at an inappreciable distance out from the body of the shell, the surrounding contiguous impulses act in upon the shell, in an inappreciable expansion of each, enabling all to surround and fully ensphere the shell, but in no action and reaction laterally each with each, and so constituting a shell of impulses, not bodily force, and yet in i's aggregate intensity pressing upon the atomic bodily shell to an equal amount as that pressed upon the core of the atom, and equally also as the intensity of all the forces is in the core of the atom ; so that the intensity of this shell of expanding impulses is, in the aggregate, as the aggregate intensity of the shell of the atom, and the whole expanded shell of impulses together presses upon the shell of the atom with the same intensity as that whole shell presses upon the core.   And in the same way, at any inappreciable remove from the last contemplated shell, there is contemplated another concentric shell ensphering the former with an intensity in the aggregate equal to that in the aggregate of each interior shell, and acting directly upon the shell next within it, with the same intensity in the aggregate as that inner shell has, in the aggregate, acted upon its next interior shell.   In this manner, all the surrounding impulses counterworking at the central core constitute an indefinite number of concentric shells, and each one receiving the whole energy towards the centre in an equal degree of aggregate intensity with every other shell.   The intensity of impulse at each point in any shell, or surface of points, is of course inversely as the surface.   But the surfaces of spheres are directly as the squares of their distances from their centres; therefore the amount of intensity of impulse at each point of a shell, or surface, is inversely as the square of its distance from the centre. And as this intensity of impulse is but another name for gravity, therefore gravity must be inversely as the square of the distance.

The law of gravity being such, in the very constitution of the atom itself, the results of the action of the atoms among themselves are alike necessary and readily determined. The gravitating simple impulses around all atoms, for an indefinite distance, must secure that any two atoms shall each be affected by the other according to the universal laws of motion. As the solid atoms stand each within the other's gravitating energy, and the single impulses of each come into itself from beyond the other, and these impulses must be cut off from working on its own atom, and converted to an impulsive action upon the other in each case so far as the impulses reach beyond the other, and such working must be according to their energies directly and inversely as the square of the distance one from the other, the result must be that the atoms shall be pushed towards each other, and finally meet, at some point determined by the compounding of their momenta, and which must be between their original positions, and then the atoms must stand at rest in contact with each other. Freely moving in space, the gravitating energy, in many atoms combined, must bring them together equally about some common centre, and ensphere them; and in the case of rigid bodies in masses, each will have somewhere its own centre of gravity, and act upon others in the line of their centres of gravity, and the whole on coming together must collocate in such place as their own fixed forms shall allow them to fill. The Atom has in its constitution every fact of Gravity.

8. THE ATOM FROM ITS CONSTITUTION IS A MAGNET. —The construction of the atom in circular movement of the component impulses on their points of antagonism, and by a slight deflection at the start making the circular motion to be spiral, and in the contrary movements of the opposing impulses making the whole movement to be also helical, secured the shutting the atom in upon itself, and thereby rendering its intrinsic integrity inviolable; and also set the impulses in positions to act every way in upon its centre, and thereby determining to its perpetual gravity. A further result, for its subsequent utility in the ends of creation which we are now to notice, is the bi-polar agency in the atom which is thus made persistent in it.

The gravitating impulses as spiritual activities come in to their central core with a returnless flow, and thus perpetuate the solid matter of the atom in their central place of mutual action and reaction, while external to the solid body of the atom, the impulses are in flowing energies that can reveal themselves to sense, only by their effect upon palpable matter which may come within their sphere of action. So now, also, we are to notice another form of energy, which has no bodily consistency, and is purely spiritual activity in persistent flowing progression, with no set-back upon its originating source ; even as the spiritual activity which impels the stone I throw, never returns in reaction upon the source it sprang from. The antagonizing impulses constituting the overt forces in the atom, and the energy turning them as they are created in their helical circuits, are the products respectively of two distinct wills in the Absolute Reason, and this helical turning of the bi-polar energy, distinct from the gravitating energy, is that which exclusively we now contemplate. This acts upon the gravitating energies in turning them, but does not augment, nor diminish, nor divert from their central incoming, the energies of the gravitating impulses. It carries them through the helical circuits, but does not identify itself with them, and may be of less or greater energy without at all modifying the degrees of the gravitating energies. Relatively to the sphere of the atom, the bi-polar energy and the gravitating energies would seem necessarily to be of equal ratios, but relatively to each other the bi-polar and gravitating energies may differ in any intensity of the wills making them. The bi-polar energies must find their balance not as the gravitating, in direct antagonist action and reaction, but in the crowding contiguity of the impulses at the

atomic polar diameters, and can thus never constitute the poles to be solid bodies as the gravitating
impulses do the atom at the centre.

In further noting determined results from the atomic construction, it is plain that the bi-polar energy,
which we henceforth know as Magnetism, must stand
neutral in polar tendencies in the equatorial plane,
inasmuch as each way from it the polarity proceeds
in opposite bearings, and in the completion of the
atom will crowd the helical circuits more or less
closely together from the equator to the poles; and
at each polar point it must crowd with an intensity
which equilibrates the energy of its whole hemisphere,
and be directly proportional in any point of any magnetic meridian as is the approach from the equator to
the poles. As the magnetic energy reaches the poles
in the opposite hemispheres by opposite-handed helices, there must be specific distinction of polarities,
and as attained in experience, they have already been
discriminated as *Austral* and *Boreal* polarities.

The contrary working of the polarities must determine the mutual action of separate atoms, standing
within the respective spheres of their magnetic influences operating through opposing hemispheres.
In such cases of mutual approach, in reference respectively to each other, when two hemispheres of
different atoms act concurrently in their polar energies, they must work in to each other, and draw the
atoms together; but when they act adversely, they
must work to exclude each other, and throw the

atoms apart. And as the boreal is in opposite-handed helicity to the austral, the polarities presented on the approach of two atoms must determine their *attractions* and *repulsions*. When the similar poles of each atom are presented each to each, their magnetic circuits come in contact on their opposite atomic sides, and, of course, with opposite magnetic courses, and so running against each other, they must push each the other off, and hence the universal law is determined that like poles must repel each other; but when unlike poles approach each other, the course of polarity runs in to each other, and pulls the atoms together, and the universal law is determined that unlike poles attract each other. When either pole is applied to the magnetic equator, its neutrality can effect neither, and the polarities pass on in their own courses.

This bi-polar energy in opposing currents must also give its determinations to the magnetic Dip. Two atoms standing near to each other with their equators in the same plane will attract or repel equally in their respective opposite hemispheres, and their polar diameters must stand parallel each to each. But when atoms are combined in larger and smaller bodies, and the bodies stand to each other in such disparity of Mass that their polar action appears only in the smaller body, if then the smaller body be suspended on its centre of gravity, thereby holding in check the gravitating results, the magnetic energy will alone work and determine

13

its dip or inclination to the larger magnet. When put between the equator and the pole of the larger, the magnetic axis of the smaller most incline to that of the larger, from the inequality of attractions or repulsions mutually between their respective hemispheres; and the inclination must be the greater as the smaller magnet approaches the pole of the larger magnet, and perpendicular to the axis when brought to the pole.

Such combinations of free atoms will make the bodies magnetic; and if the atomic polarity is hindered by the gravitating energy, or by cohesion, the bodies may be in *a quiescent* state when their polarity is neutralized, and *indifferent* when their atoms are fixed. The presence of an acting magnet may disturb the equilibrium, and the quiescent magnet then becomes active by *induction*. The body holding its atoms so fixed as to move by induction tardily, and hold its magnetism in protracted action when the inducing magnet is withdrawn, is said to have *coercive force*, and the more ready induction by repeated shocks, like strokes upon a steel bar, is well explained by so freeing the atoms When the induction is immediate, and quiescence comes at once on removing the inducing magnet, the body is said to have *no coercive force*, and the giving coercive force by condensing, as hammering a soft iron bar, is explained by the fixing of the component atoms. And so bodies with different degrees of coercive force in patches, may by the inducing magnet give *consecutive polarity* — as the patches may favor. The polarity of the inducing magnet must determine the different poles in the induced by the control given to its inner atoms. As the atoms freely determine the body to be a magnet, so the breaking the body in fragments will by its atoms make each piece a magnet. Equalities of gravitating and magnetic energies must give coincident gravitating, magnetic, and geometric axes; and any inequalities among the atoms, in this way, must make these axes discordant.

SECOND DIVISION.

DIREMPTIVE FORCE.

1. THE CONSTITUTION OF THE DIREMPTIVE ATOM. — The creative process in diremption is the reverse of that in antagonism. An explosion from one source would give distinct diremptive forces, each of which would be an outsending of two expulses in contrary directions, and all of which would fill a sphere with expulses from a centre in every direction. The ejecting source is a spiritual agency, and yet the expulses ejected must be contemplated as reciprocal in their outworking, and that the two opposite ex-pulses make force only as they mutually expel each other.

In the contemplation of antagonist Force we assisted ourselves by figuring the activity which casts a stone from the earth, and we may here help ourselves further by continuing to use the same figure. The muscular activity in the hand against the stone is balanced by the muscular activity of the foot against the earth, and the earth and stone are expelled from each other in equilibrated momentum by the same spiritual agency, and the mutual disparting of the expulses in that source is one force in two outgoing directions. As, then, the man's spirit works both ways from the mid-source in disparting the stone and the earth, so we now contemplate the Absolute Spirit putting forth two simple activities balancing themselves in mutual expulsiveness. In the diremptive limit is force, and each expulse has an energy measured by the central force. We contemplate, also, the expulses as sent out from the manifesting Agency constantly in one and the same place, and as created, to be turned also out of this place, by the forming Agency, in revolving upon their diremptive limit, as the antagonist forces were perpetually created and moved. The forming spirit so directs them at the start, that in making a complete revolution, the expulses of the first made force just pass those of the last made, and then proceed each on opposite sides of the plane formed, and in contrary directions respectively, till they fill the hemispheres, and finish a completed sphere, whose polar diameter is then these first made diremptive expulses, standing exactly perpendicular to their first position in the plane. The expulses are thus all balanced, and constitute a *diremptive* Atom, independent and complete as the former *antagonist* Atom.

In diremption the expulses go out, as in antagonism the impulses came in, and they interpulsate by their action and reaction as the impulses interpenetrated by their action and reaction; and so the limit of diremption is not a plane, but a bodily plate, through and through implicated by the expulses commingling from opposite sides. As the antagonist atom was a sphere with central intenser core and peripheral less intense shell, so the diremptive atom in reverse working will be an impervious sphere of intenser diremption at the core, and less diremptive energy in the shell, and the expulses going off from the shell in every direction indefinitely, in the same inverse ratio to the distance as the impulses came gravitating inward. The antagonist we shall know as *Material*, and the diremptive as *Ethereal* Atom; and while material atoms have weight, the ethereal atoms will be imponderable. The body of the ethereal atom from its implicated interpulsations is the common source for the outgoing expulses, and any hinderance to the expulsion on any side will proportionally augment the expulsion in all other sides, with the perpetual tendency to restore the equilibrium by the same energy as that of the assailing obstacle, and must thereby be made thoroughly *elastic;* while the material atom can give no expulsions, and must thus be utterly non-elastic. Unmingled with material atoms, the pure ether any way stricken must perpetually vibrate through all its sphere, while interposed material atoms will obstruct vibrations. Two Atoms of opposite kinds and equal energies will impel and expel each other in equal measure, and thus lie together at rest side by side, and any amount of ether tending to diffusion will be held in place by equal external material energies. The ethereal atom is the converse of the material, and they may drive or dead-lock each other according to their unequal or equal energies.

2. ETHEREAL ATOMS OCCASION HEAT AND LIGHT. — As the still Air has no sound, and while in vibration is yet noiseless, except as the vibrations strike the ear, so the ether has neither warmth nor color, except as its vibrations strike the organ, and put its living apparatus in operation. The objective is qualified in our subjective sensation, and it is of the subjective affection we speak when talking of sound, or of heat and light. Still the stroke upon the bell or a strained cord modifies the medium of sound, though there be no ear to catch the modulations and make them audible; and so the ethereal vibrations modify the medium of heat and light where there are no organs to be affected and made sensible. It is this efficiency to modify the media of heat and light which we here contemplate quite irrespective of the affection in the organ; even that to which we apply our thermome-

ters and photometers, to test the intensity of the energy before there is any action upon our senses. This outer causative of inner sensation is what we put beneath the insight of the reason as known heat and light, prior to all sensible warmth and color. The diffused ethereal Atoms constitute the Ether, and this in rapid vibration is the heat which will become sensible to touch, and the light which will affect the visual organ. In our future contemplation of matter as compounded in bodies, we shall find these bodies so constituted as everywhere to permit the diffusion of the ether through them, and thus giving occasion for the vibratory action to send heat or light to every part. The slower vibrations wake the less quick sense of touch, and the quicker and shorter vibrations affect the more sensitive organ of vision, and the same body may be impervious to one, although readily transmitting the other.

Vibration of the Ether must differ from vibration of molecular matter, since the ethereal atom as diremptive must compress the expulses, when stricken, in the line of impact, and augment the energies of those expulses standing perpendicularly to the line of impact, and thus as the wave progresses, the swelling must be transverse the course, as if the atoms were so many bubbles alternately pressed and relaxed in their journey. But an Antagonist atom can have no compression and dilatation which may elongate its diameter transverse its line of movement, and hence the rhythmical oscillations of matter must be an advance and return longitudinally with the line of travel. The distinction in vibratory velocity expounds the thermal motion to the touch, and the illuminating movement to the vision, when we have the temperature of a metal ball heated to the touch while yet dark to the sight, and rising in intensity through a dusky red, and a bright red, to the highest white heat. Bodies which quickly catch and check vibrations must as readily transmit them, and thus as they absorb they equally radiate, and where they fix and latently compress, they must again start into vibration when freed from their static equilibrium; just as the coal-measures give out on combustion their latent intensity of vibratory energy compressed within them. And so all the phenomena of the spectrum, including the thermal, colored, and chemical rays, find their determinations in the motion of the ethereal vibrations through certain media.

We shall further on see the determined diffusions and relative arrangements of material and ethereal atoms; we here need only to anticipate, that they will be multiplied and mingled in varied ways and proportions. As everywhere interfused amid material bodies and entering into their construction, the Ether, as all-pervasive, will give to its vibrations the energy of the mass, and be sufficient to stretch the toughest metals and break the strongest bands. Continued material friction, or strong compression, or percussion gives proportional ethereal agitation, and sensible heat or light is determined by the motion. Even congealed bodies have their diffused ether, which may be put in motion sufficient to work their liquefaction. The more rapid vibrations are luminous, and have in them all the determinate laws of optical science. Reflection, diffraction, double-refraction, polarization, chromatic aberration, luminous interference, &c., may all be comprehended in the reason, by an insight into the forces which underlie and condition all phenomena of vision, as giving rise to all the varied affections of the sentient organism for light and shade, and all the phenomena of feeling in varied sensations of heat, and its absence, as cold.

Thus far we have attained a speculative insight into the essential being of force, in its two varieties of antagonism and diremption; and with little danger of mistaking have found the laws of motion, inertia, gravity, and magnetism in material atoms, and the determinations of heat and light in ethereal atoms. But in contemplating in advance the compositions and conversions of these distinguishable forces according to their mechanical laws of interworking, modifications and combinations come in, so widely changing inner connections and outer appearances, that the increasing complications soon reach beyond clear discrimination. The simple compositions of forces, empirically beyond explanation, holding the elemental facts of physical science, may rationally be satisfactorily expounded, and admitted as philosophically known, because reasonably interpreted. But as we now further proceed, under this Second Division, to more complex combinations, we choose the speculation should rather be taken as tentative than final; deemed probable, but not in full insight to be said infallible; awaiting further and fuller comprehension, and to which by others may be added the determination of more facts, as occasion shall be taken.

3. ETHEREAL ATOMS ARE THE MEDIA OF COHESION. —The impulses of an antagonist force implicate themselves in action and reaction in their place of antagonism, and are there not mere impulse, but space-filling force. All the impulses of the atom so implicate themselves at their common central place of antagonism, and thus constitute the atom a solid sphere with intenser central core and less intense superficial shell, outside of which the impulses are coming in from every side. Should an additional impulse be sent in upon the shell at any part of the atom, it must directly antagonize therewith in action and reaction, and there, in its implication with the old shell, begin the formation of a new exterior shell, and so far as other added impulses should contiguously implicate themselves with the old, a new outer shell would thereby be constituted, and the diameter of the atom on that side be so much elongated. The new shell would cohere with the old, and become an incorporation with the solid atom.

But no material atom may so work its impulses into another, since they each work in upon themselves respectively; and when the impulses come in to each from beyond the other, they can only crowd the atoms together as gravity without incorporating them cohesively.   An ethereal atom, however, may stand between two material atoms, and its expulses will each way incorporate in their implications, and the two material atoms with the intervening ethereal atom will be made firmly coherent, proportioned to the energy of the implicating expulses and the intensity of the old shells.   Any number of such cohering atoms may be brought and held together by their mutual attractions, or by external pressure; and if some so shield the ethereal by the surrounding material atoms as to exclude all heat vibration, there will be a *molecule* indissoluble by outer violence.   These atomic implications may well be conceived to be in such peculiar primitive methods as to constitute the sixty-six, or whatever number there may be, of the "simple substances," so called, as the elementary bases of all cohering bodies.   When those component molecules firmly cohere, they will constitute *solid bodies*; when they admit of rolling one upon another, they will be in a *fluid state*; and when more widely separated by interposed ethereal atoms, they will be *gaseous*.   So may be formed all kinds of coherency in the varieties of density, porosity, hardness, brittleness, flexibility, ductility, malleability, and capacity for welding.   In mere cohesion, the body is made up of the component ingredients, and is what the molecules are, whether of a single kind, or of blended substances.

4. MOLECULES, RECIPROCALLY NEUTRALIZING THEIR FORCES IN COHESION, DETERMINE CHEMICAL COMBINATIONS. — The Atom is indivisible and essentially unchangeable, but one differs from others in intensity, and thus in gravity, or weight, and magnetic energy. These unite, material and ethereal, to form the primitive molecules; and inasmuch as the atoms of the same intensity, respectively, must enter into the composition of the same kind of primitive molecules, so all primitive molecules, that are the same in substance, must be of equal weight; and it is with these *primitive molecules* that chemistry is chiefly conversant, and when secondary molecules are formed of the primitive and brought in composition, they, too, must have those of like substance to be of the same weight. Chemical compounds must therefore be formed upon the general principles of *isometry*, determining the same measures to the same compounds in all cases. If, sometimes, the same primitive molecule modifies its own intensity by exposure to light-vibrations, or enters in composition with others by interposing the ethereal atoms differently, such comparatively rare exceptions will furnish instances of what has been called *allotropism*, as in the conversion of oxygen to ozone, or the altered capacity of chlorine to combine with hydrogen in darkness, when it has been exposed a while to strong sunlight; and also of changed com-

position, like charcoal and graphite, from the same primitive substance, carbon; but in such cases the modification makes, for the time, the molecule to be of a different nature. The change in ethereal composition determines the allotropism, and such exceptions, so determined, need not be here further regarded.

The composition of the molecule from the atoms determines that unlike poles must attract and hold the atoms together from *within* the molecule, and thus the opposite polarities must stand *out* in the surface of the molecule in contrary directions respectively, giving opposite polarities to the constituted molecule. Such molecules, therefore, as attract each other by their concurrent polarities, will determine their *affinity*, and as they can enter into composition permanently only so far as they balance in gravity and magnetism, the molecules in affinity must also stand to each other in composition as exact *equivalents*, and the proportions in weight with which any two bodies come in composition is that in which they must respectively be compounded with every other. Thus, inasmuch as the proportioned weight of oxygen is 8, and that of carbon 6, the carbon must always take the oxygen in composition in the proportion of 8, or some equal multiple of 8, since the primitive molecule of oxygen cannot be broken into any fractions; and then the carbon at each varying multiple of the oxygen must give a different substance. So carbon and oxygen in their primary proportions give carbonic oxide; and carbon with another proportion of oxygen, as first multiple or double in composition, is carbonic acid. So always, when two substances combine with a third, the two must be equivalent with the third, and the like compound must always have the like equivalent proportions. As 1 of hydrogen is equivalent to 8 oxygen, and 35 chlorine also to 8 oxygen, so 1 of hydrogen and 35 of chlorine must be equivalents. The law of equivalents is determined from the atomic forces, both in the primitive molecules and all subsequent compounds.

When molecules simply cohere, they stand unchanged in their sensible properties, for they are only the same forces joined in extension. But when they come together in chemical affinity, and stand to each other as balancing equivalents, they mutually neutralize each other in their old energies, whether of gravity or magnetism, and the compound must, therefore, stand forth in determined new energies, and be a third thing, unlike either of its constituents. This is known as peculiarly *chemical combination*, in distinction from mere cohesion. Composition may be applied generically to both, but the composition must neutralize the component elements, and make them to be wholly lost in a new substance, in order to become chemical combination. When the elements stand together as joined only by affinity, but not so as completely to neutralize their separate energies, it is known as a state of *indefinite* combination; and only when the unity is to the complete nullification of old energies is it known as a state of *definite* combination.

So is it with the elements of nitrogen and oxygen; they stand together in affinity in the common air we breathe, yet do they not completely neutralize their respective energies, and thus the atmosphere of our earth is but an instance of indefinite combination. So the proportions of hy. 1 and ox. 8 may stand in an indefinite combination by their mere attraction; but by the violent agitation of an electric shock they are completely neutralized, and become a definite combination in the wholly new substance of water. In given cases the ingredients may separately be noxious and the compound salutary, or the reverse order may occur. Combination of the elements can occur only as they are in dissolution, though in frequent cases the affinity may have sufficient force to dissolve their previous combination.

In cases of definite action of affinity, the combining elements rush in contact with more or less violence, and the concussion must induce proportional molecular vibration, agitating the ether, and thus converting the force of affinity into heat; and hence is determined the general law of chemical combination, that the definite action of affinity induces heat. But, on the other hand, as we shall soon more fully notice, the point of solution requires an additional interfusion of ethereal atoms between the molecules, that they may flow over, or turn one upon another, and which ethereal atoms are there so held as to check their heat-vibration, and thus render so much heat-energy to stand neutralized or latent, thereby inducing so much negation of sensible heat, which is so much positive cold, and which a mere indefinite combination of the solved molecules does not release; and thereby is determined the general law, that the indefinite action of chemical affinity must induce cold. The heat in definite action of affinity is a positive generation, by the conversion to it of another force; but in indefinite action, the suspended heat necessary for fluid solution is so much cold still held unrelieved.

So, in all cases of chemical combination, the forces necessarily inducing and determining it are already in the elements, and wherever occasion is given by their solution and approach within the sphere of the action of their affinities, the complementary elements as chemical equivalents must come together, neutralizing their old action, and passing into a new form must thereby become another substance.

5. Thermal Vibrations determine Solidity or Fluidity. — The ethereal atoms, as media of cohesion in solid bodies, are susceptible to the vibrations of applied heat, and in the consequent agitation the cohesive texture of the body is loosed and weakened. As the applied heat-vibrations intensify, and the thermometer rises, the body expands proportionally up to a certain point; but just as the molecules of the body are coming in solution, portions of the vibrating ethereal atoms are taken in to the dissolving molecules, and held there in static equilibration, thereby giving occasion for these material molecules to roll, one

molecule upon another, in incipient fluidity. This interfusion of the ethereal atoms checks and neutralizes so much sensible heat-vibration, and the point is known as *point of fusion*, and the suspended heat-vibration is known as *latent heat of fusion*.

Different substances, of course, will have their points of fusion at different degrees of temperature, but for the same substance this mid-point between fluid and solid must ever be of the same temperature; and to maintain the substance in its fluidity at that point, so much heat-energy is necessarily there suspended in the interposed ethereal atoms. Other molecular cohesions are then dissolved in the body, and ethereal atoms further interposed : and these, with all the former dissolved molecules, are free to flow one over another, and thus the body enters into a fluid state. The augmenting degrees of applied heat liquefy in succession the cohering molecules, till the whole body becomes dissolved, and the mass is made fluid.

When, on the other hand, abstraction of heat is made persistently from the fluid state, and the molecules approach the point between fusion and solidity, the interposed ethereal atoms are there found, with their suspended heat-vibration, held as latent heat of fusion; and as the heat-energy diminishes, the molecular attractions avail to bring the material elements violently together, and disengage the ethereal atoms, to return to their vibratory activity, from their latent suspended energy, and which continues till the whole latent heat of fusion is released, and all the

14

molecules cohere in solidity. The latent heat may be measured as released, and the different degrees for different substances ascertained. The mid-point between solidity and fusion is fixed for the same substance; but in careful quiet, the ethereal atoms may not find release till the abstraction of heat has been carried some below this mid-point of temperature, when the slightest shock throws them out, and brings the mass at once to the normal mid-point of temperature. A body slow, and as if obstinate in its melting and cooling, is said to be *refractory;* but few only resist all degrees of applied heat. Carbon is found insoluble practically, but its crystallization in the Diamond must have occurred in a state near to fusion by application of intense heat from some quarter. Oils loose and fix their cohering molecules slowly, and have a considerable interval for softening and hardening between their solid and fluid states, while Mercury passes almost instantly from one state to another. The semi-fluid state of iron at a given temperature makes it capable of *welding,* by a forcible interpenetration of two detached pieces.

Two different substances which decompose each other by their molecular attractions when brought in contact, and yet do not recombine, may take from themselves the heat necessary to supply the latent heat of fusion when so placed that it cannot otherwise be attained; and by a succession of such contacts and solutions the sensible heat may be withdrawn and fixed in a latent state, and the most intense cold ultimately induced. Such are known as *freezing mixtures;* and the most refractory substances become in this way solidified, as alcohol has been solidly congealed at a temperature of −150° Fahr.

The liberation of the latent heat of fusion, radiating in a sensible form, is an exclusion of so much diremptive force from the body as standing in its solid state, and which must determine that matter in ordinary solidification shall be of less volume than when in fusion. In mere cohesion, with no crystallization, the molecules come in contact, and their impulses become mutually implicated, with the media of fewer ethereal atoms than when they stand as fluid, and the vibratory action, which kept them so separate that they readily rolled upon each other, has also so diminished in their solid state, that they now interlock each with each; and hence they must occupy less space for the same mass, and the solid is a contraction from its fluid form. Some substances will part with more ethereal atoms in solidifying than others, and some require less intense vibration to be neutralized in the latent heat of fusion than others; hence different substances contract differently in solidifying, but the same substance has the same contraction at all times of cooling.

6. Heat and peculiar Polarity determine Crystallogeny. — Dana's System of Mineralogy has a Section divided into Practical and Speculative Crystallogeny; and from the varieties of crystals occasion

is taken, speculatively, to show what form and polar action the molecule must originally possess to induce the geometrical solids which the real crystals in nature present, and also the modified conditions which may secure blended and compound crystals, both paragenic and metagenic. An acuteness and clearness of insight are herein exhibited that may scarcely find a parallel in the whole range of theoretic science. From the observed phenomena it determines what forces the molecules must intrinsically possess, in order that they should build themselves up in such solid geometrical figures. But with the speculative knowledge of force in its own essence as already attained, both autagonist and diremptive, and also the essential constitution of magnetic polarity, we are in a position to contemplate the facts of crystallogeny still more clearly, and know their law more profoundly and comprehensively.

Mere cohesion of molecules may occur under all varieties of force or partially constrained action of their polarities, and thus bodies must widely differ in internal arrangement of their component molecules. Ordinary solidification will present the material body with no indices of inner selection and formal arrangement, for the molecules have come together in promiscuous compression from violence or their own gravitating attraction only. But if some combination of atoms secure special configuration of molecules, it may readily be determined how the atomic forces may be so combined, in the molecules of some specific substances as to secure their self-construction of regular solids in various forms of crystallization, when the substances strike together from a state of solution according to the polarities of their molecules; and such polar action must give the law to the crystallogeny of the specific substances.

We may contemplate, as a distinct case, four material atoms encircling an ethereal atom, and as pairs the lines of their polar diameters intersecting each other at right angles in the centre of the ethereal atom, and we shall have a molecule of two lateral axes, and their opposite terminations of dissimilar polarities. The solidity may be completed by another pair of material atoms with their lines of polarity intersecting these lateral axes perpendicularly in their common point, and this will constitute a vertical axis with dissimilar polarities of the opposite extremities. Such completed molecule would be circumscribed by a sphere having three equal axes, all at right angles. Such molecules in solution would so pile themselves together by their polarities, as would freely-moving magnetic buck-shot, equilibrating both their gravitating and magnetic energies. The determined form must be a cubic geometrical solid, and such cubic base will be the nucleus of the forming crystal. Should the escaping heat, or an intenser polarity, favor the taking of a molecule at each terminus of the vertical axis at the same time, and thereby neutralizing and so far suppressing the working of the attractions in the termini of the lateral axes, the result, instead of a cubic solid, must be the cutting off the cubic faces to the converging faces of a pyramid on each side of the common base, and building up the crystal to a regular octahedron; or in another modification of balanced polarities, the normal cubic faces may have their twelve edges suppressed and cut into the twelve faces of a regular dodecahedron. The controlling polarities will determine the modifications of the accumulations about the termini of the axes, and all possible peculiarities of regular growth, from two lateral axes and one vertical axis mutually perpendicular, will come within one Division of scientific crystallogeny which may be known as the Monometric System.

Or, again, there may be contemplated two ethereal atoms in the midst of surrounding material atoms, so making a vertical axis, through their line, longer than the two lateral axes which should intersect, perpendicularly thereto, in a common point at the contact of the two mid ethereal atoms; and such completed molecule would be circumscribed by an ellipsoid, and the ellipse which any axial bisection would make on revolving upon the axis would describe an ellipsoid of revolution, and having a vertical axis longer than the two equal lateral axes, and all the axes at right angles with each other. Such molecules freely piling themselves together by their equal polarities at the axial termini, instead of constituting cubic crystals, as before, would build up-right square prisms; and by modified polarities, as in the former case, the right square prism would be changed for a right square octahedron. Another Division of scientific crystallizing will here include all its varieties of crystalline form, and may be known as the Diametric System.

Other modes of combined ethereal and material atoms constitute the molecules of peculiar shape and attraction that determine all other Divisions of crystallogenic systems. The energies are in the molecules which reciprocally each with each, and under the conditions of outlying forces, determine the geometrical solids of all forms of crystals. Circumstantial interferences and inequalities induce the abnormal varieties of double crystals, truncated angles, bevelled edges, and secondary faces; but all follow as the determined resultants in the composition and resolution of their working forces. Many crystals have one form with one set of molecular substances, and other forms if the substances are blended; and in some cases crystallization cannot come into any form of a geometrical solid in the absence of specific conditional ingredients. Universal law is manifest, though complications often run beyond the discriminating insight.

This reciprocity and neutralization of inhering energies determine the varieties of the joined axes to sides, or edges, or angles; and the meeting of the molecules where there is least intervention of mediating ethereal atoms determines the lines of cleavage, while the peculiar interfusions of the ethereal atoms in the interstices between the molecules determine all the optical modifications of transparency, translucency, refraction, diffraction, and chromatic blendings of colors in different crystals. Solidification of uncrystallizable substances, as above noticed, part with heat-vibration and some of their ethereal atoms, and thus contract their volume; but in crystallization there is the necessary interposition of new ethereal atoms through all the interstices of the regularly arranged molecules, and thus the volume is expanded. The amount of ether thus used differs in different substances, and thus different crystals have different degrees of expansion; but in all cases the expansion from the introduction, and the vibratory energy given from the pressure of the universal ether, is sufficient to burst the hardest rocks and toughest metals, if they stand in resistance. All the phenomena of crystallization stand expounded in its determining forces.

7. HEAT-VIBRATION DETERMINES VAPORIZATION. — When a solid becomes fluid, we have seen that the heat-vibrations dissolve the fixed cohesions made by the solid implications of the impulses and expulses of the joint forces, and that ethereal atoms have additionally been interposed between the material molecules sufficient to hold them separate in their point of fusion, and where has been suspended the latent heat of fusion; but now we note from this state of fusion the augmented expansions of the heat-energy in the fluid onward to the state of vapor. The fluid

mass rolls easily upon its own molecules, and portions break off readily even by their own gravity; but the whole matter flowing or sundering in parts is still held at the point of fusion. The increasing heat-vibrations, however, induce wider molecular expansions silently and thoroughly. When by heat-solution the fluid has been carried to the point for vaporization, the dissolved molecules from their fluidity to this point demand the interposition, further, of other ethereal atoms to fix and hold them in their state as vapor. In such interposition of heat-atoms, a specific degree of heat-vibration is held suspended, and which is retained in perpetuating the state of vaporization; and so much as is demanded for keeping the molecules apart as vapor is known as the *latent heat of vapor;* and this amount differs, not only in different substances largely, but also in small degrees in the same substance.

Why the latent heat of vapor is not a fixed quantity, in the same substance, is determined by the inequality of the spheres of vibration surrounding the molecules to be vaporized, at the different temperatures of the fluid when the vaporization occurs. Water evaporates not only in all degrees of temperature as water, but also when in congelation at a temperature below zero. Enough energy of heat-vibration is made to surround some molecules, even in congelation, to send them apart as vapor. But these spheres of heat-vibration, surrounding the evaporating molecules, must be of less or greater diameter according to the temperature in the fluid outside of them. The larger sphere will be within the higher temperature, and the smaller sphere within the lower temperature, and these unequal spheres will exhaust unequal degrees of heat-energy in equilibrating with the molecular attractions, which is the amount of the latent heat of vapor.

If the heat-vibrations are persistently maintained while the volume of vapor is being compressed, the intensity of the vibrations must be augmented as the volume diminishes; and so it must be, that temperature, volume, and density of vapor shall be reciprocal equivalents. If portions of vapor be separated from the mass, and heat be added or subtracted, the pressure and volume must vary in accordance. Abstraction of heat beyond the normal degree of vaporization and retention of latent heat of fusion must return some molecules to a liquid state, and the abstraction sufficiently continued must reduce at length all vapor to a fluid, and which process is known as *condensation*. The volume of the vapor lessens as heat is withdrawn, but when the vapor is all condensed the volume of water is very small compared with that of the preceding vapor. The elastic spring and expansive energy of the ethereal vibrations in their augmenting tension soon become enormous, raising immense weights, and overcoming the cohesiveness of any known material. The application of steam-power might be indefinite if the cohesiveness of the boiler-material could be found adequate; but earthquakes and volcanoes attest that nothing terrestrial is tough enough to confine it.

8. HEAT-VIBRATION DETERMINES COMBUSTION. — Two Atoms, one material, the other ethereal, of equal energy in their impulses and expulses, and put together in a void, would reciprocally equilibrate, and stand static side by side. Primitive molecules may also stand statically balanced in their equal energies one alongside of the other. Their respective polarities, also, may bring and hold them together in more or less fixed connection, and their implication of impulses and expulses hold them in firm cohesion. Heat-vibrations may then be induced sufficient to separate these conjoined or coherent forces, and put their static energies in active collision, the violence of which will augment in rapid ratio,' as the number and intensity of the clashing bodies in concussion shall be increased. The energies of gravity, magnetism, and chemical cohesion may thus be converted into heat-vibrations, making the molecular derangements destructively violent. When such agitation suffices to make the ether luminous, the phenomenon is known as *combustion;* and while the burning substance retains its form it is said to be *on fire,* and when flying apart as luminous vapor it is said to be *in flame,* or in *a blaze.*

Bodies capable of being so luminously dissolved and diffused are known as *combustibles;* and such substances as in their strong affinities set free the combustible molecules are termed *supporters of combustion*. Some bodies so strongly cohere as to resist all ordinary applications of heat-energy, and are called *non-combustible*, while perhaps no compound bodies, above the primitive molecules, are so coherent, or in fixed chemical combination, that some possible heat-vibrations may not sunder them. The energies generating heat-vibrations are the essence of the material and ethereal forces of nature itself; and when conditions favor, ordinary non-combustibles become inflammable, and the elementary air and ether are on fire, and the face of the world is changed from former to new combinations. Solid masses part in the conflagration to smoke, cinders, and ashes; and then the conflicting forces settle again in quiet balance in those new forms of combination.

In our most advanced modern science we have the very interesting description of the process of combustion in the blaze of a common candle. On lighting the wick, the tallow melts, and is made inflammable according to the following philosophical explanation. Carbon and hydrogen are constituent elements in the tallow, and oxygen is an element in the air which surrounds the candle-flame. The oxygen and hydrogen have strong reciprocal affinities, and their molecules come together in clashes of great violence, and put the vapor in intense molecular vibration, and this " mode of motion " is the candle-blaze. The molecules of carbon and oxygen, also, have strong affinities, and strike violently together, constituting in their conflict the intense white heat of the blaze in its most brilliant portion. This collision is going on in the outer flame, while the yet undissolved carbon and hydrogen constitute the dark core within the blaze, and which is continually being decomposed and so perpetually feeds the flame; the hydrogen and oxygen combine anew, and go off in watery vapor, and other portions of oxygen combine with the carbon, and go off in carbonic acid, and so the flame is lost in the outer while steadily renewed from the inner matter.

But this interest ceases so soon as we strive to look within the empty terms, and find ultimately that they have no meaning beyond the mere appearance. "Affinities" inducing "percussions" and "vibrations," and thereby making heat as "a mode of motion," is certainly saying little for science, and nothing at all for philosophy. Not only is heat a mode of motion, but so are light and sound, and the phenomenal in every sense-organ is a mode of motion; and we know nothing beyond the naked appearance from all the set words we use, till in the insight of reason we truly find the distinctive forces which modify the motions. No words can expound what the mode of motion is, till we know what force is, and what the distinctive form of force does, and in the insight of the essential forces we can clearly determine what must be the phenomenal sequences. Carbon and the inflammable gases are substantial forces, and they dissolve and recombine accordingly as their distinc-

tive energies in their impulses and expulses interwork
with each other. The carbon in the tallow candle
decomposes in complete combination; but an intensely heated diamond, plunged in a volume of oxygen,
becomes luminous in stars of white light, with no
decomposition in its stronger carbonic combination.
The forces in solar vibration fixed in fossil coal-beds
loose and strike together in new fires, in myriad
furnaces. The forces alone determine and expound
the appearances.

9. SUPERFICIAL MAGNETISM, MADE FREE, DETERMINES
ELECTRICITY. — The composition of molecules into
larger bodies, fixing them more or less firmly in
cohesion, will in proportion to the cohesion hinder
their magnetic action. It can be anticipated of few
bodies, so molecularly constructed, that they shall
give free scope to the unhindered working of the
polarity of their component atoms. But if by any
interposing forces, such as that occasioned by heat-
vibrations, there may be the loosing or dissolving
of the cohesion, in the case of the superficial molecules of the body, so as to give to them the comparatively free exercise of their magnetic energy,
we shall then have them, so far, acting according to
their inherent mechanical forces, and in obedience to
the eternal laws of motion. With such freedom for
the magnetic energy in the surface molecules only of
the body, while the deeper ones remain fixed in cohesion, there must be a wide modification of the polar

action, even so far as at first to appear to be quite another force than that of magnetism; and with so much change in the application of its laws, it may readily be mistaken as an open field for wholly another science than that of bringing phenomena within the determinations of magnetic action. Such bi-polar energy, working only in the surface molecules of material bodies or molecules merely in contact, is *electricity;* and all the phenomena presented in electrical agency will find their complete comprehension in such restricted application of magnetic forces.

Such freed surface-molecules are independent magnets, according to the polarities which their component atoms give to them, as turned in their outer direction opposite to their inner polar unities. They reciprocally attract and repel, and mutually arrange themselves in polar directions, proportioned to their freedom, according to the working of their magnetic energy. They still, so far, cohere as to retain each its local position, but are so far free as to permit oscillation on their centres in their places. The magnetic now known as the Electric impulse flows on in the extended bodily surface of molecules, transmitting itself from one to another from the first movement, and only reaches one beyond except as it has worked through the one preceding. Should the superficial molecules in a body be not so freed from their cohesion, they can neither take nor impart polar impulses, and can therefore be excited by no applied energies to exhibit any electrical phenomena. Bodies capable of such excitement may be known as *electrics;* and if so far freed in their molecules as to oscillate to and fro sufficient to take and transmit the polar energy, they will be known as *conductors;* but if the molecules are only so far freed as to answer polar influences passing over its surface without sufficient swing to transmit, the body, though an electric, would be a *non-conductor.* A conductor entirely surrounded by non-conductors will be known as *insulated.*

When we contemplate a large body, like our earth, in its polar impulses, we note the flow of energy from the equator each way to the poles, through all the body, and so each point in each semi-magnetic axis is a polar point for its own spherical stratum; but when we contemplate the surface-flow only, it finds its static rest in the axial extremities as its poles. The flow towards the pole, when pressing directly across the filled helical circuits, will be direct in meridional lines, and any concurring polar energy in that direction will find an unhindered movement, until it and the polar flow in the body itself statically rest in the polar point. But, should any reverse polarity running occurrent to the flow supervene, there must at once be an encountered resistance, and the occurrent polarity be brought to static rest in the speedily balanced antagonism. There must, thus, be two kinds of electricity, both in the earth, and in all freed superficial molecules belonging to smaller bodies connected with the earth. That which in the earth flows directly to the pole, and in any body near the earth is concurrent with the earth's polarity, may be known as *positive* electricity, and that which is occurrent to the polar flow of the earth may be known as *negative* electricity. In all cases near our earth, the distinction must be in the concurrent or occurrent polarities.

Electricity is thus a force, and not a fluid put in motion by some assumed agency. A positive and negative fluid supposed leaves the whole in its mystery, for we must at length inquire with equal interest as at first, What moves the fluids? and why do they move in opposite directions? The force is the essential molecule, and the flowing energies constituting it determine the movement. This method of contemplating electricity will comprehend all methods of exciting it, and expound all the phenomena attending it.

1. *Electricity as excited by friction.* Strong molecular percussion, we have already seen, converts itself into light and heat in the induced ethereal vibrations. All collision of material bodies must in this way generate heat; and even so small an amount as that generated in the friction of pouring quicksilver from one vessel to another may be artificially measured. The friction of two bodies rubbed against each other, and thus converted into heat-vibration, will induce an agitation of the ethereal forces, involved in the molecular composition of the body on its surface, sufficient to free these superficial molecules for

the play of their polar energies, and which is but an excitement of electricity. The common electrical machine has in this its determination, and an accompanying explanation of all the phenomena of its action. There is the glass plate or glass cylinder with its prepared and applied amalgam rubber, and the movement of the glass beneath the rubber sets free the molecules in both surfaces. The surface-molecules in the glass body are only so freed as to become electrically excited, but not so as to transmit the energy from one to another, and thus glass is found to be a non-conductor; while the amalgam rubber transmits the energy over its surface, and is a conductor. The direction of their polar energy in the glass surface is found to be occurrent to the earth's polar energy, and thus the electricity of the molecules is negative, while that of the rubber is positive. Here, as glass, the electricity excited is ever negative; but some substances change their direction of polarity according to the more or less determined form which they or their rubber may constitutionally possess.

As a non-conductor, the glass has an artificially arranged row of conducting points placed within the sphere of action of the non-conducting molecules, and which, as points, receive and transmit the excited energy so finely and evenly as not to disturb the medium through which it passes. The glass or the rubber has a conducting connection with the earth, as the great static regulator of all smaller electric bodies in its connection; and whichever it may be that is thus connected, the opposite one must stand insulated. If the glass be thus connected and the rubber insulated, the negative electricity will balance itself through the connection, by at once standing as a static against the earth's polarity in the flow of energy towards the pole; or if the rubber be so connected and the glass insulated, then must the positive electricity balance itself in the earth's magnetic meridian, which it meets, as that stands static in the polar point. The kind of electricity thus held in static rest must crowd its opposite kind, from the limiting point between the glass and rubber, out over the connected conducting surface indefinitely. Such conducting surface is then said to be *charged* with electricity. The *quantity* of the charge is as the conducting surface, and the *intensity* or tendency to find its balance must be equal over a spherical surface, greatly augmented at the edges of a plane surface, and most of all where the surface is pointed.

As the polar energies of the molecules determine the mode of making the electrical machine, so also they expound all the experiments in exciting electricity by the machine. Among the more prominent and controlling cases may be adduced the following: An insulated conductor, in an unexcited and thus a *natural* state, may be placed near to the charged conductor so that the impulses of their molecules shall reciprocally interact, when, at once, the molecules in the surface of the uncharged conductor must be excited, and moved in position according to the polar energies imparted; and thus this conductor becomes itself charged by *induction* from the former. This induced charge, having no way of escape on account of its insulation, must have the kinds of electricity in the action of the poles of the molecules both concurrent and occurrent, and which must balance themselves in their own superficial area, thus making a neutral mid-line across the conductor, and the dissimilar kind to the exciting electricity attracted to the hither, and the similar kind expelled to the further side of the neutral line. So long as excited and insulated, these induced electricities must maintain their places, but must fall back to their natural state on removing the inducing conductor; or, if the induced conductor be connected with the earth, then must the invading energy of the inducing kind of electricity balance itself in the earth, and leave to the induced charge only the dissimilar kind in action.

And still further; such induced charge of unlike electricity to that which induced it must react upon the inducing conductor, so far neutralizing that which in it is like itself, and repelling this to the remotest side of the first inducing conductor, thereby bringing the kind dissimilar to itself to the nearest side, and augmenting the first inducing energy, and increasing the charge in the second induced conductor.

These alternately induced and augmenting charges in the two conductors must effect what is known as

condensation of electricity, and which remains steadfast on the last conductor as in a *latent* state, and is
sometimes called *dissimilar* electricity.   This falls immediately to a natural state on the removal or a discharge of the first conductor.   The Leyden Jar, or
the multiplication of Jars to a Battery, is thus effected, and heavy charges of electricity are accumulated.
A connection with the earth discharges the battery,
and when, through points in the connecting conduct-
or, as before shown, it must go off equably and still,
balancing in the earth with no molecular or ethereal
vibration.   But if the termination of the approaching
conductor be a ball, or expanded surface, the discharge
meets and makes a violent percussion with the intervening forces, and notifies itself in the commotion.
This is by sound to the ear in the agitation of the atmosphere, and by light to the eye in the vibration of
the surrounding ether.   Both the sound and the light
or heat are cases of conversion from one form of
force to another.   Thus a cloud of many square miles'
surface may so be connected at some point with the
earth by its mist or falling rain as to balance one kind
of its electricity with the electrical currents of the
earth, and thereby give occasion for its friction in the
winds to charge the whole with the dissimilar kind,
which may a while stand quiet in its insulation; but
it can have no safe rest till balanced in the earth in
both electricities.   If taken off by points, the air
knows no commotion; if taken off by explosive shocks,
the molecular vibration becomes converted into light-

ning through the eye, and into thunder on the ear. And so may be determined all the phenomena of electricity excited by friction; with like and unlike kinds; insulated and uninsulated conductors; charged and discharged; all is in the constitutional energy of the polar activity of freed superficial molecules that compose material bodies. Some substances are easily excited, and some with great difficulty, or not at all; but the force to give all the movements of electrical agency is constitutionally in the very construction of material atoms, and retained in the molecules of all material bodies.

When an electric battery is made to work its current in an exhausted glass receiver, a luminous stream is sent from either the positive or the negative end of the pointed conductor; the positive electricity in lines slightly diverging from the point into a brush of light, while from the negative point the stream flatly radiates in a star-shaped spark about it. So it should have been anticipated. The molecules of atmospheric matter are mainly abstracted, but the ethereal atoms at least are there filling the air-exhausted space, and though they only oscillate on their centres as the polar action goes from one to the next, the converted fire-flash from the polarizing stroke is perpetuated from atom to atom, and the light is truly in motion. The positive stream is continuous, and when in it is also concurrent with the earth's magnetic meridian towards the pole, and can find little impediment from anything; but the negative current meets the earth's magnetic current flatly in the face, and must scatter itself in star-shaped atomic polarities.

So, again, with electric perforations of pasteboard, or other substance favorable for the trial; the hole made is not as if pierced from one side with a bodkin — indented at the entrance, and burred at the exit. The molecules have been made to vibrate and sunder their cohesion from within outward, and so have burred both sides.

2. *Thermal Electricity.* — There are substances found, that when connected according to a certain arrangement, and heated in a certain way, give out their different currents of electrical energy. Alternate bars of bismuth and antimony, soldered together at their ends in divergent and convergent directions, respectively and successively, making a row standing in more or less acute angles at both ends of the bars, and the beginning and terminal ends, which are single, connected by a conductor, will constitute the arrangement for a thermal electric battery. When the bars are heated at one end through the range, an electric current passes from bismuth to antimony; and if cooled at this end below the temperature of the opposite, or the opposite be more heated than this, then the flow reverses itself, and proceeds from antimony to bismuth. The bars are comparatively heated and cooled in their opposite ends, and the positive flow is in the heated end, whichever it may be, and from bismuth to antimony bars respectively;

but when both ends are of like temperature, the electric energy is quiescent.

The polar energies in the molecules of the bars determine the whole process and results, as before in electricity, by friction; varying only as the changed conditions require. At the heated ends through one side of the range, the molecules in all the bars are the most fully liberated, and in each bar the molecules are less and less free as they approach the cooled end in the other side of the range, and thus the electric energy will be greatest in the heated, and least in the cooled ends. The movement must therefore be from the heated end of the bar to the cooled, and thence through the cooled end of the alternate bar to the heated end of the next, making the positive flow in that direction, and the negative action in the opposite direction. When the ends in the other side of the range are heated, conditions are reversed, and the positive current has a reversed direction, making also the negative energy the opposite in direction from its former course. The whole passes, in contrary directions of positive and negative each to each, in a closed circuit. The particulars of the polarities are like the voltaic currents, and can best be noted in that stronger flow.

3. *Electricity chemically excited.* — Some substances of different force of affinities in their molecules, and especially such as are in different degrees oxidizable, must chemically affect each other in coming in contact, and may thus free their superficial mole-

cules so as to admit of their polar arrangement, and
thereby excite electrical action.   The least oxidizable,
and thus of greater force of affinity and stronger
combination in itself, will ordinarily give the positive
direction towards and through the more oxidizable
body, and the oxidizable bodies will be specially
minerals.   The mere contact can induce but slight
excitement, while constant contact, within a chemically
active solvent, may much more effectually free the
surface molecules, and greatly augment the electrical
action.   Acids, alkalis, and saline solutions may so act
upon different metals as to excite their surface molecules in strong polar attractions and repulsions reciprocally.   Electricity, so excited, has circumstantial
peculiarities, and is known as Galvanism, from the
name of its first observer ; or more recently as
Voltaic electricity, from a later more thorough experi-
mentalist.

This voltaic electricity is still the same essential
polar energy as in the cases already contemplated;
and the artificial arrangements for exciting it, and all
the phenomena of its working, are determined and
expounded by the necessary laws of mechanical force
and motion, as contemplated in the free magnetic action of the molecules that lie in the surface of material bodies.   We may carefully apply these laws, as
we pass, to the arrangements and results, in their facts,
under the insight of the reason, and we cannot fail to
see their strictly determined conformity.

When two metals, as zinc and copper, are conveniently shaped and joined at their ends, they mutually act on each other in freeing their surface molecules and awakening their polar impulses. As the more coherent and less oxidizable, the copper sends the positive current through the zinc, while the negative current goes from the zinc through the copper. When these are immersed in a chemical solvent, the molecules are more thoroughly and extensively loosened, and the electro-motive energy is greatly augmented. A series of such metal plates being arranged and immersed, their quantity of voltaic electricity will be as the aggregate surfaces of all the plates; and the intensity of the current will be as the number of pairs of metal plates, each one super-inducing its own current upon that of all the former. The poles of the pile of plates will be as the outgoing currents, the positive at the end from which the positive flow of energy proceeds, and the negative at the end from which flows the negative current. Attached conductors at these poles receive and perpetuate the flow according to their respective attachments.

These conductors have their superficial molecules electrically excited, and thus the poles are carried to the extremities of these conductors respectively, and when insulated by the atmosphere, though put in polar directions there is no perpetuated flow, but if one pole of the conductors be connected with the earth, its electrical action will be neutralized by the earth's dissimilar polarity, and the electric energy of the voltaic battery must then be wholly of the unlike kind of electricity. When both poles are connected with the earth, they must both be balanced; and if all are insulated, and the poles be connected not with the earth, but in contact with each other, there will then be a closed circuit, and the currents will pass, each in its own direction, as constant as the continued arrangement. When the communication is with the earth, each separate stroke from the pile and its flow to the earth is therein balanced, and thus every electric shock is truly a new one; but when the insulated poles are connected in the closed circuit, there is no balance of either pole, and the old current fills and repeats continually. When the current, as in the former case, flows perpetually new to its balance in the earth, it must act upon an applied electrometer; but in the other case of a closed circuit and the same old current, the electrometer can have no strokes from the current.

This constitution of the molecular polarity determines all the phenomena of *electro-magnetism*. A pole of a magnet so placed that its action shall reciprocate with a voltaic current, all the movements must at once be determined by the magnetic attractions and repulsions upon the surface molecules, in which is the electric flow. The magnetic impulse and the electric current are but one polar energy. As the north magnetic pole is directed to an ascending or descending current, or as a south magnetic pole is thus directed, so the movements must be in each of an opposite-handed character. A fixed current may have movable magnetic poles, and a fixed pole movable voltaic currents; and the courses in each must be the resultants of the compound attractions and repulsions.

And so we have also the like clear determination for all factitious magnets. As soft-iron has no co-ercive-force, it comes under, and falls from, the polar energy, as applied and removed, instantly. When, then, a conveniently shaped bar of soft-iron is sur-rounded by opposite-handed helical conductors, the voltaic currents passing in the opposite-handed helices instantly put the molecules of the soft-iron bar into a complete magnet, with its neutral equator, its opposite-handed hemispheres, and its opposite polar-ities. Such factitious or artificial magnet, being con-stituted and used in connection with the telegraph wire of no coercive-force, all the wonderful facilities of telegraphic communication, will be at once deter-mined. The insulated soft-wire in the atmosphere, or by its coating at the bottom of the ocean, has its surface molecules put in vibration at every touch of the magnet, and fall in quiescence at every withdraw-ment. The connection of one pole with the earth, and balanced, gives to the other the working im-pulse, and the capacity to spell any message.

THIRD DIVISION.

REVOLVING FORCE.

In the constitution of the Atom, we noted a revolving agency, which turned each component force as created upon its limit of antagonism, and thus made all to turn spirally, and in helical circuits opposite-handed in opposite hemispheres, till in the completion of the atom it had become a sphere, locked within itself and excluding further revolution from its own inner counteraction. Thus far, we have found such a constituted atom subserving its ends in material nature by its magnetic and electric energy, and revealing the design of the Creator, in so constructing the atom, by the results of its own agency. But now we come to a much more extended use for such construction, in the very revolving agency itself, which not only secures to the completed atom its bi-polar action, but ministers directly to the fashioning of the Universe, and the determining of a Common Space and Time as Absolute for all worlds.

1. A REVOLVING FORCE DETERMINES THE UNIVERSE AND ITS ABSOLUTE SPACE AND TIME. — That there

may be a common space, in the experience of many,
demands that a fixed position be taken and maintained by a perpetual filling it with substantial force;
for if the one fixed position be once lost, the possibility of determining the one space must thereby
be lost. And so also, that there may be a common
time for the experience of many, there must be continuous movement from the one fixed position; for
should the motion stop or be cut off from connection
with the fixed position, the possibility of putting all
their times into one time would be gone. But rectilineal movement from a fixed position cannot measure itself; the movement must return into itself in
cycles, and thereby have its own measure, and be
also an occasion for comparatively determining all
periods. While, thus, revolving movement will give
determined common space and time, it will also be
found to .determine the forms and positions of material worlds, and the construction of the entire
universe.

The threefold agency in creation, as before found
necessary to make either the Creator or his creating
work intelligible, will here be noted as indispensable
for comprehending the facts of nature, as far as all
experience has yet gained them. The conscious will
of the First Person must hold within itself the universal Idea; the conscious will of the Second Person
must overtly express, and hold in stable reality, the
substantial Forces elemental for this universal Idea;
and the conscious will of the Third Person must turn

all the elemental forces together, and hold them in Unity. The constituent Forces in the two varieties of antagonist and diremptive have all that is elemental in material and ethereal substances, as they have already been contemplated; and we now seek to know how they may be shaped and bound in the complete unity of the original Idea. This is to be accomplished in the contemplation of a distinctive revolving Force overtly acting upon the material and ethereal forces, and so, other than in any thinking-process, an actual willing energy is to determine the universe as palpable thing transcending all stated thought: centrally fixed in itself, and turning in its place, in the one common space and time for all rational Intelligences.

Were we to begin with the elementary material and ethereal mass, and attempt to account by the logical Judgment for the separation into parts, and the sorting and putting them together in a universal whole, one method we might take, as some do, in explanation of the universal forming process would be, to assume the being of a personal Creator who had in his own way overtly fixed the hard material, and now fashions it in many worlds at his pleasure; and while it is supposed that *he* knows all thoroughly and comprehensively, it must be taken that *we* can know nothing about the manner how, and are forced to content ourselves with the study of the mere appearances. If, however, we should see it to be illogical to assume the being of a Creator and fashioner of the universe, and will begin as others have in facts, and not assumption, we may carefully study the appearances as they come in experience, noting how they stand together or succeed each other, and how the many later have come from the fewer which were more early, and may talk of this as "development" and "evolution;" and then may imagine that if we could go far enough back, we might fall upon one simple being needing nothing further back; and could there say, inasmuch as "genetic production," after the law of "like from like," with "occasional deviations," has been given in experience, this first simple being in the millions of ages has begotten all "varieties of species," and preserved all "consecutive gradations" by "natural selection." But then, this primitive simple is the "absolutely unknowable," and indeterminate whether person or thing, and so our science and our religion vanish in blank "nescience." The upshot of all philosophy of experience is, — God knows, but we cannot know; or, — we attain an absolutely simple, which we cannot say if it be God or not.

But the case is far otherwise, when we can give the carefully collected facts of experience over to the insight of an acknowledged faculty which reads the certain meaning in empirical appearances, and knows this to be *force* in nature, and *free personality* as Author of force above nature. We thus intelligently enter nature in her very essence, and in "the things that are made" we "clearly see the power and Godhead" of their Maker. We can then legitimately begin with the making, and follow the process of fixing the realities which determine all our observed appearances. We know God as independent of time, and that his knowledge of the universe is timeless, and thus, to him, the making of the atoms, and moulding them in worlds, and turning the worlds on one centre, were as if instantaneously accomplished ; while to bring the work into our finite comprehension, we must follow through the process, item by item, and see the work go on atom by atom, that at last we may attain to the consummation, when the working will of the Spirit, by a revolving force, has taken the atoms in their formless state and void of all inter-consistency, and turned them into solid worlds, and lit them up in the brightness by which he hath "garnished the heavens."

With the insight of reason, then, we now go back to the commencing work of creation, and there contemplate the interposition and results of this revolving Force as the direct product of the Spirit's agency. When the Logos, as realizing Will, made overtly stable the first substantial Force, the Spirit as fashioning Will, revolved it on its antagonizing point that the next created Force should occupy the exact place which the first had ; and creating and forming agencies so continued their work, till the first completed atom filled its place, and in its own fulness could take in no further forces. And now, that the creating and revolving processes may go on, the Spirit must move not merely the successive forces, but the created atom from its place ; and doing this to the extent of half the diameter of the solid atom, the precise old position for a new created force is thereby vacated, wherein a new atom may begin, and here a second is made and fashioned as was the first atom. But while the second atom is being formed, it and the first compound their moving energies, and the resultant is quite a modified movement.

The first atom, completed and moved in a right line to the extent of half its diameter from its original position, must carry with it the excess of energy given on one side, and have in it the momentum of its own mass multiplied into this excess, thus determining a continued rate of moving; but this continued movement cannot be rectilineal, since the moving energy is at once compounded with the energies essentially in the newly forming atom. These energies of the forming hold on to those of the first formed atom by their mutually gravitating impulses, and also turn the first atom, by their own constituent revolution, out of its direct line of departure from its old position, and the resultant must be a movement of the first atom about the position in which is the forming second atom. This second being completed, and removed as was the first, gives the same original place for the created force which begins a third atom, and the second and first are then acted upon by the forming third atom, and the resultants become increasingly complicated with every new formed atom. Each atom and the forces of all kinds in all the atoms come within the mechanical laws of composition and resultant, and while the whole is clear in the Absolute Reason, the compositions soon run beyond all finite insight. Nor is it important here that we accurately determine anything further than the general result of all the movements.

All created atoms thrown out of their original place must at once begin revolving about that place, from the revolving movement of the impulses in the forming atom, together with the revolving movement given to all the preceding atoms. These outgoing and revolving atoms also act upon each other magnetically, and thus we have the central revolving force, the ejecting force, and the polar forces acting in composition, the resultant of which must be a movement in opposite-handed helical circuits, forming a hemisphere of atoms on each side of an equatorial plane, and constituting thereby a revolving sphere which must also have its own magnetic polarities. So, in the universal result, there must be an augmenting mass of created atoms ensphering themselves in the aggregate magnetically, and revolving concentrically. The aggregation can at no time make the mass a complete sphere, since the atoms approach each other in the poles of the mass with similar polarities together, and which must make at the poles mutual repellencies, thus keeping the polar points of the mass open, and making the universal mass of atoms rather a broad spherical ring than a completed sphere. The revolving force from the fashioning Will at the centre goes out with and works in every atom, and so reaches every portion of the aggregate mass; and such revolving energy may be intensified, and the revolutionary velocity augmented at pleasure. The original Idea in the Absolute Reason is in this way brought out and attained in full overt expression, and what the universe comes to be determines what that primitive Idea was, and we may speculatively follow out the process, and note the mode of movement, which has secured for the constituent forces of the universe the present distribution, arrangement, and orbital movement.

In the fulness of material, place, and period known in the divine wisdom, the last antagonist atom completed the material elements needed, and the next force made was diremptive, beginning the construction of a diremptive atom. The new diremptive force took the same place in which all the antagonist forces had been created, as the last antagonist atom had been moved off, and this diremptive force was revolved on its mid-limit of expulses, by the fashioning Will, and in like helical circuits as in the antagonist impulses, till the two hemispheres together filled the space and finished the first ethereal atom now at the centre of the aggregated and revolving material atoms. Thenceforward were made and sent off successively ethereal atoms continuously, keeping the one central place fixed and filled, and the movement out from it incessantly continuous; thus steadily determining a common universal place and period in the one Space and one Time.

So the ethereal atoms were multiplied and accumulated as a revolving mass within the expanding material envelopment, and interfusing themselves among the material atoms as their mass expands, till at length the outpressing ether and the impressing matter equilibrate; and in this balance of diremption and antagonism the creative work ceases, and the overt real is the copy of the inner ideal. As two equal antagonist and diremptive atoms side by side would hold each other in balance, so the equal accumulation of each kind in this concentric ensphering will hold each in its general place respectively by the unbroken equilibration. The heavens and the earth were thus created in their elements, but with neither outer distinctive form nor inner consistency. Cohesions, chemical combinations, and crystallizations begin, but as yet the universal forces hold together as a whole by the outgoing central diremption balancing the incoming gravity. The inner sphere is pure ether; the outer envelope is chaotic matter; but through the matter the ether has become interfused sufficiently to give occasion for universal heat- and light-vibrations. The pure ether has perfect elasticity, and thus unhindered vibratory movement; but where antagonist atoms intermingle, vibratory motion is impeded. Mechanical law everywhere prevails and controls in keeping the whole steadfast, and the parts interacting in full correlation and equivalence. Nothing is fortuitous nor capricious, but all forces are within the central sway of Eternal Reason, insuring the coming of universal beauty and order.

2. THE REVOLVING FORCE DETERMINES THE SEPARATION AND DISTRIBUTION OF THE UNIVERSAL MATTER. — The last made diremptive force, finishing the last Ethereal Atom, stands with its expulses in the same position the first and each succeeding force has occupied. The creating Will has rested from his work, but the fashioning Will still maintains his energy, and keeps the last force, and thus also the last atom perpetually revolving, and which may be of any conceivable velocity. The atoms act on each other, but as vapor or fluid, and not as a cohering solid. The central movement must thus be the most rapid and extending outward in broader and thus slower circuits, making the whole movement as a vortex from centre to periphery. The entire spherical annulus is thus in measured motion about its centre, at ratios proportioned to the distance of the moving atoms from the centre ; and as the central motion goes on, the periphery, though always slower than the centre, must still be with augmenting velocity, and both from the revolving impulse, and polar repulsions, there must follow equatorial accumulations and an axial revolving. In process of the persistent central working there must come at length the starting-off of large vapory masses from the periphery of the

spherical annulus, some nearer the poles, but most nearest the equator.

In speaking of this revolving universal mass, which from the similar polarities of the atoms to each other at the extremities of the polar diameter must repel each other, and thus open and expand the polar regions so far as to make the whole a spherical annulus of material atoms, yet as we are to contemplate it, will the whole mass of matter enveloping the interior ether be so near to a thick spherical shell about it, that it will not lead astray to use the term sphere, rather than the longer but more exact expression of spherical annulus. In the augmenting rapidity of revolution, and thus ejection of large superficial portions of this so called universal sphere, should the ejecting impetus be equable in every part, the particular ejected portion would move off on its separate way with no one part moved round another, and thereby forming an axis of revolution within itself. But such exact equality of impetus would seldom, if ever, occur. The natural process must be, that in the ejected portion, that part which was moving further and faster in the surface of the universal sphere than the part moving shorter and slower a little within this surface, will on ejection run beyond and overlap the latter; and further, that the less superficial part must leave the universal sphere latest, and somewhat adhering to and slackened in departure from the sphere, and must thereby augment the tendency of the former to overwrap the latter;

and so the ejected portion will begin its separate journey by turning upon itself and forming for itself an inward axis of rotation. The general ejecting impetus tangential to the universal sphere is compounded with the direct attraction of the sphere, giving the resultant in an Orbit around the old sphere, or around any central world into which the parts may subsequently be distributed. The rotation of the ejected portion on its own axis will accumulate from the polar parts about the equatorial region, making the new world an oblate spheroid, and so steadying the movements in its orbit by its rotation on its own axis, that this axis will be held parallel with itself in all places.

Other superficial portions successively pass off in the same way till the material shell is exhausted in its pieces, and yet the whole is a universe still; the distributed worlds are as stable on their old centre as when in mass together. The Ether fills all interspaces, and by its diremptive energy equilibrates all gravitating impulses, while the superintending hand of Absolute wisdom and power is on the centre, managing every movement.

3. Single and Compound Worlds. — The masses into which the universal sphere breaks up will at the first be detached, fleecy forms, with no similarity or regularity of outline, as masses of cloud break up and drift apart one from another. Slowly they gather into their more condensed and rounded

shape, as their gravitating and rotating forces fashion them.

There could hardly be such a conjunction of distinguishable antagonist, diremptive, and revolving forces working at the separating and ejected world, as to send it off with an equal and direct impulse in every part; nor can we see a reason why the Creator's hand should seek so to adjust the forces; but should such equable impetus strike off a superficial mass, and leave it to its own action, it would pass on its solitary way, a single world with no attendant. We cannot say such worlds are not; we can only say that the forces, in their determinate action, give no occasion to anticipate that such will somewhere be constituted.

But should some masses be so unequal in impulse and movement of parts as to break asunder on their separation from the great sphere, or should two or three separate masses move off from the surface nearly at once, their imparted motion and their mutual attractions might very well determine for them, at the start, a tendency to arrange themselves about some common centre of gravity and of revolution, while the whole combination would have its grand movement about the great sphere, and each its distinct path about the common centre. Such may be *binary* or *ternary* worlds, or perhaps so combine as to be *quaternary*, and all will have their determinate laws, and harmonious and safe movements. As viewed from other worlds, they will stand to the spectator in the direction of their own common orbital plane, and there appear alternately to approach and then recede from each other; or as perpendicular to their orbital plane, when their full revolutions will have no change of distance, respectively, from each other; or they may stand at any intervening inclination of their plane, and appear with corresponding obliquities of revolution.

Viewed from our terrestrial stand-point, the stars are of different magnitudes, and the numbers greater as the magnitudes diminish. If it be taken for a probable fact that the smaller are proportionally more distant, two stars of unequal magnitudes may readily appear as if joined in system, and constituting a compound world. But when lying in nearly the same line of vision, while one may be at a great remove beyond the other, they are only *apparent* double-stars, and as two bodies they have no common connection. More than six thousand double-stars have been noticed, taken in both hemispheres, which have no more probable relation than other stars, except as it happens that they lie to us nearly in the same line of vision. But all cases of double-stars are not merely so in optical appearance. Taking stars to the seventh magnitude, and the chance that they should appear within 4″ of each other, and so be binary, it has been computed would be but 1 to 9870, and that they should appear ternary, but as 1 to 173524; and yet of ternary combination there have been observed at least three, and of binary more than six hundred.

There is, however, more direct evidence of compound worlds, than that they appear beyond their proper number from chances. There are more than six hundred and fifty that have been noticed as having relative motions, and not by parallax from our change of position; and of these, sixteen, at least, have had their orbits determined, and some have completed more than one revolution since their discovery. The periodical times of these *physically* double-stars differ from thirty to six hundred and thirty years. Their distance and their non-polarized light determine them to be suns shining by their own light, and not planetary bodies. Whether such compound worlds have their planetary accompaniments can be known by no present methods of observation; all we can say is, they have communion each with each in their revolutions.

4. SYSTEMS OF WORLDS. — A large nebulous mass thrown off from the universal sphere must soon assume a spherical form in its rotatory movement, and begin to acquire consistency from its gravitation and incipient cohesion. The condensation will be comparatively great at the centre; and if the surface be of a comparative levity proportioned to its distance, the result, in many cases, will be that the superficial gravity will be less than the force of revolution, when the newly-formed sphere will give off a portion of its equatorial surface, and this ejected portion will also turn on an axis of its own, and revolve about its

primary, and be carried by the primary around the original centre. This primary becomes a Sun to its smaller globe, and that a planet revolving around it.

The rotation of a planet on its own axis must be in the direction of that of the primal sun, and an exact force of revolution and balance of gravity would put the planet's equator in the plane of its orbit, and this orbit would also be in the plane of the sun's equator. Disturbing forces must be anticipated as sure to interrupt such regularity. The unequal affinities, and cohesions, and gravities will induce unequal accumulations about the sun's equator, and the planets will be sent off in directions intersecting its plane; and if this had been at a considerable angle, when the sun's revolutions should have brought up to its equator the superficial matter for another planet, the excess from one hemisphere before will be probably balanced by a corresponding excess from the other now, and this planet must thus go off at an angle inclined to the plane of the sun's equator on the opposite side. Such oscillation from side to side, in planetary inclinations of orbit, would be *à priori* probable, and also that their axes should be in lines variously inclined to each other. Should a planetary axis of revolution be so formed, by unequal force of ejectment on one side of its centre, or the unequal quantity of matter and its gravity on one side, as to carry its inclination more than 90° from the normal plane, in such case its rotation on its axis would be reversed, and the movement be retrograde.

This rotating planet, again, carries its superficial portions to its equatorial region, making the planet oblate; and in some cases of a planet the force of revolution may be sufficient to eject portions of its surface at the equator once, or repeatedly, and the planet thus have one satellite or more which it carries with it about the sun. The planets and their satellites condense gradually to comparatively small dimensions compared with their first sizes, but their orbits must be of much the same diameter from the first. It may sometimes be, that the conditions shall accumulate so homogeneous and equable equatorial surface about the planet, and the revolving force be so assisted by satellite attractions, that the matter shall not separate itself, but be raised from the body of the planet, which also condenses beneath, and this equatorial portion become a ring entirely about the planet. While it retains its vaporous or fluid state, it may revolve about the planet, and adjust itself to any unequal attractions; but should it become cohesive and unyielding, a violent disturbing force must rupture it, or throw down one part of it upon the body of the planet.

At any subsequent times, the then present state of the worlds must indicate what has been their cosmological history. As we now look on, we may read that the sun has passed from its superficial accumulation about the great sphere, and at the time of its ejection was a nebulous mass that filled the whole place within the orbit of its outside planet, and its periodic time of rotation on its axis then was the periodic time of this farthest planet in its orbital revolution. The planetary bodies have since been successively thrown off in their vaporous or fluid state, and they have thrown off their satellites, and all have condensed and settled into their present positions, from volumes of matter that was filling the whole place within their orbits, and revolving on their own axes at the periodic times of these present worlds in their orbits, and which periodic times these bodies have from the first observed.

An older history is still further back, when the suns and systems were a contiguous collection of atoms filling all the place within the grand range of the furthest star, and when the ether, that is now diffused through all the interstellary spaces as the medium for light- and heat-vibrations, was then an inner sphere beneath the superincumbent shell of universal matter, expanding and revolving this shell till by installments it became disrupted and thrown into the suns and systems which we call fixed stars, because their distance forbids that we should find for them either apparent size or motion. The universal law of mechanics was inherent in these forces at their first constitution, and all the resultant facts of planetary systems have been determined by it. The necessary laws of gravity and universal motion contain within them Kepler's laws of planetary revolution, and all go back to the Absolute thought and will which fixed the first simple impulses in their antagonism, and set them in revolving movement on their central limit by the repetitions of similar creations.

5. THE REVOLVING FORCE HAS DETERMINED SEVERAL PHENOMENA OTHERWISE INEXPLICABLE. — The general results in these cases should so be as before given, while inequalities and varieties are such as different conditions might well be supposed to have occasioned, and sometimes the modifying conditions are quite patent. These phenomena occur in our own system, and may be taken as indices of similar phenomena in other systems.

1. *Gradations in planetary density.* Varied densities, and of wholly irregular measures, would result from planetary formations by independent Causes; but if they have been successively thrown off from the same solar mass, they must gradually have a general increase of density from the further or outside planets. And such is the general fact, with irregularities slightly occurring, that might readily be expected from peculiar circumstances slightly modifying the condensations. The most noticeable is the specific gravity of the sun itself, which is but about the density of Jupiter, when as central it should be denser than any planet. The immense photosphere of imponderable flame greatly enlarging the sun's apparent volume, and which, as the divisor

of the mass in attaining density will give too small a quotient, is a sufficient explanation.

2. *Gradation of interplanetary spaces.* A regular gradation of spaces between the planets would not happen from independent causes of separation; but thrown off from one solar body successively as that body successively diminished, the spaces between would gradually diminish from the outer inward. The facts are, that the interplanetary spaces are a near approach to a duplicate ratio on each remove from the inner planet.

3. *Inclination of planetary orbits.* If the planets were thrown from the solar sphere by a revolving force, we should expect a general conformity of orbit to the plane of the solar equator, with varieties occasioned by circumstantial unequal accumulations about the equatorial region before the planetary ejection. If we suppose the plane of the sun's equator to have been between the orbits of Neptune and Uranus when they successively were thrown off, we shall have balancing alternations from side to side of from half a degree to three and a half, till we come to Mercury, whose ejection was on an advance, and not return swing, and then we have the sun's present equator still a trifle in advance of the orbit of Mercury. Nothing would seem to account for such near conformity of orbits so well as revolving projections from the solar sphere.

4. *Periodic times and heliocentric movement.* On the supposition of successive ejections from the sun's

body, the periodic times of revolution by the planets should bear a general proportion to their distance from the centre; and so also with their heliocentric motions, the greater periodic time and the less heliocentric movement should be in the further planet. And these gradations are, in fact, so in accordance with revolving-force requisition that no other cause need be sought in explanation. And with the sun's present rate of revolution and heliocentric motion in the equatorial periphery, were another planet now to be thrown off inside of Mercury, there would be corresponding shortened revolution and accelerated movement.

5. *The orbits of the satellites should present greater irregularities than those of the planets.*   Exactly balanced material would give exact motion, and throw all orbits in the plane of the sun's equator. But the planets should have been anticipated to be thrown off as excess of accumulation from side to side of the solar equator, and so with some but not large inequalities in the inclinations of their orbits. Then their own unbalanced matter at first about their centres will more widely derange the inclinations of their respective axes, and thus furnish occasion for quite wide varieties in the movements of the satellites they shall eject in their own revolutions. Should such occasions of disparity conspire, in a particular case, to make the inclination of the satellite orbits more than 90° from a normal plane, it would reverse the order

of their revolution, and make the satellite-movements to be retrograde.

Taking the earth's orbit as in the normal plane, and looking out from the sun's centre, and then taking the right hand to be our northern hemisphere, and the eye directly in the plane looking westward, as we have our face, we shall there view the revolutions of the system passing on from westward to eastward, and such as are in and parallel with the ecliptic will move squarely direct, and such as may vary from the plane, inclined on either hand, will move obliquely direct according to the degree of inclination, and when such inclination shall pass beyond a perpendicular to the plane, the movement of the body in such orbit will be reversed, and become obliquely retrograde.

The earth is the first from the sun among the planets having a satellite, and the moon's orbit has an inclination of about 5° to the ecliptic, and is thus direct with little obliquity; while the equatorial plane of the earth inclines to the ecliptic about $23\frac{1}{2}$°, with a direct motion indeed on its own axis, but largely oblique.

Jupiter is the next with satellites, of which there are four. nearly in the same plane, and this common plane of the satellites also nearly in the same plane as the planet's equator and orbit, and all less than $1\frac{1}{2}$° inclined to the ecliptic; and thus all the movements of Jupiter and his satellites are very nearly squarely direct.

Saturn is next, with eight satellites and a ring, all moving nearly in the same plane, except the exterior satellite, which varies from the common plane about 12°, and this common plane is about 28° inclined to the ecliptic; and so the Saturnian movements are all direct, though largely oblique.

We then have Uranus, known to have four satellites with orbits nearly in a common plane, and which stands inclined to the ecliptic about 69°; and yet the Uranian satellites are retrograde in their revolutions though quite considerably within 90° inclination to the ecliptic. Here is an anomaly, long noticed and hitherto inexplicable. It would still remain inexplicable if we were obliged to take the pole of the Uranian axis, which is at the right of the ecliptic, as the end of the axis which was thrown up from its normal position perpendicular to the ecliptic, on the same side, in the forming and rotating process; since, as so affording less than 90° inclination, there could not be a reversal of its movement. But, if this right hand pole were advanced to its present position, from its normal perpendicular position on the left hand, then would the inclination pass beyond 90° to about 101°, and make the movement very decidedly retrograde. Such is to be the contemplation, if we consider the axis of the plane of the satellite-revolution to be also the axis of the planet; but as such Uranian axis is not known, and which perhaps may be as oblique as the earth's axis to that of the moon's orbital plane, or about 18½°, this would leave the rotation of Saturn direct on its own axis, while its satellites have gone to a degree of inclination reversing their movement.

6. *Planetoids and Saturnian ring.* The first discovery of a Planetoid was on the first day of the year 1801, and in 1870 there had been found one hundred and ten planetoids. They are all within the appropriate region between Mars and Jupiter for a single planet, and have general conformity and characteristics with the planets, differing most in diminutive volume, and varied ellipticity and inclination of their orbits. The largest is about five hundred miles in diameter, and the smallest may be no more than fifty miles diameter; the aggregate volume of all is equal only to a small planet. Their movements are direct, but their diversity from the planets and among themselves in inclination and eccentricity of orbits, longitude of ascending node, and longitude of perihelion, have been inexplicable. The determinations of a revolving force consistently account for all these peculiarities.

When the great planet Jupiter, whose mass is more than three hundred and thirty-eight times that of the earth, had been just separated from the solar sphere, its attraction of the portion of the sphere close beneath must have given to the equatorial accumulations upon it a very peculiar state and position for constituting the next planet, and specially fitted for forming the planetoids. As the solar sphere revolved on its axis under so large an attracting body, its equatorial gathering must have been much hastened, and this protuberance must have been much disturbed and drawn away from an equable diffusion about the whole equatorial part to a rising tide following along under the moving planet. This equatorial accumulation could not thus be retained till it should ultimately be sent off in a large mass; but on the collection becoming somewhat considerable, and rising up directly beneath the large planet Jupiter, the revolving force must have seized its crest and taken off the tide-wave, so to speak, in detached portions. The first planetoid was thus prematurely formed, and then followed others in successive installments, till the least distant from the sun was taken in the same way, and sent revolving round it at quite a delayed period, and at last the balancing relief was attained, as if all had been expelled in one planet. The ordinary accumulations afterwards went on, with a density too great and an attraction too small, that they should thenceforth be taken off piecemeal; and Mars came next — a regular but smaller planet.

This tide-crest under Jupiter must have been perpetually passing round the whole equatorial circle of the solar sphere, and thus determining the wide differences respectively of longitude of perihelion and longitude of ascending node; and the unequal attractions of Jupiter, as in his revolutions he passed on opposite sides of the solar equator, must have occasioned wide disparities in orbital inclinations. With such a planet as Jupiter, his next inferior planet could not have been matured and thrown off in one projection; nor, on the other hand, could the peculiar planetoid formations have taken place without just such preponderances of planetary attractions and tidal elevations. The planetoids must have occurred between Jupiter and Mars, and could have been constituted between no other planets of the system.

The rings of Saturn are the opposites of the planetoids, and are an unbroken satellite, inasmuch as they are a separation from the planet on all sides. Saturn is the least dense of all the planets, and has sent off from his own body a larger proportion of equatorial accumulations than any other. He has eight satellites, and a ring in the equatorial plane about the planet and between its own body and the orbit of the inferior satellite. This ring has two main divisions concentrically by a comparatively narrow space between them, and a transparent portion of the inner ring stretches downward as a veil towards the surface of the planet. The exterior ring is about ten thousand five hundred miles in depth, and the interior is more than seventeen thousand miles deep, and their dividing space is about eighteen hundred miles, and exclusive of the pending veil, the lower edge of the interior ring is about nineteen thousand miles above the surface of the planet. These main rings have also apparent slight subdivisions. The edge of the ring in direct line of vision is barely perceptible, and cannot be more than fifty miles in thickness. The ring is together slightly eccentric, and thus balances itself on a moving point about the centre of Saturn, and must be a vapor or a fluid, or, as some deem, an accumulation of separate granular bodies. Such a phenomenon nowhere else in the heavens presents itself.

But the peculiar conditions readily supposable explain why there was this flat ring rather than a spherical satellite. If the eight satellites of Saturn were, at a favorable state of the equatorial accumulation, pretty evenly distributed, in their respective orbits, about the body of the planet, their attraction in composition with the even revolving-force all through the equatorial surface, instead of throwing the whole out and off at one place, would raise the whole in all places, and permit the body of Saturn to condense and revolve on its axis beneath the ring thus formed, while the ring would revolve in its own place with the force it had when on the body, and has retained since its separation. Such a revolving ring must throw its vaporous or fluid matter into a thin plane, and might very probably be expected to make a permanent separation between a denser part thrown furthest and highest, and a lighter part with a thin veil hanging from it below, and thus by its own action to work itself into what is its present shape and position. So long as the condensation is not a solid, it may have its revolving flow unbroken, and accommodate itself to any limited disturbing attractions. Nothing could determine such a ring but such equable attraction and force of revolution, and with such its formation was a necessary result. No other planet has the rarity of matter, and the number of satellites, to permit that it encircle itself with such a revolving ring, anywhere else in the system.

7. *The same matter is co-extensive with the universe.* It has been found that a sodium flame gives a yellow band across the spectrum, at the same relative place in it as a dark line is given in the solar spectrum, and which, from special observations made by him in obtaining this and other relative spectral lines, has been known as the line of Fraunhofer. Further experiment reveals, that an intense white light put behind the yellow sodium-flame gives a spectrum with a dark band in the place of the yellow, the sodium yellow having absorbed the yellow that was blended in the white light put behind it. The general conclusion is, "A flame absorbs rays of the same refrangibility as those which itself emits."

Applying this generalization to particular flames determines particular substances. The incandescent body of the sun, with its yellow vaporous flame before it, gives the dark Fraunhofer line in the solar spectrum just where it is by the sodium-blaze with the white light behind, and thus evincing the presence of sodium in the substance of the solar body. Appropriating the different Fraunhofer lines in the solar spectrum, with those of different substances in the lines made by their respective flames in their particular spectrum, each with each, it has been concluded that the substance of the sun has also the metals calcium, magnesium, barium, iron, nickel, copper, chromium, and zinc added to the sodium first found; and similar experiments with the fixed stars find a portion of the same substances entering into their composition. Such experiments find, what the formation of the systems by revolving forces determines must be, the same matter everywhere universally diffused. A careful examination of the sun's spots determines a luminous atmosphere about the body of the sun, of much more intense brightness than the body itself; it is not thus the sun's substance that is white beneath the outer flame, but the intenser lower portion of the photosphere has its rays stricken down in passing through the colored flame above, which absorbs as it emits, and determines the Fraunhofer lines, and gives the substance of the flame, and not that of the sun.

This photosphere is gaseous, inasmuch as its light has no polarization; and whether induced by meteoric matter impinging by gravity upon the sun, or other cause, the same efficiency for perpetual light- and heat-vibrations will apply to all centres of systems.

6. COMETS COME INTO THE SYSTEM FROM WITHOUT. — Matter both atomic and molecular will still be diffused through the interstellary spaces when the systems have been constituted by the central revolving force. It will ordinarily be too rare to interrupt and reflect the light-vibrations, but in some collected

masses it may be expected to have consistency sufficient to retain form, and be made luminous.   As
separate from the systems it may be known as meteoric matter, and must move in the general revolution
of the central force, and portions of it must also feel
and obey the interactions of stellar attraction, and
fall within the eddies and cross-tides which must be
induced between the moving forces. Some portions
may move wholly outside of any system, and remain
unknown to observers within; others may come in
and pass out of a system; and a few of the many may
be caught and retained permanently by the attractions of the system. Such meteoric matter appearing within a system, of considerable volume and determinable movement, is known as a Comet, whether
once passing through and off, or revolving statedly
within it. Those of the former may pass in hyper-
bolic or parabolic curves; the latter will have full
orbits more or less elliptical; and the movements of
either may be direct or retrograde, inasmuch as they
may enter the system from any direction.

The facts as observed correspond with such speculative liabilities. They are so rare in consistency,
that a fixed star before which the comet has moved
shines through the most central part of it with undi-
minished lustre, and though the motion of the planets
is not appreciably obstructed by the ethereal media,
that of the comets has a noticeable retardation.
Some have come into the system, and made more
than one regular revolution in it, and then have been

lost to any further observation ; and another has part-ed into two within full observation, and the two for months visibly receded from each other, and on their periodic return both again appeared, but they were a million and an half miles asunder. Of two hundred comets whose elements were determined, the largest portion were found to be parabolic, and nearly equal in direct and retrograde movements, while forty of the number only were of elliptical orbits. Of these forty revolving within the system, thirteen have their mean distances within the orbit of Saturn, six within the orbit of Uranus, and twenty-one beyond any known planet. The least of these cometary orbits whose mean dis-tances are beyond Neptune is thirty-three times larger than that of the earth, and the greatest is two thousand one hundred and thirty-eight times larger than the earth's orbit. Of.the thirteen within Saturn there is an approach to planetary conformity in inclina-tion and eccentricity, and they are all alike in direct movement. Of the six within Uranus, there is great diversity of inclination from 18° nearly to a perpen-dicular, greatly augmented eccentricity, and one of them has retrograde movement. Of the twenty-one beyond Neptune there are similar varieties of inclina-tion, great eccentricity making the opposite sides of the orbit for a long distance nearly parallel, and as nearly equally divided as possible in movement, hav-ing ten direct and eleven retrograde.

While these diversities forbid the supposition that the comets have been thrown from a common central

source with the planets, those within the system may
find the determinations of conformity to planetary
movement from forces acting upon them since their
introduction. The less velocity, which permitted
them on entering to be retained, would secure diminished eccentricity generally proportioned to their
confinement within the system; but especially the
orbital inclinations, and the *direct and retrograde
movements,* may be referred for their classified differences to forces acting upon the comets within the
system, but which do not reach them when beyond
the system. Thus all the comets, whose mean distance is within the orbit of Saturn, must perpetually
move within the sphere of Saturn's attraction, added
to the aggregate attraction of all the planets within
Saturn's orbit. Let, then, a comet commence its
revolution at any extreme degree of inclination, and
the aggregate attractions in the plane of the comet's
orbit will have their excess on one side of it, and
draw the comet in its course to that side; and such
conspiring attractions must bring the plane of the
comet's orbit in nearer conformity to the mean
plane of the planetary orbits; hence the inclinations
of orbit with this class of comets are, with one little augmented exception, less than the most inclined
orbit of the planetoids. Such gradually changing orbit
must at length find its place of general equilibrium
from one perihelion passage to another, and henceforth oscillate back and forth as any excesses or
deficiencies in particular revolutions may induce, and

each comet in its orbit will find its own balance in its own aggregate attractions. Those revolving beyond the range of such attractions will keep their original orbital places.

And in reference to direct and retrograde movement, a comet moving concurrently with the planets will have more attraction from them in its revolution than when more quickly passing them in occurrent movement. A retrograde movement will have its concurrence with the planets in that part of its orbit which is most remote from them while they are in the most remote part of their orbits, and occurrent with the planets in that part of its orbit which is nearest to them while they are in the nearest part of their orbits. The retrograde comet must thus be drawn in opposite directions in the opposite portions of its orbit, and thus augmenting its longitude with every revolution, till it shall reach its culmination, and turn from its westing to its easting movement, and which will be its change from retrograde to direct movement. Afterwards the comet and planet move concurrent in the parts of their orbits nearest each other, and all further change of longitude ceases, except as occasional modifications occur in particular revolutions back and forward. Hence all comets within the system are now direct, except Halley's comet, and which may be with every revolution approaching its climacteric from a westward to an eastward movement.

7. GEOLOGICAL FORMATIONS. — Geology, as the name imports, is the science of the internal constitution of the earth. We can know little of the inner construction of any of the worlds of our system except that of the earth. Yet what we know of our world may be applied by analogy to the other worlds of the solar system, and our system may also be taken as analogous to all systems of worlds. But even of our earth, almost its whole interior is hidden from observation, and by no human process as yet has more than eight or ten miles deep of some portions of its superficial construction been examined. What we do know is, however, directly in accordance with the determinations of our speculative philosophy, in its revolving force for the world-formations.

The immediate leading facts relative to this superficial crust of the earth are, that it has extensively and repeatedly been broken through and turned up by internal forces, and that large portions of the fractured strata have been set edgewise to the surface, dipping less or more towards the horizon; and such upturned edges disclose the contents of the several strata and the order of their superposition in their previous horizontal state, and thus by analogy disclosing the state of the earth's crust which has had no upheaval.

As found underlying the other strata is the Granite of an unknown thickness, and which unmistakably evinces the earlier and wide action of intense heat from its sub-crystallized composition in its cooled and solid form. Above the granite is the Gneiss, of great thickness, and on this rests the stratum of Mica schist many thousand feet in its depth. All these compose what has been known as the Cumbrian Formation, and in which nothing but the mechanical forces of inorganic matter appear.

The Cambrian system of old Slate stone, a mile in thickness through all its stratifications, overlies the Cumbrian; and here begin the indices that atmospheric air and water were contemporaneous with their formation, and that with the earliest fossil remains they must have been deposited beneath the water on the cooled crust above the fire. Then comes the Silurian system, of a mile and an half in its depth, with hundreds of extinct species of fossil organizations. Above is the Secondary Formation, with its old red sandstone, made up of older rocks fractured and disintegrated, and anew deposited, of a depth of many thousand feet, with many old fossil remains; and on which again are interposed layers of limestone and coal formation, the new red sandstone, the oolite, and chalk beds; all filling a space several miles deep. Higher still towards the surface is the Tertiary Formation, of lime, and clay, and sand, on which are diluvial deposits: when we come to the comparatively recent period of the oldest satisfactory traces of man on the earth, and the opening of human history. All this is naturally consequential upon the rolling firemist sent off by the solar revolving forces, and left to ensphere itself, and cool down, and condense a crust upon the shut-in fires beneath. The silicious mass of granite, and gneiss, and mica schist takes its ordered position, and thereby is in preparation for collecting vapors, and an atmosphere, and condensed water; and then is introduced the life-power, building up its organisms of plants and animals through their successive and rising species.

But still below all this, chemical examination carries our knowledge deeper, and yet perfectly in accordance with, and confirmatory of, our speculative knowledge, from revolving forces. The granites and porphyrites which underlie the stratified and fossiliferous rocks are largely composed of silica, and are thence termed silicious rocks, and have a specific gravity of 2.4. Another class of rocks, as the trap and basalt, have much less silica, and more lime and iron, and whose specific gravity is 2.72 — a ratio to the other greater than that between water and oil, and which have been forced through and lie in position upon the older formed silicious and sedimentary strata. The silicious cooled first, and then the other termed basic rocks, as in their fluid state lying lower, have been since pressed through the fractures, and cooled upon the surfaces and in the crevices of the lighter and originally superior material. This latter kind of basic rock is very sparsely found in positions upon the silicious and primitive rocks, but appears in increased frequency among the fossiliferous rocks of the palæozoic era, and is the product mainly of all modern volcanoes, while the silicious rocks were more common from old subterranean eruptions, but are now very rarely found among modern volcanic lavas. This would seem to indicate that the granitic matter has become fixed, and that present volcanic eruptions throw out the heavier matter still melted in the lower positions. The whole mass of the earth is 5.5 of specific gravity, and as so much of water and silicious rock that is lighter occupies the superficial portion, the interior must be mainly of the heavier bases and metals ranging from 6.0 and upwards; and thus is evinced that the heavy metals, as arsenic, antimony, copper, and gold, however located in the rocky veins or mines, were originally quite below all granitic matter, and may most probably have been sublimed from the interior as chemical salts.

So manifestly with our earth. A solid crust cooled first, which had its fractures, disintegrations, and decompositions; then arose vapors, waters, and an atmosphere; then the detritus of primitive rock would be deposited in successive layers; organized bodies appeared, and as life departed they took their fossil state amid the depositions; and frequent upheavals, and successive submersions, and occasional eruptions have given to the earth's superficial portion just what the geologist now witnesses. And so far as observation reaches, we have sphericity and equatorial protuberance in other planets, an atmosphere with its twilight in Mercury and Venus, and not only air, but clouds and polar snows, in Mars, and a dense and little elevated atmosphere in Jupiter, and bare mountains with their shadows and volcanic craters in the Moon. The revolving forces have determined these geological phenomena.

8. From Facts found in the Universal Stellar Distribution, we determine our Terrestrial Relative Position. — The general configuration which the completed speculation assigns to the material Universe is a broad, spherical Annulus of distinct stars, as the central suns of separate systems, over-arching on all sides except at the polar extremities, an inner sphere of pure ether, which is composed of perfectly elastic diremptive Atoms, all revolving on one fixed point at the creating source from which all originated. The stellar worlds fill the place of a spherical Annulus, and not a complete globe, both because the mass of material atoms, which have been distributed in them, was open at the polar region from their reciprocal magnetic repulsions, and because the revolving force which distributed them could detach them from the mass at its surface only as it gained an augmentation of impetus on its approach towards the equatorial plane. All along the universal Axis there is a vacuum of stellar worlds, thinly distributed some way back from the poles, and thickly studded through the equatorial region. At the equatorial mid-plane, the unequal accumulations of the original mass gave an excess of impetus from side to side which threw off the stars obliquely, this side and that, and so in the mid-plane the stars are

sparse and unequally arranged, but greatly though irregularly accumulated in ranks each side the mid-plane. Clusters were occasionally sent off that fill patches in the heavens, and nebulous portions floated away at different places, presenting different forms as they stand in their respective lines of vision. The universe may be as large, and its suns as distant from each other, as the Maker wills, but it is finite in space and time; it had its origin, and perpetually has a balancing centre and a balanced periphery. The central ether presses out, and the gravitating matter presses in, and though the ethereal atoms diffuse themselves everywhere through the stellar spaces, yet is the ether so balanced by the gravitating matter, that the latter does not permit the former to go off and exhaust itself in the matterless void, nor does the former permit the latter to aggregate within the central ethereal sphere, though the material annulus gravitates towards the ethereal centre, in all its parts, as if the matter itself reached and filled the whole interior sphere.

This equatorial belt of stars, standing in two irregular ranks on each side the equatorial plane, may be known as the Galaxy. A line through its centre, perpendicular to the plane of the belt, may be known as the galactic Axis; and the extremities of the axis may be known as the galactic Poles. Standing at the centre of the Universe, the galaxy would be a great circle equally dividing the heavens; and the galactic poles would be in opposite regions of the heavens, where there were, in both, the entire absence of stars; and from a few degrees back of both poles, the stars would thinly appear and increase in density greatly and continually up to the equatorial belt. But such central vision is for no material organ, and the only stand-point for sensible observation is on some world among the material systems. The starry heavens must have their peculiar phase from each separate world, and from distant worlds their particular phases must greatly differ from each other; and taking the universe as we have speculatively contemplated it, the astronomical phenomena to our vision must determine for us our terrestial stand-point, and fix the position of our solar system relatively to the other Suns of the universe.

Among these phenomena, a galactic fact *first* applicable for this purpose is, that the galaxy to us is not exactly a great celestial circle, but it divides the heavens unequally, about proportional as eight to nine. Our point of observation, then, must be out from the centre, and within the larger portion, so far as to foreshorten the galactic circle in the ratio of one out of nine.

A *second* fact is, the gauges made of the stars, in equal Zones each side the circle, increase in about equal ratios up towards the circle, but in each gauge invariably the number is some larger on one side than on the other. Our system is, thus, out of the galactic equatorial plane, and within that area where the stars in the gauges are the smaller number.

A *third* fact is, that stars of different magnitudes increase in number in the gauges very disproportionately. Stars to the eighth magnitude make no increase as the gauges rise towards the circle; stars· of the ninth and tenth magnitudes increase in number only from about 30° each way out of the circle; stars of the eleventh magnitude increase from near the galactic poles; and from the twelfth magnitude and more, the increase appears as if quite from the poles. These disproportioned numbers in the stars of different magnitudes demand for our system a place above the pure ethereal inner sphere, and so far within the material stellar envelope, that stars to the eighth magnitude may stand between that position and the pure ether towards the centre, and that no stars stand there beyond that magnitude. Of course, at a longer radius from our position, stars of the ninth and tenth magnitudes will appear in the lower edges of the stellar envelope towards each galactic pole, and begin from that degree below the circle to increase towards the circle; the eleventh magnitude will appear at a radius reaching near the pole, and increase upwards from it; the twelfth and higher magnitudes will stand between the spectator and the poles, the higher the further on in the polar direction, and all increasing at once as the gauge rises towards the galactic circle. Our solar system must be so far imbedded in the stellar annulus, that stars to the eighth magnitude may stand all about it, but not those of the ninth and tenth magnitude, between it and the grand centre.

A *fourth* fact is, that portions of the galaxy have never been penetrated through to open space beyond, by the highest magnifying glasses. It was a conjecture which Sir William Herschel once expressed in his early astronomical writings, that our system lay imbedded in the milky-way, and that this was but one among the many nebulæ, others of which might fill as large a space as the galaxy itself. This notion is still indulged solely from Herschel's expressed conjecture. But later in Herschel's observations, he came to find that the most powerful telescopes could not reach to the extent of the furthest stars of the milky way, and thus that no nebula was provable to be further from us than some portion of the galaxy, and therefore the conjecture that the galaxy was itself one of the nebulæ would be absurd. Says Humboldt, Cosmos, Vol. III. p. 149, " William Herschel, in his last works, expressed himself strongly in favor of the assumption of an annulus of stars; a view which he had contested in the talented treatise he had composed in 1784. The most recent observations have favored the hypothesis of a system of separate *concentric rings*. The thickness of these rings seems very unequal; and the different strata, whose combined stronger or fainter light we receive, are undoubtedly situated at very different altitudes."

A *fifth* fact is, that the Galactic Circle is inclined

about 40° to the ecliptic, and its plane inclines about 63° to that of the celestial equator, intersecting this last on each side of the centre at about 10° from the equinoctial points; and thus determines the varied positions and directions of our terrestrial abode in the system, and the heavenly objects seen from it. The plane of the terrestrial equator is $23\frac{1}{2}$° inclined to the ecliptic; and thus the earth's axis is $66\frac{1}{2}$° inclined to the ecliptic; and which puts the earth's north pole nearly in the direction of the north star among the celestial constellations, and the south terrestrial pole in the direction of the constellation Octans. The north galactic pole, as perpendicular to the plane of the galactic circle, will be from us nearly in the direction of the constellation Coma Berenices, and the southern galactic pole between the tail of Cetus and Apparatus Sculptoris.

A *sixth* application of facts relates to the position and distance of nebular and stellar clusters. The largest glasses pierce the heavens to more than two thousand times the distance of stars of the first magnitude; and from which, as estimated by experiment of the sun's rays, light would be more than twelve thousand years in making its passage. In the galactic circle, at some portions, stars of the first magnitude stand in front of the deeper brightness, and while in places we look through to dark, open space beyond, in others the background is so completely studded with stars as to be wholly unbroken in its brightness. Nebulæ are none, or almost so, in the galaxy; but clusters of stars and nebulæ are numerous at distances from it. The place of greatest number is a region above the north galactic pole, and some remarkable ones are about the south galactic pole; but the most important fact for present use is their resolvability relatively to their positions in the heavens. Those which are irresolvable are in directions admitting of the largest distance, while in directions admitting only of least extreme distance there are none irresolvable. Taking the relative position above ascertained for our System in the great Universal sphere, it is easy to determine the direction and bearing, through the constellations on the celestial sphere in which the clusters and nebulæ are found, towards the points from which the longest radii may be drawn. The nearest part of the periphery of the universal sphere to our system must be the region about the north galactic pole, and a little back from this pole are the numerous clusters found in the constellations Leo Major, Coma Berenices, and the head and wings of Virgo, and all resolvable by large telescopes. At a longer radius to the furthest stars from our system, in the sword-handle of Orion, is the long noticed and remarkable nebula, which, with Lord Ross's great telescope, was barely resolved, the stars being still too close to be counted; and about an equal distance from the outer universal surface is another nebula in the girdle of Andromeda, and which is resolved with the like difficulty. There are also the Magellanic clouds, known

as Nubecula Major and Minor, standing about 12°
apart, and from 26° to 30° back from the south celestial pole, thus admitting of their being from us at
nearly the greatest possible distance, and which
are among the most remarkable phenomena of the
heavens. They have their distinct clusters and nebulæ of various magnitudes, but the base of all is
a brightness hitherto utterly unresolved. There
should be also added the large nebula in the constellation Argo, admitting from direction of being
also at greatest possible distance, and which shows
no tendency to resolution through the most powerful glasses. We cannot say of these unresolved
nebulæ that they are the furthest possible from
us; it is much that they stand in direction, from the
position above attained for our system, in which the
longest lines may be drawn to the periphery of the
universal sphere.

A *seventh*, and now last noticed galactic fact, is the
peculiar bifurcation of the galactic circle. This circle is narrowest, and yet brightest, when viewed near
the constellation of the Southern Cross and the hind
feet of Centaurus, being about 3° in breadth. In its
broadest undivided portions, it reaches to 15°. In
some parts the circle seems nearly broken; but the
more notable peculiarity is a remarkable separation,
or forking into two distinct belts, which again come
together. Starting in the southern terrestrial hemisphere, the bifurcation begins near the constellation
Circinus and the fore feet of Centaurus. The more

southerly fork passes unbroken through the constellations Aquila, Sagitta, Vulpecula, and more irregularly, on to Cygnus. The northerly fork loses itself near the foot of Serpentarius, but appears again further on, and joins the southerly fork about 130° from their separation. The two forks nowhere but slightly diverge from a mid-line, but in their widest portion they fill about 22° from the outsides. The certainty of a separation of the galaxy throughout cannot be affirmed, as with the planets in our system is the fact, of from 30′ to 3° 30′ from a mid-line between Neptune and Uranus; but if there is, it could not be observed from our eccentric position to a greater distance than is the galactic bifurcation. The divided ranks opening over us would appear to join both ways considerably short of half their complete circle. At least, the irregularities, cessations, and separations in the galactic circle indicate the stars about the mid-plane to have had oblique projections, from unequal accumulations about a common revolving sphere, and a probability that the same continues through the equatorial plane.

So, our solar system has its determinable place among the stars, and the universe of stars has its fixed centre and definite periphery. Every world has its exact balance and harmonious movement. The whole is of such extent that the rapidity of light traverses the broader interstellar spaces only after a flight of many thousand years; yet is the ethereal light-medium everywhere diffused, and the light-vibrations, from all surrounding solar systems, come down through the pure ether upon the centre, in unrefracted clearness. Here is the source of creative Power and eternal Wisdom, hiding itself in light to which no mortal eye approaches. Not planets around suns, and suns and systems around some greater orb, and the highest with no ultimate support; but an independent Spiritual source originating all, and sending out all, and holding all in equipoise, through this one fixed centre. Matter can never give a first of either motion or rest, nor either one from the other, and without the spiritual the material is wholly inexplicable. A sentimental fancy may please itself a while in fleeing from sun to sun to get hold on something stable ; but a necessity comes at length to all to stop and rest; and materialism *has* no resting-place. It cannot find whence it comes nor whither it goes; and only as we hold in reason can we know an origin, a progress, or a consummation.

CHAPTER III.

LIFE.

1. LIFE DISTINGUISHED FROM FORCE, IN THAT IT DE-
TERMINES HIGHER UNITIES. — Distinguishable unities
mark distinctive kinds of Being, and in nothing can
we note the distinction between Force and Life,
and in Life the distinctions between Organizing
Instinct, Sense-consciousness, and Spiritual Personality, so clearly and comprehensively as in the
respective unities which each is severally competent to determine.

The phenomena gained in experience can have
no intrinsic unity. They are singles which may be
outwardly conjoined, but not inherently connected.
The handful of sand or the bundle of rods is still
so many singles; and the chain is but so many single
links, and as destitute of essential unity when the
links shut within, as if they were joined outside of
each other. The Building is so many pieces, still
as single when framed and mortised as when lying
loose from each other. They may be externally
joined, never essentially united. Yet of such outside joining of singles there is a made-up whole;
and to distinguish the conjoined from the separate

singularity, it may be allowable to speak of it as a *factitious unity.*

Phenomenal qualities frequently standing together, and events frequently occurring in the same order of succession, are universally spoken of as having some necessary connection, and the notion of substance is put as the connective of the qualities, and the notion of cause as connective of the events, and so nature is bound together in what is assumed to be laws of experience; but when we discard the insight of reason, and refer such connection to the judgment of the logical understanding, we can find nothing to justify our use of the notions of substance and cause, and are forced to a scepticism of all necessary connection, and admit that we know only single qualities grouped together, and single events as sequents to each other. The laws of connection are mere facts of occurrence, and we have no other warrant for any inherent unity, save that in our experience they have in fact so stood together in place, and so followed each other in period. Yet because an unrecognized rationality urges the assumption of such connections, as if there were somehow a unity, we may term it a *quasi-unity.*

When, however, the recognition of the distinctive reason-intelligence enables us to contemplate forces in their essential constitution and working, we know how singles come to lose their singularity, and stand in veritable unity, in which the component singles neutralize themselves in a third single unlike to either constituent. So the insight of reason contemplates two spiritual impulses, working in antagonism at a common limit, and becoming united action and reaction, as losing their distinctive energies in a third thing which is itself single, and therein knows essentially the existence of Force. So, again, we contemplate the single forces, shutting themselves together at the centre by their gravitating and bi-polar energies, as losing their singularities in a third single, which we then essentia'ly know as an independent Atom. And so, again, single material and ethereal atoms are contemplated, as shutting themselves in cohesion by the implications of their respective impulses and expulses, and in this lose their distinctive atomic singularities, and become another single as a primitive molecule, and which henceforth we know as simple Substance. So far as we may get insight of the neutralizing working of the component atoms, we know the essence of the simple substance, the distinct varieties of which present experience numbers sixty-six.

Finally, two simple substances in affinity come in chemical combination, completely neutralizing their old forces, and working in unison as a single new force, and thus make a *new* single substance unlike either ingredient. So oxygen and hydrogen in due proportions combine as water, in which the component singles are lost, and the new thing is as truly a single as was either the oxygen or hydrogen.

Nature's forces are seen by reason to be continually converting themselves into new substances while cancelling the old, and yet the old is not annihilated, for the new may be again resolved to the old. The neutralized action and reaction of the two has become wholly another action in the third, manifesting itself in experience in new qualities, and inducing other effects.

In all the above cases the old elements negate themselves, and appear as wholly a new single thing; and such essential unity of component singles into a new single is known as *negative unity* — not as if opposed to positive unity, but the posited unit has been constituted by the negation of the elementary units. The elementary units in their affinities are properly complementary each to each, and when apart may, in a sense, be said mutually to need each the other; they cannot fill out their combined action apart one from the other; but neither has any efficiency to supply the other. The need is a lack, and wholly empty and helpless in affording to itself the complementary relief. So an acid may be said to need its alkaline base, but wholly outside of itself must come the efficiency that supplies the base and complements itself thereby in the neutral salt. The elements, brought together within the spheres of their several energies, complete themselves by cancelling their old energies in essentially another kind of substantial force. We thus comprehend the very essence of a negative unity. The energies of complemental forces neutralize themselves and become another kind of force, but the unity is effected only within the sphere of the elementary action, and when the new unit is constituted, it has no need to go out of itself in complement with any other. The negative unity is henceforth a static in its place, and does nothing to work new combinations and extend unities beyond its place. Let the combinations in negative unity fill place to any extent, yet each point has its own unity in its own neutralized energies. Every part of the salt has its own saltness, and no unit goes out of itself in communication with another. Every unit perpetuates its cancelling within itself, but is wholly dead to all participation in the cancelling of units beyond itself.

If, however, we should speculatively contemplate the deficient element to have some way within itself *a feeling of its deficiency*, and which thereby attains to a craving want instead of a bare lack, the *deficiency* will from its self-feeling have become an *efficiency*, and go out in longing to find its complement, and consummate its unity in so cancelling the two that they become another one. Once endowed with this craving want, the element will no longer be held in its inertia, but will have an intrinsic prompting to go over of its own accord to its complement and satisfy its longing. A simple want, however, prompts only to an immediate outgoing, with no inducement for a returning; spontaneously tending to its end, with no reflex action back upon itself; it can, therefore, never come to any self-recognition. It cannot be conscious of the impulsive prompting urging on, nor have any remembrance of the activity when past, but is solely a *thrusting in* to its direct issue: and this is literally an *instinct.* An appetite involves a recognition of the fitness of the object to the want; and a desire involves a remembrance of previous gratification; but an instinct thrusts through to its end in pure unconscious spontaneity. The element with the want, of its own accord, communicates with its complemental element, and secures the negative unity : but the want still urges on to further communion, and goes over into other complemental combinations, thereby putting negative unities themselves in unity. This spontaneous uniting of negative unities themselves is wholly the product of the want, and could never be produced by the complemental elements alone, which of themselves must ever rest in their neutralization, with no going beyond to a further union. And now, in this spontaneous uniting of negative unities, we have the higher unity which has passed beyond all the combinations of dead mechanical forces, and stands within the sphere of living agencies. We have contemplated it in its simplest state, and have it in speculation as pure unconscious instinct, but still a spontaneous agency competent to multiply negative unities all about the first unity, and to diffuse itself all through the body of unities which it thus holds together in complete individuality. No one unit of all the individualized unities can be taken away without sundering the diffused bond which holds all in common.

19

Thus the life-power determines the distinctive *unity
of individuality.*

2. The Contemplation of an Agency competent to
work Individualities. — In contemplating cohesion,
we saw the necessity that ethereal atoms should be interposed amid material atoms. Material impulses hold
together as attraction, but cannot implicate themselves in fixed connection, since those of each atom
work towards its own centre, and not to act and react
with the impulses of other atoms. But the diremptive action of ethereal atoms works directly in implication with the impulses of material atoms, and when
the ethereal stands between material atoms the action
of the expulses and impulses must interpenetrate in
mutual cohesion. And still further, when matter is
in cohesion, it is the vibratory agitation of the interposed ethereal forces which breaks up the cohesion,
and puts solid matter in solution. As media for combination, and also for dissolution that there may be
recombinations, the interposition of ethereal forces is
indispensable; and where their agency can be controlled and applied for this purpose, the ethereal medium is a sufficient interposition. A spontaneous user
of diremptive forces is a competent agent to assimi-
late complemental elements, to combine them in negative unities, and to go out of the effected unity, in
communication with other complemental elements,
and add their unity to former combinations.

The ethereal expulses must thus become the instrument for effecting this higher unity of negative unities, and bringing them into individuality. The expulses are themselves spiritual activities, but we now contemplate them as receiving a more sublimated spiritual agency than that of their original energy. The instinctive want to combine complemental elements is now contemplated as infused into the expulses of the ethereal atom, and it becomes instinct with the spontaneous prompting to put itself in composition with congenial material elements, and work their combination, and to go over from the combination already brought in negative unity, to neutralize further complemental elements, and thereby build up an extended body of unities which shall be held in individuality by its own thorough diffusion and connection with every part. The superinduction of the instinctive want upon the diremptive expulse is also a reciprocal intussusception of their respective energies. The expulsive energy takes in the want, and the spontaneous want takes the mechanical energy, and a new existence is begun hitherto unknown among mechanical forces. The craving want is utterly a creation, and its superinduction upon an already created existence puts a new being into nature as really from the Creator's act, as in the primal origination of force itself. The atoms, on whose expulses this instinctive want is superinduced, now stand out amid the ethereal and material atoms distinct in essence from all else the universe contains. Such atom has pure spontaneity, forever separating it from all the mere push and pull of mechanical movement. Herein is the real *Proto-Bion*, and the Light of the world becomes literally Life in the world. No ethereal atom can wake within itself such instinctive prompting, nor can it be an impartation from any physical forces, antagonist, diremptive, or revolving; it overrules and uses physical force, and can have existence only from the Absolute Source of all origination.

Such superinduction of the instinctive want upon ethereal force by the absolute Creator evinces, in the reason of the case itself, that it must have been for the attainment of ends beyond what could have been secured by the latter alone. If mechanical forces could have answered the purposes of spontaneous instincts, the latter must have been brought into existence for no reason; the life-instinct is made in vain. It is not made from force, but is added to force, that it may use force in subserviency to its own end; and in this only is the wisdom of the making and superinducing, that thereby the expulses may serve new purposes.

The expulses of the ethereal atom are on this account put under the control of the life-instinct, and it is competent for it to direct them for its own interest by changing their balance, and giving an excess of expulse on one side, thus inducing and directing movement, and thereby modifying and appropriating to its own use both ethereal and material atoms about it. The instinctive want is not force; nor is it competent for it to give any new force; but it uses the forces already in being upon which it has been super-induced. When it has taken and used force, and thereby exhausted it, the spontaneous want communicates itself to other forces, and assimilates and incorporates, and then dissolves and eliminates them. In mechanics, the force controlling other forces is called *a power*; and though not itself force, yet in its use of the forces it infuses, this life-want may be properly termed *life-power*. Taking advantage of physical forces, the life-power serves its ends by the help of nature, or uses one part of nature's forces to counteract others, and convert opposing forces to its want, and so works its way, even against nature, in putting negative unities together in an individual body which it builds up as its own dwelling, and which is indivisible except in violent dismemberment, and is therefore an agency *producing* strict individualities.

3. THE LIFE-POWER IS AN ASSIMILATIVE AGENT. — The life-want is a spontaneous longing or craving for its own satisfying, and it controls the ethereal energies it has pervaded so that they work *on* and *in* dead matter, in some of its substantial forces, and render it complemental, in particular elements, for new and largely extended combinations beyond what the mere mechanical action of forces can effect. It separates existing cohesions, dissolves old combinations, changes inner antagonisms to other polarities and attractions, and thus induces new affinities, and thereby introduces into nature a vital chemistry pe-

culiar to its own working, having new equivalents constituting new substances. It thus assimilates new elements to its own ends, and fits them together for constituting its needed incorporations. Not all the complemental elements which mechanical chemistry works in combination is used by the life-power, and but four simple substances are made by it to enter into complete combination. Carbon and the three elementary gases — oxygen, hydrogen, and nitrogen — it assimilates and completely incorporates, and these only. Sometimes in the ternary combinations of carbon, oxygen, and hydrogen, and sometimes in the quaternary combination when nitrogen is added. Carbonic acid is the union in chemical proportions of carbon and oxygen; water is the like union of hydrogen and oxygen; and ammonia the like union of nitrogen and hydrogen; and with these three substances at hand, the life-power can supply itself with all the simple elements it ever completely assimilates. If either were wanting in our world, it would not yet be ready for the introduction of the life-instinct. Many other elements mingle in with these when building up living bodies, such as phosphor, sulphur, iron, silex. &c.; but they are supplementary only, filling in and supporting the structure, but not complementary as neutralized in the new product. Ethereal vibration, as sensible light and heat, is necessary to living assimilation as really as the presence of the ethereal atoms themselves; and except in excess, the growth and vigor of the living body is as the measure of light and heat; but these light- and heat-vibrations are but preparative and conditional, and not the efficient powers in the work of assimilation. And how it is, that the insight of reason determines the life-want to be the efficient power in assimilating the complementary elements, may be manifested in putting together the following facts.

By strongly assisted vision careful observers followed up the phenomenal process of vital growth to the life-cell, and found this to consist of a covering membrane with an inner film about a minute globule of viscous fluid, in which floated lesser particles that were colored, yet partially transparent. The elementary constituents of all bodies, vegetable and animal, were chemically in this cell-matter; and whatever the living body might be, its base was a multiplication of such life-cells, with similar appearance in all. The cells were found to multiply and enlarge themselves by various methods, and the aggregates of cell-production were known as *cellulose;* which standing in consistency was known as *tissue;* if only a superficial expansion it is *cellular tissue,* and if cylindrical in extension it is *vascular tissue.*

A more protracted and careful examination found the membraneous envelope and the inner film to be a product of the inside viscous fluid; and passing over the peculiarities of the outside tissue, the interest was restricted to the primitive inside matter as the essential constituent in all cell-life, and the one common substance out of which all forms of living bodies in plants and animals are constructed. As a compound of the elements known as combined in living structures, and thus as the pabulum and nutriment for organic existences, and competent to take on all the fabled forms of Proteus, it was called *protein;* but as assumed to be one and the same thing in itself, and passing out in equivocal generation into all varieties of organic existence from its own plastic nature and tendency, it was known as *protoplasm.* Eminent physicists take this as the ultimate that is reached in the domain of life; and that it is not needful we should attempt to attain a deeper fact or apply a broader law; but just as water is the product of its constituent elements in favoring conditions, and crystals have their solid forms and angles from the nature of their ingredients when the occasion for their combination is given, so living bodies have all their peculiarities from the intrinsic nature of the protoplastic matter out of which they are constructed. Protoplasm first is, and all forms of life spring up out of it. Further experience by equally eminent observers finds facts which render it wholly unscientific to suppose all forms of life to spring from one protoplastic substance. Plant-formations spring directly from the mineral kingdom, and in them is produced the protoplasm which makes animal life possible. The animal organism cannot be till first the plant has been, and so the vegetable and animal body cannot each have the same protoplastic origin. In the animal body, each organ and distinctive product has its appropriate protoplasm, which cannot be made interchangeable. The protoplasm of a muscle cannot produce a nerve, nor can that of either a muscle or a nerve produce a bone; nor can an eye grow from the protoplasm of an ear; nor can the protoplasm of an unicellular plant grow out in the body of another species of plant; and so of all vegetation. The fruit of one tree cannot produce itself into the life of another specifically different tree. Some protoplasm appropriates as already living, and some can only be appropriated by the living as itself already dead. Certainly, if all life comes from protoplasm, the protoplasm is not ultimate, for something beyond it must be making wide modifications of it.

A later and more profoundly complete and satisfactory examination of the living process of assimilation and growth has been attained by tinging certain specimens in a carmine solution. The mildew, yeast, and sugar plant; the mucous, and white-blood corpuscle; the simplest life known in the yet structureless amœbæ, and the forming of the most complicated muscle and nerve organisms; all may so be subjected to direct inspection under the highest microscopic enlargement. There are thus made to appear three different forms of matter concerned in the assimilative process — the germinal or forming, the fixed or formed, and the nutrient substances. The nutrient matter is yet lifeless, the formed matter appears fixed in the vital tissue, and the germinal matter is moving through the constructing and growing process.

The germinating matter has everywhere and every way internal motion, and this movement manifestly spontaneous and diremptive from various centres, and the central points moving of their own accord any way through the mass, by no mechanical pulsation or chemical affinities. The membraneous tissue enclosing a cell, or standing any way as a fixed fibre, is the formed product, woven from the forming germinal movement, out of the assimilated nutrient matter brought within reach. So the cell-envelopment is seen in its forming process. Sometimes the germinal matter is seen protruding itself, and looping itself by a tissue with the mass left behind; and at other times spinning in its wake muscular fibres, or nerve-filaments, and laying them along a former similar construction; or again working in the germinal matter at the bulbous root of a hair, and pushing out from it the spicule already constructed. The carmine tinge does not pass over from the forming matter into the formed structure, and hence within the product no motion appears; but while in use by the life-power, the formed member must still be a living member, though portions of it may be successively becoming effete and dry, and needing elimination. No chemical combination can make cellulose from protein, nor put formed cellulose back again to protein; but here the spontaneous agency is in the germinal matter, moving and using it for an organic construction wholly after its own peculiar arrangement. The nutrient matter becomes altogether a new thing in the formed matter, and often the same nutrient is made into different tissues, and what is salutary to one is sometimes utterly destructive to another. The living instinct is here verily back of all protoplasm, and is the working chemist first making his own instruments, and with them modifying and combining the protoplasm to his own distinctive organic ends, and then abiding in the structure he makes, and serving himself of its conveniences at pleasure. Not material force, but a spontaneous user of force, is manifest in this diversified assimilating and incorporating.

The life-power in its first and lower stages barely assimilates its matter to its end in individualizing its combinations. The first and lowest life-want is just to multiply negative unities, and communicate itself all through them in individuality, and then let the individuality fall apart in unicellular productions. Each cell has many negative unities, and all held in strict individuality, and every going over to a new cell is but repeating the old process of multiplication by dichotomy; prolonging the old life by cutting it into separate individuals. So the snow-plant of Alpine and Arctic regions is unicellular, and individual in its one instinct diffused all through the cell, and this cell divides itself into other cells that break from it, and each in turn parts into others; and so in a very short period the snow-plant multiplies and covers an area of many acres. So the brittleworts abound in ocean and fresh water, and on the bare earth. They absorb carbonic acid and give out oxygen in

large measures, purifying water and air for higher
animal life, and supporting that life when it comes by
yielding their own cellulose, in exhaustless amount,
as food to' nourish these more complicated bodies.
Their single microscopic cells have neither leaf,
nor bud, nor seed, nor sex, but live and multiply
solely from the original life-want that was in the
first, and communicates itself in prolongation through
all.   The life-instinct is thus in these and other
unicellular products in perpetual activity which is
barely assimilative.

4. THE ASSIMILATIVE AGENCY MUST BE ELEVATED TO
AN ORGANIZING AGENCY. — The amount of protoplastic
or cellulose sustenance in unicellular bodies, in the
earlier geological epochs, from its rapid multiplication
must soon have opened the way for higher forms of
life.   Deleterious gases were held in combination, and
salutary elements were disengaged, and appropriate
nourishment was prepared, and thus the need must
arise from these meliorating conditions, in the ongoing
of Nature, for more complicated living structures.

Speculatively, the original assimilative want can no
more raise itself to the higher want requisite to these
meliorated conditions, than the mere mechanical force
could have raised itself to a living instinct.   All
beyond the assimilative power is a mere lack; a
helpless deficiency ; and can minister nothing to the
efficient supply which is to fill the empty need.   The
same creative source which gave the assimilative

instinct must now give this higher want, which, of its own accord, shall prompt to its own satisfying. It cannot be development from the mere assimilative instinct, but must be a direct origination of so much as reaches beyond the mere assimilative agency. Speculatively, it might be taken that the higher life-instinct needed would be produced when the meliorated conditions came, and thus the created supply be afforded successively; but as with the creation of the mechanical atoms, it may better be assumed that all needed and designed grades of instinctive life-want were, at the outset, superinduced upon ethereal energies, and that each, as primitively created, waits its appropriate occasion to do its work in the better circumstances when the period arrives. This anticipative provision would equally manifest divine power and wisdom as in a directly extemporaneous interposition, and with seemingly more comprehensive self-possession and dignity in the Author.

As, then, the occasion for more complicated assimilations shall come, there must be present, in addition to the feeling of deficiency for merely incorporating complemental elements, a feeling of deficiency for securing helps and instruments for working these more complicated assimilations, and which will be a higher life-instinct than that which has been working unicellular products.

Such advanced instinctive want is superinduced upon the light-force, and the light becomes at once a so much higher life-power, and competent to so much higher and complex assimilations. The sustenance to be appropriated lies about, different in kind and in diverse localities. The food from the earth, and water, and air, must have facile instruments for taking and using according to its condition. In unicellular life, this is at hand, and immediately imbibed and absorbed in the cell-assimilations; but now, what is in earth and water must be mingled in assimilation with that which is in the air; and root and stock, branch and leaf, must be provided to minister their subserviences accordingly. Where the food itself removes, or is already in remote places, the structure must have members for locomotion, and for grasping, carrying, and digesting while moving; and this entire apparatus must be packed in accordant consistency. While, then, the morphology of one kingdom must be of root, stem, and branches, another kingdom will have its rule over constructions in the general form of head, body, and conforming members; and in both these kingdoms, their varied general structures must have their particular conformations and arranged members according to what is to be each one's habitat and mode of life. The instinctive want must prompt in the building of the structure, and the laws of comparative anatomy and physiology will be already determined in the spontaneous instinct superinduced upon the ethereal atom. Each primitive life-power will have in it, from the Creator, its own type of construction and mode of perpetuation.

Here we rise to a higher unity than that of Individuality. The many combinations in negative unity are held in the indivisible bond of the same diffused instinct not only, but here are distinct instinctive constructions held in one by a spontaneity that runs through all. Each organ, as the leaf of the plant, or the lungs of the animal, or the ear or eye of sense, is strictly an individual, having its own instinctive want controlling its own construction, and building it up from its own exclusive protoplasm or cellulose growth; and yet all the individual organs are held subservient to a higher Individuality that controls them while they subserve it, making of all organs an organism in strict *organic unity*.

And so the distinctive and graded types of organic life are given at the start by the Creator, in the superinduction of appropriate instinctive wants upon ethereal forces, which spontaneously go out to their constructive work when the occasions open. From the unicellular plant-life there rises, through all types of plant-production in their primal grades of instinct as originally created, all vegetable forms not only, but these prepare the way for types of organism in a higher kingdom, and which are alike created at the start, and begin the construction of the lowest animal forms of life, but little subsequent to and immediately starting up from the lowest plant-formations. The brittleworts scarcely begin their multiplying ere the jelly-like forms of the protozoa are introduced, and the world of sense opens scarcely above the life of plant-instinct. In their lowest forms, the protozoa take their food without a mouth, digest without a stomach, move without muscles, and multiply with no media of embryo, or egg, or sex. There is barely assimilation with scarcely incipient organization. But soon the rising orders of the Foraminifera are found, whose fossil remains are as countless as the sands with which they are mingled. Their complex shapes, and colored shells, and incipient sense-organs, show the decidedly opening work of the organizing agency. The unicellular constructions at the base of the vegetable kingdom are the support also of the azotic cellulose of the animal kingdom, and from this ground, in graded organism, each pyramid of plant and animal life rises, with less breadth as the organism is the more elevated, in diverging lines of direction conjoined at the bottom, but wide apart in separate grandeur at their tops.

5. A HIGHER ORGANIZING INSTINCT WORKS SEX-DISTINCTIONS. — Rising above unicellular life, among the earlier plants are such as exhibit incipient organs with distinct functions, but which are yet rootless, leafless, and flowerless; and still further along are plants with root, stock, and forming leaf, utterly sexless, and which perpetuate their kind from collected grains of protein enclosed in spores, that start off in separate plants from any part of the spore's surface. And so, also, with the lower forms of animal life; they are but memberless masses of cellulose, multiplying by dividing in parts, with no sexual dis-

tinction. These separate bodies are but as separate buds of the same plant, or at most as extensions of the same plant by slips and grafts. They have no propagation of new individuals.

But for higher organization, and wider variety, and renewals in fresh vitality, and an opening way towards communion in social life, there comes the need for propagating the kind, in new individuals, through successive generations. To practically meet the empty need, there must here, as in all former cases of rising to a higher life in a higher unity, be an original addition to the instinctive life-want. The deficiency is in a higher point, and a new feeling must wake to it, and be a want for it, and a prompting instinct to fill it; and this new instinct can only come from the great creative source. In the light of reason "it is not good" that the single organism "be alone;" the "help meet for it" is, a division of the one organic life into two genders, and the begetting of descendants through this double parentage. Leaving some of the lower organic forms to perpetuate their kind, solely by separating the growing cellulose into parts, the Creator superinduces upon the organizing instinct, for other and higher forms, the further spontaneity to put that one organic life in two divisions of male and female, and give the one stock in two sexes. Such imparted formative instinct organizes the female with an ovarium, in which are the proto-plastic elements for new organizations, but which in themselves alone are wholly component organs of the female, and belong to the one female life. The organizing instinct constitutes the male with sexual organs, in which ethereal elements are infused with the life-power for new fertilization, but which is yet a component part of the male organism, and stands in its one life, and can go over into no new organization of its own, except as it shall embody itself in the protoplastic preparations of the female ovarium. In both cases, separate sexual life is fruitless, and propagation ensues only on the concurrence of the two sexual vitalities. This newly engendered life, in the incipient organizing of the female protoplasm, begins a new individual, known as an *embryo*. The life-power from the male is known as *the sperm;* and the protoplastic contribution of the female is known as *the germ;* the concrete unity of the two is a new Individual Organism. The parentage is conjoint, and the offspring several; every descendant of the dual parentage is in as distinct individuality as was either the male or the female Ancestor.

This sex-organizing instinct works in varied forms in the vegetable and animal kingdom. While the merely organizing instinct, in the plant, sets the leaf-bud in its place, that it may minister to the elongation and enlargement of stem and branch, the sex-organizing instinct, annually or so often as there is fruit-bearing, sets the seed-bud of quite another kind in place for the end of new propagations; and this in its way and season flowers and ripens into fruit, which fruit has in it the embryo of a new organic individuality. The plant itself has no sex; but its sex-organizing instinct produces in it, year by year, its sex-distinctions. These, on filling the sex-want, pass away to rise again in their period for successive propagations. Commonly, the seed-bud holds both sexes, and the opening flower in the same calyx has the male organs of stamen, anther, and pollen, and also the female arrangement of pistil and ovule. The generation of the seed is carried on within the same floral envelope. Sometimes the male organs occupy one part of the plant, and the female another and even quite distant part, as in the maize; again, a wider separation is found, as in varieties of the strawberry, with male and female flowers on their separate plants. The common form of plant-sexualization is known as *hermaphrodite*, the second form as *monœcious*, and the third as *diœcious*. The sex can hardly be said to belong to the plant, but to the flowers the sex-instinct brings from the plant.

In animal life, the lower forms can scarcely be distinguished from plants, and have had the name *zoophytes*, as though they were participants of both kingdoms. But as zoophytes multiply in their sexless varieties and numbers, there comes the need for sexual distinction, and the organizing instinct is originated and works out the kind in two genders. In the acephalous bivalve, from a necessity given by the conformation, the generating process must begin and pass within the confines of the one animal, and we have the hermaphrodite gender within the jointed valves, as in the common plant we have both pollen and ovule together in a common calyx. Another rising step is again given in the sex-forming instinct before there is reached full distinctive sex-organization. The earth-worm is hermaphrodite in a peculiar way; each individual is of both sexes; but instead of self-engendering, two together reciprocally impregnate each other. Above these, the organizing sex-instinct is given, which produces the kind in distinct male and female individuality from the origin.

Sexual distinctions in plants are in the bud; in animals, the sex is distinguished in the embryo. From the birth animals go out, as from the direction of Noah they went into the Ark, "male and female of every kind." And of man, the crown of animal being, it may be taken just as it is revealed, that God created him male and female by first forming the man, and then forming woman from that which was taken out of man. Animal life is thus constituted as a fountain, in its respective kinds, passing out in two streams, of nearly equal breadth and depth of current, in the sexes, through successive generations, whether the form of generation be oviparous or viviparous. In lowest stages, the stock is merely prolonged by cuttings, or in vegetable spores and tubers; in the higher stages, sexual generation propagates the stock in renewed life through successive individual descendants. The life runs out in the failure of the ancestry, but is renewed and runs persistently on, with ever fresh vigor, in the offspring.

6. Sexual Propagation carries in it the Unity of Species. — Propagation by cuttings, or through stored-up protein in spores or tubers, is but a prolongation of the one old stock, although reset in multiplied separate places. The willow from the reset branch, the strawberry rootlet from an advanced joint, is yet in each case as truly the old plant growing out as if there had been a growing on without separation. The tuber of the potato, planted through unnumbered series, carries out only the old stock, and the peculiarity of a new variety of the old stock can be attained only through the sexual generation of the seed in the potato-ball. The flowerless plants and the sexless protozoa multiply their parts in separate places, and those parts become independent wholes of their own; but they are still the old produced, and not a new begotten. Convenience may classify the produced wholes as the species from the old stock, but rational science can find only the old repeating itself, and not the old renewing its kind in so many generated selves.

But in sexual propagation, an instinctive want, to the same end as in the old stock, has gone over from the male, and coalesced with the congenial material elements supplied in the female, and in this generation from two sexual sources a new life begins, which process is repeated in every begotten embryo. The sperm and germ from joint congenial sources become one organic life in the descendant. The two must meet, and in coalescing they make a distinct living organism. The pollen must penetrate and fertilize the pistil; the spermatozoa must impregnate the ovarium; and in every descent from this duplex source, the new life-power has taken the same instinctive prompting to its end as was that of the parentage, and the original type-instinct of the progenitors runs down through all their posterity, and in which is a unity more widely comprehensive than any yet before reached, viz., the unity of many individual organisms in the ancestral type, and which is the true *unity of species.*

The distinctive type is in the end of the peculiar want which is given in the organizing instinct. Each instinctive prompting to organize is after an originally given pattern, or archetype, and the kinds originally here given include all the kinds that universal life-power anywhere presents. Take, then, any original organizing instinct, and which prompts to its end through sexual distinctions, and this will have its distinctive type in the end of the want after which it works, and which must constantly come out, more or less modified by the conditions of the case, in every begotten individual. The type-instinct is a constant which runs through and binds in one all the descendants, and amid all numbers and varieties of engendered descendants the one original type holds them in unity. Each individual descendant has his organic unity; all the descendants of the original type, in the accordant progenitors, have the higher unity of species.

The law regulating the propagation of species is thus found in the determined working of the inner specific instinct, according to its original type. In the individual, the organizing instinct has been in the interest and to the end of the individual only, and all the organs have been formed and placed for expediency and convenience in the one being. The root, stock, and leaf have their adaptations to the one plant; and the heart, lungs, and stomach, with eye, ear, and limb, have their teleological form and arrangement in reference to the one animal. And so in the sex-organization, the instinct has worked to the end and in the interest of the kind, in the unity of the one species. The two genders are in accordant sympathy, and are thus congenial in that they each have their mutual adaptation to the propagation of the one kind. The normal working of sex-distinctions must, therefore, be in the perpetuation of the one species, in that the congeniality of male and female controls their engendering. Both sex-conformation and sex-inclination determine the propagated posterity to be of their own accordant type. Variable conditions in the propagation will make varieties in the descendants, but there will be constancy in the parental type. The conditions may sometimes so vary, and give so wide a diversity, as to make the variety hereditary; and there will be forthwith propagated a distinct breed or race. Races may so widely vary that cohabitation between them may become reciprocally repugnant, and the blending of races be infrequent and the offspring less vigorous. The crossing of breeds in which there is no repugnance will facilitate returning conformity with the normal type, and give a more healthful and prolific progeny. It may, also, in some cases, occur, that truly distinct species may come in so near accordance of type-instinct, that there may be a promiscuous engendering induced between their sexes, yet as such hybrid progeny could bring with them no specific type, they must ordinarily be barren; and if in few cases of nearest conformity of ancestral type, the hybrid stock perpetuate itself, it will be with growing tendencies to return to the normal type in one or the other species of the abnormal parentage. The specific instinct is perpetually directed to its own end through all occurring varieties or hybridities, and thus works a persistent integrity of species through occasional modifications, and even partial interblend-ings. Speculatively, descent from one original pair for the species would be of no importance. The unity of species is in the type as given by the formative instinct, and if one or many seeds or pairs be first cre-ated, those of accordant type-instinct will propagate together the one species.

What has been called "natural development," or "law of evolution," to account for the origin and per-petuation of species, is utterly unphilosophical, be-cause wholly destitute of all reason. It starts in experience, and never attains anything to expound the experience. Single activities are found branch-ing out into multiplied varieties, and each variety running into further changes, and what is so far found to be fact is assumed everywhere to bo law, that progress is universally from the more simple to the more complex; and it gives tho law of evolution to bo "from tho homogeneous to the heterogeneous." Examining still further, it finds the heterogeneous in progress becoming the more definite; and then that the definite integrates in the concrete; and the whole law of nature's evolution is from the simplest to the most definite and concrete forms of heterogeneous elements. To the question, *Why* such order of evolution? it can answer nothing; and only assumes to have attained a knowledge of force deeper than consciousness, and that all conversions of forces stand in the persistence of the one absolute force; and of the absolute force, it affirms it to be unknowable, and that we cannot determine whether it be personal.

Now, the attainment of species from such "natural development" fancies that in infinite time we may go back to the primitively simple and homogeneous, out of which all slowly-growing orders of heterogeneous, definite, and concrete existences have come.

But suppose that fancy to be fact; and that we have come to stand face to face with that primal simple existence, and even that we know it as absolute force in its homogeneity, — how are we to know anything about its development? What right have we to say anything about development and evolution? How start from this simple to go out into the more complex, and from this to the more definite, and from this to the concrete, and thence to the specific forms of concrete being? If we first know simple forces as having already in them their gravity and polarity, then may we know that if they are multiplied they must take on other forms, and these forms be more definite, and the definite more concrete; the elements must become compound, and the compounds more cohesive. The molecules must become heaps, and the heaps harden into rocks and mountains. But if we have even the primitive force in its simplicity only, we can say nothing of its heterogeneity, or definiteness, or concretion, or any law of evolution. We have no *en*velopment, and have no logical permission to say anything about *de*velopment. And even if we grant to this theory its progressive advancement from simple forces to definite heterogeneous molecules, and thence to more definite and concrete heterogeneous rocks and mountains, these aggregated rocks and mountains, in all their varieties, have nothing of the unity of species about them. They are put together from the outside, and have neither organic growth nor genetic propagation.

But it is here urged that nature has already its organisms, and their genetic propagations, and that we may assume its original law to have been " like producing like," but with conditional exceptions; and then the theory of " natural selection " is introduced to account for the origin and perpetuation of species. Some simple organism arose and propagated its like, and in varied conditions its slightly modified varieties;

and such as were competent to endure the struggle for existence survived, and the improving modifications have come out progressively in surviving species, while myriads have been abortive, and gone down in annihilation without a record. In infinite time there has been opportunity for so originating, and preserving through the myriad abortions, all the graded species, step by step, up from the lowest to the highest.

But whence came this assumed first organism, with its law of genetic propagation? Certainly it can be no development from simple force, for it controls and uses force spontaneously. It is more than force, and cannot be evolved from any mechanical agency. But, having assumed the primal simple organism, how elevate it through all the sub-kingdoms of organic existence? Certainly, again, not in any evolution, for in the primary the simplest only is involved. Infinite time, if it may give varieties under conditions, can possibly give no elevations above what already the primal organism has. If the lower may be evolved into the higher, it may as well be in one leap as through the million ages. Besides the terrible waste in the abortive productions, even-assuming there could be the evolving of higher organisms from lower, such fortuitously occurring higher organisms must themselves perpetually modify the circumstances in the battle for life, and the coming up of a successful new species may make the persistency of any old species henceforth impossible, and so successively the conflict of all to be desperate. What sure road throughout such dangers, fortuitously arising, could any species have for gaining its passage through the chaos, and coming and permanently abiding within a rational Cosmos?

But with an organizing instinct superinduced upon mechanical forces, and using them according to the specific type in the end of its own want, we have in sex-generation a rational, and so a philosophical, determination, for the unity and persistency of all fossil and living species, till the typical instinct itself be crushed or exhausted, when the species perishes.

7. NOT SEX-INSTINCT, BUT THE ABSOLUTE IDEAL, DETERMINES THE HIGHER UNITY OF ALL SPECIES. — The organizing instinct unites the separate organs in the individual, and through sex-propagation the individuals in the species, and with this the formative life-instinct terminates. Nature will not disclose within herself the formal determinations which unite the species in their genera. The creating Logos has been guided by the Eternal Ideas in making the original types for all species; and the creating Spirit has been guided by the Absolute Ideal in comprehending all specific types of being in universal consistency and order; and thus the gradations of species are to be sought only in the supernatural arrangement of Absolute Reason. Since creation is the work of Absolute Reason, and all organic unity

has its source in Eternal wisdom, there must be a rational end in the introduction of all created Organisms; and all types of being must conspire in particular gradation towards the consummation of all in that end. And though this may be determined through many stages by unifying forces and powers put within nature, yet somewhere we must come to the link which is ultimate in nature, and has no higher connection through second causes, but is held immediately in the Creator's own hand. Even finite reason can never satisfy itself in classifying through endless categories, but must at last comprehend all its classifications in creative unity, which Absolute wisdom has conceived, and Omnipotence executed, and Essential Goodness adorned, as the completed universal work of one Supreme Being. We stop, then, here with the organizing power in nature, where the life-instinct, by sex-distinctions, has been arranging through all generations individual organisms in the unity of species. If further study of nature shall find some higher organific bond, holding her species in more generic comprehension, all very well, and most gratefully to be accepted when validly confirmed; but the deepest insight into nature cannot now read any natural unity in her productions, any further than the sexual distinctions send the unchanged parental types down through their successive generations.

We look, then, now only to the arrangement of specific types by original supernatural creation, as indicating the Eternal Archetype after which organic life has been arranged, and species graded, and do not anticipate any natural medium here between us and the Creator.

This connecting Archetype, as Eternal Ideal, will be clearly seen when we contemplate man as the consummation and crown of all terrestrial life. The human organism is the antitype, after which all types have in their gradation been fashioned ; and each rising step has been as if the succession were anticipative, and emulous to reach and rest in the completed human structure; erect in stature, expressive in attitude, look, and movement, and holding dominion over every creature on the earth. Something of the model of the man is in all lower animal forms ; and as man grows up from embryonic generation, he passes all the inferior stages. The generic orders of universal Animated Nature find their unity in the eternal Idea of Humanity.

Each rising unity has, then, its interest and end within its own comprehension. Each organ has an instinctive want working to its own completeness and preservation. Each individual has every organ in its own interest, and the one life-want working in and through them for its own end. Each peculiarity of sex-distinction is in the interest of generating a new organism from the double-parentage. The mammæ of a man is not for the man's interest, but its nerve-sympathy is wholly in the interest of the double-gender. Every law of perpetuated type, and varied race, and determined hybridity is in the interest of the species. It is not for the good of the mule that the hybrid is barren, but for the two species between which the mule stands, making it necessary that all propagation shall lie back in the one ancestral type or the other. And so, also, when we come to the original creative Ideal, which puts all species in graded unity up to man; it is not in man's, nor any lower animal species' interest, that such graded succession obtains, but "God has given to each a body as it has pleased *him*, and to every seed his own body," solely in the end of his own rational behest; obliging all to say, "For *thy* pleasure all things are, and were created." The teleological principle that all organic being shall foreshadow man, and in man's coming shall all be comprehended in man, is to be sought and found only as ending in God; and which is adequately expressed only in the God-man's own language, "Even so, O Father, because it seemed good in thy sight." The "good" is, that to Absolute Reason this was seen to be the most reasonable. So we follow up the working life-instinct, spontaneously constituting its ascending unities, till we reach ultimately the creating fiat after its Eternal Ideal; and the unity of all overt real existence, in order and harmony here, compels all finite reason to recognize the Absolute Reason as essentially a Triune Creator.

8. ORGANIC LIFE TERMINATES IN DEATH. — It would not be the proper meaning of death, to recall the life-instinct from an ethereal atom, and leave its diremptive forces again to themselves; this would rather be the annihilation of life, since the separated life-want would thus be withdrawn again to its original source. Nor would it be the meaning of death to take the living-light from matter, and then conceive this separated life, because it can show no organic embodiment, to be dead. When life is lost from a plant or an animal, we can only speculatively contemplate the lost life itself as somehow existing in an unseen state, and not itself dead, but only invisible. But when all living activity ceases in the body, and the lifeless organism begins its return to dissolution, without asking of the departed life where it has gone, it is of the dissolving organism that we speak as dead, with no reference of such meaning to the life away from the organism, wherever that life may be supposed to have gone. The organism without life we speak of as death, and conceive the death as wholly relative to the deserted tabernacle, and not to the departed inhabitant.

So, again, when the organizing instinct has matured the organism, its subsequent activity is expended in preserving the matured structure. Assimilation and dissolution are in continual succession, and the life-power works to perpetuate the body through this ceaseless flow, by introducing the new on the exclusion of the old. But here also we say, that it is not the continual dying of the changing elements that we regard when we speak of death, but the arresting of the flow at once in the cessation of all new supplies, and the falling of all the parts together into decomposition and disorganization.

And in this acceptation, organic death is to be viewed as terminating organic life from the very nature of the case. The fulness of the life-power is expended in maturing, and then in perpetuating; and while new life is being sent on in posterity, old encumbrances and burdens augment in the ancestry, and vitality and recuperative energy decline, leaving the organism to irreparable decrepitude and decay. Any shock is then dangerous, and some stroke at length will be fatal, or the necessary supply gradually and ultimately completely fail, from the wearing out of the life-power in exhausting efforts against reacting material impediments, and death will necessarily ensue.

There is nothing from this natural necessity of death, as seen in speculative philosophy to follow from the order of sexual generation, to impugn the doctrine of immortality for man as given in revelation. We may further along see how the superinduction of a rational spirit upon animal life modifies the organizing agency, and opens the way for human immortality; but it is enough here to remove all scruple to remark, that revelation itself manifestly supposes that the natural course for organic life is its termination in death. The immortality of the primitive man was viewed as a result from some special divine interference, and an exclusion of such interposition left man, of course, to disease and death. The " tree of life " was open to him in innocence as the source and pledge of perpetuated life, but the forfeiture of life by his fall, and the incurring of the curse of death, shut out all remedial interposition. What had else replenished life's waning vigor was now fenced out by " a flaming sword turning every way," lest he should " eat and live forever."

Where generated life is, there is in its very working the necessity for death. The very exuviæ which life throws out carry with them some of the energy of life's assimilations. The remains of a once living plant are the more facile food for present vegetation, and the excrements of animal life clothe the earth in richer verdure. There is a change in the very exhalations of the living body, and a power goes out from the instinctive life-want which not only builds up organic structures, but modifies inorganic nature, and leaves its traces on the material world; and this outgo from working life must exhaust the vitality in the ancestry that the posterity may have more genial conditions. Natural death must come not only, but it is needed. It is no evil, but the death is as sure a good as the precedent life. The meliorations wrought by the living generation can come to the next only through previous dissolution. The species matures, and more elevated species originate, and the animal kingdom rises on the vegetable, and human personality and culture crowns brute appetite, only as the death and dissolution of that below gives possibility for that which is higher. Only to this crown of all life, as it is in man, can death be a curse; and this only as a reclaiming of an imparted prerogative which his sin had forfeited. And even to him the curse opens into a blessing, through a gracious redemption and promised resurrection.

Through all organic being, the growth and preservation of the organism is by the death and departure of the successive assimilated elements, and the melioration and perpetuation of the species is by the birth and death of its individuals. Through unmeasured eras before man was made, and cursed, and redeemed, the changes of vegetable and animal life to death, and the passing of the vegetable into the animal life by death, have been steadily moving onward, preparing a dwelling-place for man, and opening a theatre for his probationary discipline, and this quite as much by the dying as by the living. The Fossil Rocks and broad Coal Beds, and deep Petroleum Fountains, owe their present ministrations to human want as really to the subsequent taking as to the original imparting of life. Nature could no more have run her normal course in subserviency to man without the intervention of death than without the incoming of life. Her first seeds had in them the law of coming dissolution as truly as that of previous germination.

So life flows and death ensues, and yet with the conservation of the essential life-power through all the vicissitudes of generation and dissolution. The young life opens fresh and vigorous, but the generating of the new is in the exhausting of the old, and the more prolific the stock, the sooner the flowering and the earlier the fruitage, and so the more rapid the stream by the quickened exhausting and dissolving, but with no diminution of the vital essence. As one force flows into another, and all is still correlation and conservation, with nothing lost, so one life goes and others come, but all is but conversion from one material combination to another. One portion of matter succeeds to another in the same individual, and one individual to another in the same species, and one species runs out and another is brought in as the material elements ripen; for the rational life must be superinduced before the individuality can be immortal.

As we now have the formative life-instinct in contemplation, we will, in a summary manner, speculatively follow its action in building up its particular structures in the several rising kingdoms of organic life, and more particularly and discriminatingly notice the different modes of activity which the rising grades of organism give occasion for exhibiting within the completed bodily structures of the successively advanced kingdoms.

THE REIGN OF LIFE IN THE VEGETABLE KINGDOM.

The *cryptogamous* or flowerless plants are the lowest and least complete organisms which the life-instinct constructs, opening with unicellular formations, which multiply by an inner growth and outer expulsion, rising to bodies of expanded tissues with fronds and thalli, and then to stems of firmer texture, with leaves and spores which vegetate from any part of their surface. All these varieties are with no distinctions of sex, destitute of flowers and seed, and yet accumulate an immense amount of cellulose as nourishment for higher forms of living existence.

At a more advanced stage, the life-instinct builds the more complex and complete organisms in the series of *phenogamous* or flowering plants with full distinctions of sex, and flowers and seed after their kind, and with the complete plant-organism of root, stem, and leaf. The aliment of the plant must come mainly from the earth, become assimilated in the light and air, and hence the vegetable must be on the general plan of striking its root in the ground, throwing up a rising stem, and spreading abroad branches and leaves.

The *root* has the varied forms of bulbous, tuberous, and fibrous; which last are elongated by adding new spongiole cells at their tips, and in their multiplying rootlets; and in the root is often stored the pabulum of starch, sugar, and oils for coming exigencies. The root also supports and holds the stem firm, in the conflict of the branches and leaves with the winds.

The *stem*, as longer or shorter, gives to vegetation the distinctions of herb, shrub, and tree. At the salient points of the embryo, where the life-instinct works downward in the root and upward in the stem, is the *yoke* which holds root and stem together, and through which the circulation passes, with no fixed centre, from root to branch, and again from leafy branch to the root. When the vascular tissues are sent down from the leaves within the pulpy pith of the stem, and there harden into firmer fibre, as in the palms, the botanic distinction of *endogenous* plants is given; and when the tissues form the ligueous growth out from the stem and within the bark, as in all solid woods, there is the distinction of *exogenous* plants. The former have in the embryo but one rudimentary seed-leaf, or cotyledon, and the latter have the embryo enclosed between two cotyledons, and these cotyledons are from the life-instinct of the ancestral plant filled with protein for the sustenance of the new plant in its opening germination.

The upshoot has then its forming *buds* and *leaves*, and in which the formative life-work is of the highest interest, more specially in the exogenous class. The leaf is wanted for oxygenating and elaborating the sap sent into it, and in which assimilative process the appropriate elements of the air and sunlight are conditional. The leaf is an extension of the tissues of

the stock in the upper and lower surfaces, and these
surfaces spread out by ribs and veins of firmer texture. The upper surface catches the light, and the
green-colored protoplasm proximate to it becomes the
chlorophyll, so peculiarly distinguishing it from the
fainter green of the lower surface. Between the
stem and foot-stalk of the leaf is the *axillary* bud, as
an embryo, which at any favoring time may grow out
in a branch; and the stalk itself has its *terminal*
bud, elongating the stem from one leaf-node to another. The received sap, prepared in the leaf, goes
down in the vascular cellulose of the branches, and
thence in the stem, and through the yoke into the
roots, carrying nourishment and forming in them their
ligneous substance. The stem and branches need
their uniform nourishment on all sides, and the life-
instinct secures this by giving to the vascular cellulose of the forming stem and branch a spiral growth,
that throws out the leaves and buds evenly on all
sides, whether as relatively to each other they stand
opposite, alternate, or verticillate, and in their regular
supply from higher to lower keep the woody part of
a cylindrical shape, tapering from the bottom upwards, and so securing for the tree the highest
strength and symmetry.

And here we have a special manifestation of the
life-instinct spontaneously using nature for its own
ends. It facilitates this spiral formation by using the
force of gravity in its assistance. An air-bubble,
working up against the downward pressure through

the water, necessarily rises in a spiral course; and the forming cellulose in the growing branches has almost universally attained for itself this advantage. The terminal buds are turned upwards from horizontal or pendent positions, and the cellulose is made to form itself against gravitating pressure. The plant regards its need of light more than this advantage from atmospheric pressure, and for the sake of the sun-light will turn towards it, though it may be in the direction with gravity.

That this upturned direction of all branches is instinctive for such natural assistance, has been tested by ingenious experiments. In Gray's Botanical Text Book we find the following statement: "The seeds of a bean-plant were made to germinate in a quantity of moss fastened to the circumference of a wheel, which was made to revolve at a rapid rate; where the seeds were subjected to the centrifugal force alone, acting like that of gravitation, but in the opposite direction. On examination, after some days, the young root and stem were found to have taken the direction of the axis of rotation, the former being turned towards the circumference, and the latter towards the centre of the wheel. The same result took place when the wheel was made to revolve horizontally with considerable rapidity; but when the velocity was moderate, the roots were directed obliquely downwards and outwards, and the stem obliquely upwards and inwards, in obedience to the centrifugal force and the power of gravity acting at right angles to each other." But the seeds would not regard such offered advantage to the attainment of a spiral vegetation against the higher want of light, for " when caused to germinate in moss so arranged that the only light they could receive was reflected from a mirror which threw the solar rays upon them directly from below, in such case their roots were sent upwards into the moss, and their stems downwards towards the light."

This instinctive spiral tendency prevails in the growing flower as well as in the leaves and branches. The cellular tissue which in the leaf-bud would become a stem with spiral leaves, in the seed-bud is made successively, first a whorl of sepals in a calyx, then of petals in a corolla, then of stamens and their anthers, and lastly the pistillate whorl of circling ovules in an ovary. The parts of the flower are but the transformed spirals from the leaves, and are inci. dent to the instinctive working of the life-want for its cylindrical stem and branches. And this general law admits of many varieties in the flowering as in the foliage. If we should assume the apple-blossom as a normal type among flowers, having five sepals in a calyx, alternating with five petals in a corolla, and then five stamens followed by five pistils, all regularly alternating, the abnormal varieties would be a multitude, making their distinctive differences to appear in every portion of the floral combination.

So the life-want reigns through all the vegetable kingdom; everywhere it is exhibiting its instinctive working to its ends, and adapting a change of means

in new circumstances. From its lowest unicellular
products to its tallest oaks and cedars, and in the
monstrous sequoise trees of California, near forty feet
in diameter and four hundred feet in height, it is
everywhere spontaneously and unconsciously reaching onward to its ends, and directing its assimilating
and formative energy, by the help of nature where it
may, and against the hinderances of nature where it
must. If any lesion in the parts of the bodily structure occur, it will work to repair; if deficiencies are
found, it will work to supply; if obstacles are met, it
works to remove or surmount them. In changing
conditions, it modifies its means to its wants. It
sends the roots or the branches in the way to its
nourishment; turns the leaves to the light; and the
tree, sheltered in the forest by its fellows, spreads its
roots upon the surface soil, but when standing alone,
it sends its tap-root deep in the ground to hold itself
against the tempest.

But it has no other agency than in spontaneously
constructing. It comes to no consciousness in the
body it inhabits, and builds up its cellulose that other
and higher organisms may enjoy it. Vegetable life is
not for itself, and only as an instinctive worker from
the mineral, that the sentient may afterwards appropriate and enjoy. Its whole activity is in forming
and maintaining its organism; but it has no capacity
to use its organism, or live in it, for its own interests.
There is neither loco-motion nor conscious mental
action.

THE REIGN OF SENSE IN THE ANIMAL KINGDOM.

Vegetable life absorbs carbon, and sends off its excess of oxygen, and prepares an atmosphere, and secures in itself the aliment for higher organic existences. The occasion is the need for a more elevated formative instinct, which may take the cellulose of the plant and combine it anew into the nerve, and muscle, and bone of the animal. Plant life has simply instinctive craving, and an agency solely in the direction of its longing, and only builds up its organism and repairs its waste, with nothing further to work for. But animal-life is essentially nerve-irritability, with a central organ to which the irritability comes, and from which a complementary irritability departs, and in which is the source of self-feeling and self-finding, and therein the capacity for recognizing its own want and directing its own agency. This conscious sensation is wholly another reign than plant-instinct, and introduces altogether a new and more elevated kingdom. When the instinct has constructed the organism, the sense lives and acts in it for the ends of its own gratification.

The animal organism is the product of an unconscious agency, as truly as in the vegetable kingdom is the production of plants and trees; but the formative instinct here works to another and further end, that it may raise up a structure in which sentient life may have its dwelling-place, and the members of which the sense may use in subserviency to its own happiness; and yet, until the organism is thus instinctively constituted, the animal reign of sentient irritability cannot begin. As the mineral could not develop itself to the vegetable, since mechanical forces have within them no spontaneity, so the vegetable cannot develop to the animal, since in the vegetable is no sentient irritability. It might, perhaps, even in theologic consistency, be urged that divine wisdom and power would equally be manifested by an original endowment of the life-want to rise, on occasion, to an instinctive animal construction, as they have been by a new creation of the higher life-want when the occasion came. But inasmuch as the organizing instinct in the animal economy carries plant-cellulose to nervous irritability, there must be a power given to it which the plant-instinct has not; and then, in the nervous system, this power is to be a sentient agency and a conscious user of the organism; and in both respects it is made manifest that animal-life cannot be evolved from plant-life. The consideration of the period in creating is of no speculative importance; and it may as well be supposed that ethereal atoms had their nerve-want superinduced when others had their plant-want, as that the former was posterior to the latter; and then each works in assimilating and organizing after its own kind, as the conditions of their respective combinations are given. The animal instinct must wait upon the vegetable, for the animal cannot be directly constructed from the mineral; but the lower organisms of each may have no long period between; and the animal forms, as meliorating conditions open, will rise in completeness of nerve-irritability, and muscular excitement, and conscious sensation, and directed loco-motion, to their higher gradations.

The distinctive sentient organization is essentially in the irritability of the nervous system, and the whole bodily structure, with its varied organs and members, is determined in consistency with the nervous arrangement. The centres of nervous irritability are the ganglionic portions.

A *ganglion* is an ash-gray mass of unequal cells, irregularly rounded in their single outlines, and imbedded in a granular matter which fills the interspaces. Filaments of a dull white color extend out from the gray ganglia, and constitute the *fibrous* tissue of the nervous system. The filamentary often interfuse or envelop the ganglionic portions, and the fibres go off from the ganglia in bundles to their communicating parts of the body. The bundles divide, branch off, and inosculate with other bundles in their course, but the single fibre maintains its own continuity throughout. They are of two kinds, and subserve two purposes; one bringing communications to the ganglion, and is an *afferent* nerve, the other carrying an executive communication from the ganglion, and is an *efferent* nerve. The ganglia have broader tissues of connection also, and which are known as *commissures*, and through which the system has accordant sympathy and activity. This nervous arrangement has its stages from incipiency to maturity. Close upon the primitive vegetable *algæ*, and *diatomacea*, come the *protozoa* and infusorial *animalculæ*; and as vegetation rises from unicellular form to complete root, stem, and leafy branches, so the animal forms rise in gradation through all the sub-kingdoms.

The lowest subdivision of the animal kingdom, in its higher forms of sentient life, has five ganglia encircling a mouth, and connected, by their commissures, with afferent or *sensor* nerve, and efferent or *motor* nerve; and the whole division is known as *Radiata*, with its protozoa sexless, and senseless except in touch and taste. Then come the *Mollusca* of higher nervous organization, just touching the point of possession for all the special senses with the most advanced species, and yet the best only slightly awake to sentient consciousness. The *Articulata* rise to a symmetrical arrangement of ganglia in a mid-line of the body, and side-branches for moving members on each side; and then we come to the complete animal structure in the *Vertebrata*, with its classes of Fish, Reptile, Fowl, and Mammifer. Here, at last, is the Brain with cerebrum and cerebellum, at the head of the spinal cord of anterior and posterior portions, and the sensor and motor nerves in their connections with the surface to the limbs, and the special sense-organs. Connected with these, through the sensorium, are the sympathetic and pneumogastric nerves for controlling digestion, circulation, and respiration. As there is more or less air in the lungs, blood in the heart, or food in the stomach, so respiration, pulsation, secretion, and peristaltic motion, are quickened or retarded.

Here is the full arrangement for stimulating and directing nervous irritability; and the method of movement is always direct at first in the afferent, and then reflex in the efferent nerves. Not only is the building up of the nervous system instinctive, but very much of the nervous action in the organism is wholly in unconsciousness. Digestion, circulation, secretion, in their healthy action, are all below consciousness, and wholly involuntary ; and though we may, temporarily, repress respiration, and become conscious of partial control of our breath, yet soon the instinctive impulse will control and force down all factitious resolution. Even the special senses often guide the action in the absence of all conscious recognition. Habitual movements, activity in reverie, and the strange and sometimes dangerous feats of somnambulism, are all guided by sense-impressions, though destitute of conscious volition. The vegetable-instinct is mere spontaneous want, ever going out and not back. The sense-instinct has nerve irritability, working direct and reflex in its organism in mere spontaneous activity, leaving no recognized traces in the ganglionic centres. Much of animated activity is merely sense-instinct.

Rising from simpler to more complex nerve-organisms, we have ganglionic centres held in connection by their commissures, and the whole acting in concert; and then we find one ganglion as an organic centre regulating all its subservient ganglia, and each organic centre supervising others, and there-by enabling one sense to correct others; and in the highest sub-kingdom of the vertebrates, and its high-est class of mammals, we have the perfection of sense-regulation in a central sensorium, and in this a central coördinating ganglion, that may recognize and regu-late all nerve-irritability which comes within the general sensorium, and give a unity of conscious intelligence and sentient agency to the individual. The spinal cord sends its fibres in striated lines up through all the cerebral portion; here, again, are the two hemispheres of the cerebrum with their gangli-onic convolutions, and the cerebellum with its gangli-onic envelope; and then, in the most central position possible for spinal cord, cerebrum, and cerebellum, is a distinct ganglion known as that of the *tuber-annulare*, which experiment has shown is the co-ordinating ganglion of all ganglia. Other portions of the brain may be disturbed or removed in some animals, especially some birds, and life still continue, but with deranged sentient activity according to the respective point of injury; but if the tuber-annulare be undisturbed, sensation, and motion, and directing judgment, may recover from the shock of amputation to their normal activity; yet when this ganglion is broken up, and the rest of the brain left uninjured, the vital functions may a while instinctively operate, but consciousness and voluntary motion cease from all man-ifestation, and every sentient function is paralyzed.

We may thus speculatively determine the mode of sentient consciousness, and all animal intelligence.

The nervous organism gives occasion for central direct and reflex irritability; one centre can have its communion with others in the common sensorium; and one coördinating centre is occasion for supervising, and distinguishing, and in this consciously recognizing, every impression which is made on the sensorium. The life-instinct in one part of the organism catches its own agency in another part, and as feeling reciprocates feeling in the common sensorium, so in the coördinating centre the life-instinct wakes in sentiency, and comes to conscious recognition of nerve-irritation.

Full provision is here for all sense-affections, and capability to distinguish and define them and bring them within conscious apprehension. Instinct at once guides itself by sense, as a deeper instinct had guided in forming the nerve-organism; and experience soon begins learning how phenomena are grouped and how they succeed each other. and therein a judgment according to sense opens. The brute retains, and associates according to retained experience; and the parts of the groups and successions, that have been invariably together are the predicates of which the group or the series is the subject. Experience finds agreeable and disagreeable sensations, and from this all animal appetites and desires awaken. These prompt to executive movement in gratifying or in shunning, and a brute-will, ever as highest happiness dictates, is called up in exercise. Comparison and contrast, association and abstraction, analysis and combination, can

22

all go as far as sense has preceded, and the brute makes his inductions and conclusions according to his experience. Some species of animals have extraordinary practical sagacity. A fox, about two thirds grown, was so chained as to permit his descent to the bottom of a burrow made for him. The fowls were picking up the corn which dropped from the cart on its unloading, when an ear of corn tumbled from the basket and fell within his reach. He suddenly caught and carried it within his burrow. Awakened curiosity led the men to watch what a fox might do with corn. He was seen to nibble off a few kernels at the mouth of his hole, and returning the ear, he stealthily lay back in concealment. But no sooner did the chicken pick his corn than the fox picked the chicken, and to save the poultry they were forced to uncover the burrow and take the ear of corn away. This case, among other instances of brute intelligence scarcely less striking, has in it abstraction, and generalization, and logical conclusion from sense-data, followed by executive action with design, in the end of motive, as completely as in the adaptation of means in human economy. But the judgment is wholly within sense-experience. It is conclusion from former observation of the order of occurring facts, but with no insight of reason which catches the connecting bond that holds the facts necessarily together. Uniformity of experience induces conclusion and designed action, but there is no attainment of a universal principle determining the order of experience, nor of a moral imperative which must control appetitive indulgence. The cunning fox can inductively philosophize as really as the man, but he cannot get truth beyond sense and speculatively philosophize. All arises in organized nerve-irritability, and all vanishes when the nerve-organism is dissolved.

THE REIGN OF REASON IN HUMANITY.

The vegetable kingdom is ruled by the mere life-instinct, the animal kingdom is ruled by conscious sensation, but its highest intelligence rests in what has appeared in experience. There is nothing to rise above experience and comprehend the universe, much less to recognize the God of the universe as absolute Creator and Governor. What we have in these two kingdoms of organic existence must be a preparation only for something further. Sentient being has in it no rights of sovereignty, and rules only by the necessities of nature as already constituted. Its sensibility is made for it, and the means for pleasure or pain are put about it, and the process to its highest happiness is a fixed destiny within it, and there is no alternative in the case, but the sense-activity must put itself through the course which opens before it. In attaining its end of enjoyment in the highest practicable degree, it knows only a perpetual subserviency to the fixed relations of nature which determine for it how only it may be happy, with no known rights by which he may in personality govern himself and attain conscious dignity and self-respect.

It is as clear that the intrinsic excellency which inspires dignity and demands respect is not in sense, and can never be a development of it, as it was that life was not in force, and could never come out of it. Sense only prompts to conscious action through desire, and its highest good is gratified appetite, and it is not thus possible that the good of satisfying an imperative should come in to its experience. There is nothing in it that can make anything due to it, and hence we can say nothing of duty about it. It can assert no rights and feel no claims. That it should come to conscious dignity and self-respect, it must have that which has intrinsic excellence superinduced upon it. In no other possible way can the animal rise to conscious sovereignty over its own agency than by an endowment of reason. In the light of reason he can then say when he ought to be happy, and when he ought to suffer. But from no quarter can this endowment come except from the creative source in the Absolute. It has been expressed in every kingdom, mineral, vegetable, and animal; but in neither has it been a conscious possession, and thus in neither has there been anything which might wear the crown or hold the sceptre of sovereign authority. So far as we have yet contemplated it, the created universe has nothing in it which may rule itself, or rule others in its own right, and can stand only amid the necessitated connections of nature.

There must here be done just what revelation declares man's Creator did — give to him a living soul in a peculiar way, distinguishing his life from the merely sentient animal life. As he did not to the animal, God breathed into Adam the breath of life, and this breathing his living soul into him made him a spiritual intelligence distinct from all brute-perception. "There is a spirit in man, and the inspiration of the Almighty giveth them understanding." (Job xxxii. 8.) Both plant and animal live as organizing instinct, and the animal life has conscious sentiency; but only in the supernatural inspiration of reason is man elevated to the prerogatives and responsibilities of spiritual life and action. The sentient soul of Adam took within itself also the rational spirit which God's inspiration superinduced, and in this supernatural endowment man stands above nature in the likeness of the Deity. Instinctive life and sentient soul belong to nature, but rational spirit crowns nature, and of right takes dominion over it.

As creative origination in an outer expression, there is nothing peculiar in this divine endowment of man with reason to distinguish it from other creative acts, except as it is an impartation of the Divine Image. Material and ethereal forces originate in God, and are put out from him in overt expression by his immediate creative act, but they are not in his likeness. God is not force, neither antagonist nor diremptive, though he is the direct Maker of them both. And so both instinctive and sentient life find their origination in outer expression direct from the Creator's hand, but they bring with them no likeness to him, for God is neither instinctive want nor sentient prompting. And so, in the same way of direct production and expression, the rationality of man is immediately from God's creative agency, and is his product in man as truly as force in nature, and life in plants, and sense in animals; but here the created product comes, bearing the very image and superscription of the Creator. The finite rational spirit is not God, but as really an outer created expression from God as force, or life, or sense; only that the former is like, while the latter are unlike, the Maker. The manifesting in outer expression is the creating work, and this is alike to be contemplated in all creative acts as originating in God.

This supernatural endowment of sentient life with reason is an impartation from God of a self-intelligent and self-determining essence, which, as superinduced upon life and sense, is competent to use them in its own ends and purposes. The formative instinct is made unconsciously to do the work of reason in the organization of the human body, making it to comport with the dignity and designs of the human spirit. Where reason is, instinct and sense both act under higher control and for further ends than the mere organism, or than the sense-gratification. When, in the absence of reason, the sentient life-instinct constructed the nervous arrangement of central ganglion and communicating filaments, and in the nerve-irritability controlled the unconscious sense-instinct, and then through the coördinating sensorium managed the special senses in conscious direction to the ends of sense-gratification, it did nothing that reached beyond the ends of the organism itself and its appetitive indulgence, and was held wholly subservient to mere organic preservation and enjoyment; but the rational spirit knows what is due to its own dignity, and works for the ends of self-approbation and the respect of others. When the organism dissolves, sense vanishes; and even while the nerve-organism lasts, the elementary composition and conscious activities are perpetually passing and recurring, and so both sense-existence and sense-experience are a continual flow of appearance and disappearance, with nothing steadfast. Such fleeting show cannot comport with nor satisfy the intrinsic dignity of the abiding spirit. Animal life merely both may and must exist as fleeting, renewing wasted forces and departed indulgences that can remain for no two moments the same: but the life of reason should and must be abiding in principle and purpose. When superinduced upon the life-instinct, it infuses its energy through the living ethereal forces it inhabits, and makes them to be for it an abiding tabernacle as a "spiritual body;" and when superinduced upon sense, it fixes the material forces in which sense resides in balanced and unchanging combination, and the perpetuated sentiency becomes a perduring soul in a changeless soul-body. For all the ends of sustenance and growth, and organic perception, and reproduction, the flowing assimilated forces, which come on and pass off from this perduring basis as the soul-body, supply every need; while constantly the rational spirit in its spiritual body holds both its own ethereal forces steadfast, and reaches over the material forces of the soul-body, holding them stable, and keeping both spirit-body and soul-body in firm alliance. The spirit-essence in the spiritual body is, in human life, never "unclothed," but "clothed upon" by the material soul-body.

This alliance of soul and spirit constitutes *Humanity*. However in other worlds spirit may be "clothed upon" in corporeal existence, in this our world it is by superinducing reason upon sense, and the reason in its body of ethereal forces incarnates the spiritual in the material basis of all sentient life as soul-body; and such union of soul in soul-body and spirit in spirit-body constitutes the human being, man. Not sentient soul and rational spirit incorporeal constitute man; for except as abiding in substantial force, either ethereal or material, neither spirit nor soul can have expression away from their creative source; but spirit in ethereal and soul in material corporeity constitute humanity, and the two combined in one by the energy of the reason which presides over both. While the conscious disposing of the spirit in voluntary execution of its end in life is a moral power, standing in its own responsibility, the instinctive, unconscious agency which carries on the vital functions is involuntary and irresponsible, though spontaneously guided by reason.

In the sphere of instinctive working, the reason in the human spontaneously makes many new modifications and arrangements for its own ends and uses, which mere animal sense does not want, and which brute consciousness could not use. Organs of speech are fashioned in flexibility for sounds, and in facility for tones, expressive of thought and sentiment in man, wherein no brute participates, and for which animal life can find no occasion for utterance. The human hand is formed in the interest of reason, unlike the corresponding member for brute instrumentality, readily becoming skilled to work the ideals of human invention on to solid matter, whether of the useful or beautiful creations of genius. The erect stature is given man, whereby he attains and holds dominion over the animal kingdom, subduing nature, cultivating the ground, and distributing the productions for universal consumption. And yet more wonderfully, this spontaneity of reason works its own stability out in expression on the human organism in its erect stature, self-poised attitude, symmetrical figure, and its authority on the open brow, and the light of its own majesty shining in every feature. The inner spirit uses the ethereal forces of its spiritual body, spontaneously, in building up the tabernacle for the sentient soul, that itself may control and use the sentient life for higher purposes than any animal consciousness can recognize. Such infusion of the rational spirit in its spiritual body everywhere through the sentient soul in its soul-body, and this in the instinctive construction of the human organism for rational action and moral probation, makes a peculiar being, so far as we know from observation or revelation unlike any other, and is the distinctively *human*, which the Absolute Reason knew it behooved him to create.

This comprehending bond of the spiritual holding all the sentient within it determines *human Individu-*

ality. As before seen, that which the insight of reason detects running through the manifold, and shutting them together in one, individualizes the many, making of them an indivisible single, inclusive of itself and exclusive of all else. So with the force of chemical combination in the mineral kingdom, the life-instinct in the vegetable kingdom, and the sentient irritability in the animal kingdom. In each the individuals are determined by their peculiar bond which runs through and holds the manifold in a single. And here this infused bond of the spiritual through all the sensual determines an individuality of its own exclusively. The inbreathed spirit from God in Adam held at once the substantial ethereal and material forces of both spirit- and soul-bodies in one, and had control of all sentient appetite in executive gratification, and in this began an experience and a history of his own; one and single, distinct both from his Maker and any other creature. Put by God's inspiration into sense, and holding that sense in comprehension, it became the individual Adam, inclusive of himself as sense and spirit, and exclusive of all other. Subject still to God, and responsible to God, Adam was sole individuality in himself; originating his own action in the disposing of his own spirit, and using his own sense, so that the acts were Adam's acts, and neither the acts of the Creator nor any other creature. That rational spirit put within and infused through that sentient soul constituted the first human individual, shutting his own in, and shutting all other individuality out.

And not only was Adam so made by God at first in his one inclusive and exclusive individuality, but every descendant in sexual generation has rational spirit diffused through and binding its own sense in unity, making an individuality of its own, distinct from God, and Adam, and every other descendant. All have humanity as soul and spirit, but each its individuality as such a soul held in its own spirit; and so Adam's posterity stand out in human Individuality.

The same substantial forces, held together by the spirit, determine *human Identity*. The river is the same only as new waters flow on in the same way and the same place. The tree is the same, from germination to maturity, only as new particles have been assimilated in constant succession by the perpetually working life-instinct. When the life goes out in plant or animal, the identity is lost. But in the human individual there is the spirit holding in unity the same living ethereal forces as the spiritual body, and the same material forces as the permanent basis of the organic elements which come and go in the earthy body, and which permanent is the unchanging soul-body; and this spiritual holding in unity the same spirit-body and the same soul-body, gives an identity to the human which can be determined for no other individuality. It holds on the same through all vicissitudes of the mortal state, and will still perdure when all sense-affections and sex-distinctions shall have passed away.

The rational spirit secures for the sentient soul in the soul-body assured *Immortality*. The animal individuality is determined in the continual life-instinct working its new assimilations and old eliminations through the changing body; this life-instinct constantly holding its organic construction in form and measure about itself, and retaining and expressing its irritability and conscious sensibility through each successive moment. The living bond determines the individuality, and the continued form, though made of perpetually passing elements, is the animal identity. And man, so far as animal only, has only the individuality of being held together by the one working life-instinct, and the identity of perpetuated organic form and proportion, through his successive development. So with his whole organism of sense-nutrition and sex-distinction, which are " of the earth, earthy," and dissoluble as the brute individuality and identity. As above stated, the exhausting life-action and nature's melioration for higher existences demand dissolution as earnestly as the previous construction. When the organism has reached its end, the animality has finished its work, and in the certain dissolution the same sentient individual exists no more.

But man has rational spirit superinduced upon the life-instinct and conscious sensation, and this spirit has been set to its fleshly abode that it may control sense and hold every appetite subservient to spiritual dignity and integrity; and when having thus gained dominion over sense, there comes at length the claim of freedom from the perpetual warfare; or if having given up to carnal indulgence, there comes the equally resistless claim that it meet its deserved shame and reproach for its sensuality. In either case, sentient soul and rational spirit have been in communion in the period of probation, and they must stand together, from the reason of the case, in the coming retributions. The individual spirit can be known only as the permanent dweller in the body of ethereal forces, and the individual sentient soul can be known only in its body of material forces, and so the spirit has held steadfast its spiritual body, and infused through the sentient soul it has also held the soul-body steadfast in its balanced material forces. However the earthy animal organism may change or dissolve, its material basis of substantial forces abides for the soul, and is held identically the same forever. The soul body may cast off all its earthy trappings in animal death, and may be separated from the spirit-body in human death, but the soul-body itself cannot lose either its individuality or identity. The spirit in the spirit-body demands its reunion, and it must be kept in its integrity. That spirit-body is "a house not made with hands, eternal in the heavens," and the " earnest desire of the soul to be clothed upon with the house which is from heaven " must be gratified. The spirit-body is the sole medium for the spirit's distinction from, or its communion with, God, the Father of all spirits, and that it has been linked with soul, and soul-body, and fixed its permanent disposition and character in that connection, fixes also the certainty of their eternal communion in the world that follows all probation.

This pervading of sense by rational spirit determines *human Personality*. Personality in God is independent of all conditions from nature ; personality in angelic spirits has its connections in an unknown nature ; our natural world has no personality ; man alone has personality conditioned in known natural connections. Material nature has the necessitated connections of mechanical force ; vegetable nature has the spontaneity of instinctive want, but no alternative in consciousness ; animal nature has conscious appetite, but no alternative to a movement towards what it deems highest gratification ; and so below man there are only *things* governed by the necessary connections in nature above them, and no *persons* obedient to a voice within in spite of all without.

Man, in so far forth as he is merely sentient, is animal, with animal appetites, and subject to act under the condition of finding no alternative to the execution of the strongest propensity. But the sentient is one side only of the human ; man is rational spirit as well as sentient soul, and the human is essentially and peculiarly this union of sense and spirit. We know but only the lower half of man, and that which is wholly within nature, when we deem him the mere agent for attaining his highest happiness. The better half of man is his reason, which is agency for attaining highest dignity. Reason is itself spiritual, supernatural, competent to stand against force, and instinctive want, and sentient appetite, and hold solely and persistently to its own conscious reasonableness. Reason knows itself; its own intrinsic excellency ; and thus what is due to itself for its own sake, aside from any appetite. Nature's forces, or instincts, or appetites may urge in any direction, and with any strength, but the spirit may refuse all compliance, on the sole consideration that its own integrity is lost by yielding. Man, endowed with reason above nature, may look nature through within himself and without, and aside from all adaptations to want and appetite, he may see what the reason-idea, or principle, in nature is, and without which nature itself could not so have been. Among these Eternal Ideas and immutable principles, he may discriminate such as control in their particular sphere, and take such as an ultimate standard each in its respective sphere, and then may explore and comprehend that sphere in the light of that principle which determines it. So far as such contemplation extends, he will know that whole sphere, not merely as in sense it appears, but in the reason of the case why it should and must so appear. And in every such sphere he may stand by the eternal principle he attains, and maintain his own integrity and fidelity to it in spite of any opposing force, or want, or appetite. He can free himself against all promptings of nature in such sphere, by holding to the determinate and eternal truths of such sphere. In all such positions he has spiritual freedom, and can do as no animal can — overcome nature, and stand on the dignity and honor of his reason alone. In this, man is *Person;* other than a thing ; and at once he is open to claims and responsibilities which the presence of no force, or want, or appetite can annul.

As rational Intelligence in any or all of these distinct spheres, the man, as person, is *Philosopher ;* and as Actor in the light of the truths in any or all of these distinct spheres, he is *free Agent ;* and in the more prominent and important of these spheres we may contemplate him as Philosopher and free Agent both in one. We stand here wholly beyond all animal experience, and in a region where Sense-knowing and Sense-acting are utterly irrelevant and impertinent; and a very short consideration of man, in these respective spheres, will make conspicuous the prerogatives and responsibilities which put him above all we have yet speculatively known of creation, and make him to be truly the crowning work of the Creator's hand.

That may be known as *Science* which gathers and classifies facts as they appear in experience; but in this there is nothing of the insight and control of reason, and hence nothing of Philosophy, nor of free Responsibility.

Sense-experience may learn what appearances please the eye, or what sounds please the ear; and by careful study and trial man may attain the skill to imitate nature by finding and applying practical rules for copying nature, and so far he might know how to give forms or tones which will be generally pleasing. But in this way there can be gained nothing of the philosophy or of the freedom which belongs to the *Fine Arts.* The reason can at once see in the forms of nature the living sentiment they express, and in what blended forms the blended sentiment desired may be most perfectly and fully expressed; and such forms give the standard for beauty, or sublimity, and become a universal guide for taste in admiring, criticising, or executing in Art. In this way only can one be artist in his free personality. As following the agreeable in sense and copying nature by it, he is bound solely by the fact of constitutional sensibility and the tried forms presented to it, and he can say only what *does* please, while the reason may say what *should* please both him and all others. In the insight of reason the true artist may dispute all tastes but that which stands conformed to the Absolute Standard. He may freely guide his action, and make his selection, or set himself to the execution, in a ' work of art, by the reason's ideal, and refuse all appeals to any sensibility which would vitiate the taste, or debase the reason in repudiating the pure Ideal.

So, also, in *Geometry* and *Mechanics,* the reason sees in the pure diagrams or motions the truths of which they are the symbol, and may not only, like the sense, say so nature *does* appear; but from its own insight may know, what no sense can, that in the diagrams projected such forces nature *must* use ; and in the forces nature uses, such diagrams her movements *must* make ; and so the man reads the meaning of the Maker in both the Earth and Heavens. And here, too, the Philosopher can free himself from any demands the sense-appearance may impose, and hold to reason's claim, refusing all abatement or perversion, though he die for it.

Still more specially, by the endowment of reason

man rises into the pure region of an immutable and free *Morality*. Animal happiness is the gratification of an animal sensibility, and this is the end of all sense, that the highest practicable gratification be secured. The sensibility is the highest endowment the animal has, and its gratification is the highest good. The sensibility is a thing made, and the law of highest Happiness is found in knowing how the sensibility is constituted, and then avoiding what pains, and attaining and applying what pleases it. There can thus be no immutable rule; for a sensibility can be variedly constituted, and the rule must be as the constituted fact is found. And even if all sensibilities were found alike, this could not give an ultimate rule; for we could thence only know that the Maker was most pleased to so constitute all sensibilities, and the last fact thus gained would be, that the Maker finds he himself has such a sensibility that he must so make other sensibilities, or be unhappy. The last we here find is still a fact with no reason for it. We have, in the Maker of all other sensibilities, a constitutional sensibility with no rule to determine it.

Still further, a sensibility can only crave, and, never claim. It may ask favors, but can never demand dues. Its highest end is gratification, and it can never attain to approbation. Hence the possession of a conscience is impossible to a sensibility. Its shortcomings are losses of happiness only, and hence to it occasions for regret, but never losses of respect, and hence can never give compunctions for guilt. No possible elevation of a rule for sense can rise above prudence, and can never attain to an imperative. A sensibility cannot feel obligation in itself, nor can reason see in it any rights. Out of a sensibility it is impossible that there should, in any way, be derived a morality.

But an endowment of rationality is another and much more exalted good than being constituted with a sensibility. Here is an intrinsic excellency with conferred dignity; the highest which the Maker can give or the creature receive; even the very image and likeness of the Creator.

Sensibility has no intrinsic excellency, and so no dignity, and is merely a utility; an instrumental means to a further end, and worthless except in reference to that end beyond itself. But to know that reason has been superinduced upon sense is at the same time to know that the reason should rule and the sense should serve; and also at once in this is seen, that gratified sense may often be forbidden, and that all happiness must be reasonable or it must be rejected. And the present denial of gratifying sensibility is not at all that the sensibility may be made happier at some future time, but that reason may now and ever be honored. It can never be morality to say, " I do this that I may be happy; " but only to say, " I do this that I may be worthy."

Nor is this at all open to an inconsiderate objection that such ground of Morality involves the absurdity of making " the highest good of man to consist in his choosing as an ultimate end his own choice of an ultimate end." (President Hopkins's Lectures on Moral Science, p. 57.) There are distinctions of worthiness, and thus of good, in all consideration of Morality, and no statement should be permitted to confound them. To be endowed with reason is a dignity and a good; and so also to conform to reason is a dignity and a good; one an imparted and the other an attained worthiness and good. When the man goes back for his ultimate rule, he sees the imparted worthiness and good; and when he turns forward to an ultimate end, he looks at an attained worthiness and good; and he chooses in both cases, and with no absurdity in so doing, for the choices are as distinct as the worthiness and the good in the two cases. The former he chooses as rule, and by adopting makes it his maxim for life; the latter he chooses as end, and by conformity establishes integrity of character. Both are ultimate; the former in the direction of origin, the latter in the direction of consummation; and both are intrinsic, as thoroughly in the very reason of the case; and yet they are in themselves so inherently distinct that they cannot become identical, and if logically confounded they confound the logic. Both these forms of worthiness are good in the estimate of reason, and therein wholly different from all good in the estimate of sensation; and the proper discrimination is kept when we say of the two former, their good is that of worthiness, and of all forms of the latter, their good is that of happiness, for no possible happiness could compensate for the loss of either distinction of worthiness. The endowed worthiness must be in order that the attained worthiness may be, but the possession of each is invaluable compared with anything else in earth or heaven ; and if the endowment be, then must the attainment be, or " it had been good for that man if he had not been born."

The affections in the sensibility and those in the reason may both be known as *feeling;* but though they receive the same name, they are themselves essentially unlike. The sensibility is a constituted thing, and has its constitutional nature, and hence all its feelings are as the constitution is made to be. In many things it differs in one man from another, and might be made in each different from all ; and hence the sense-feeling is as the sense happens to be in the particular subject, and the gratification happens accordingly, and so the sense-gratification may properly be termed Happiness. But the reason is not made, and has no constitutional nature, and no difference of feeling for different subjects. It cannot be conceived to have feelings that happen to it in any way. As reason is, so it necessarily must be, and as its feeling is, so in the conditions they must have been, and no power can change it or, them. Were reason to be other than it is, it would become unreason ; and were its feelings in any case supposed to have been different from what in that case they were, they could not have been the feelings of reason. There is no nature, and no making about it ; above and beyond all of nature, reason is and must be eternally the same. When sense loves flesh, it might have been constituted to love herbs; and when it lives happily in air, it might have been made to live happily in water. But when reason feels obligation, or remorse, or self-approbation, or reverence, it cannot be conceived that, by any possibility, it should so have been constituted as to have there felt differently. They are not feelings that can happen to it, from some essential changes happening to be made in it; for its essence is absolutely changeless. It is as truly ultimate and immutable in feeling, as in knowing; and as ultimate and immutable in willing, as in knowing and feeling. It is supernatural, and hence beyond all nature's changes; and is rule for all, in all places and in all periods. The strongest obligation possible is, that the imperative is reasonable; and the highest approbation possible is, that reason is satisfied. Authority can have its investiture from nothing other than reason, and can attach its claims only to reason; and can fix approbation only to the reasonable. Man participates in all this not as sensible, but solely as reasonable.

In the last place, and higher than all, Man's endowment of reason raises him to the sphere of *Theology*. Sense can know nothing of God, nor in anything can it be brought in sympathy and communion with God in any one of his attributes. Animal being can neither know whence it comes nor whither it goes, and may only possess and enjoy what has been given to it. When sensibility is empty, it is uneasy; when fully supplied, it rests in a surfeit. It has gladness in its fulness, but knows neither gratitude for supplies, nor reverence or respect for any providential guarding and overruling. But the impartation of reason to man capacitates him to see, in the things which are made, the thoughts and intentions of the Maker, and thereby clearly to know his power and wisdom and essential Deity. Both *that* God is, and *what* God is, reason reads in his works. Communications made through any appropriate symbols can reach the reason, and the evidence that they come from God reason also can receive. Neither religious faith nor divine worship is possible, except to a person endowed with reason; and what should purport to be a revelation, opening a door for heavenly communion, could awaken only credulous superstition till it was brought to the light of reason. Any declarations it may make concerning truths beyond the reach of finite human reason, the man may accept on the strength of the divine testimony; but the ground of the testimony must come within the light of reason, and then the message declared may be rationally received, though the manner how that truth shall be explained may yet remain in utter darkness.

Reason, thus, prepares man for both natural and revealed religion, and gives to him an ultimate standard. " There be gods many, and lords many ; " and many assumed revelations; but wherein they differ, all except one must in something come short of the full claim of reason. Only that assumed religion, which fills the claim of reason, can be the true and safe source of confidence. That the Deity on which the religion rests is accordant with reason will, in all cases, constitute the very ground for our religious allegiance and devotion. Not any gratification of constitutional sensibility is to hold us in his service, but the conscientious conviction that himself and the service he requires are entirely reasonable. No service is from pious love, if it spring not more from reverence for God's reasonableness than fondness for God's kindness. Finite reason finds in the Absolute Reason the ultimate rule which is to settle for us, both the God we must choose and the service we must render, if we would gain our own and God's approbation.

So endowed with reason, man is competent to study nature, live in society, and commune with God. Creation is about him to be learned and be used: he is in the midst of his fellows to help and be helped by them; his Maker is ever present for his loving trust, and immortality opens before him an endless conscious and responsible experience. In him is the crown of all terrestrial existence, and nature has its end in subserviency to man's reason, and the end of man's finite rationality is eternal communion with the Absolute Reason. The Ultimate Unity is Unity in Reason.

NOTE. — Humanity can be comprehended in full Idea, only in the History of Man through his trial, fall, redemption, and resurrection to Eternal Life; and such a work, with the Title of Humanity Immortal, may be anticipated as speedily following the present publication.